INSIDER LAW AND POLICY

by

STEPHEN M. BAINBRIDGE

William D. Warren Distinguished Professor of Law
University of California, Los Angeles

CONCEPTS AND INSIGHTS SERIES®

FOUNDATION
PRESS

Concepts and Insights Series is a trademark registered in the U.S. Patent and Trademark Office.

© 2014 LEG, Inc. d/b/a West Academic

    444 Cedar St., Suite 700
    St. Paul, MN 55101
    1-877-888-1330

Printed in the United States of America

ISBN: 978-1-60930-430-0

Mat #41517101

As always, for Helen

PREFACE

Insider trading likely is one of the most common forms of securities fraud, yet it remains one of the most controversial aspects of securities regulation among legal (and economic) scholars. This text provides a comprehensive overview of both the law of insider trading and the contested economic analysis thereof. It adopts a historical approach to the doctrinal aspects of insider trading, beginning with turn of the 20th Century state common law, and tracing the prohibition's evolution up to the most recent U.S. Supreme Court decisions under Rule 10b–5. The text then reviews the debate between those scholars favoring deregulation of insider trading, allowing corporations to set their own insider trading policies by contract, and those who contends that the property right to inside information should be assigned to the corporation without the right of contractual reassignment.

In preparing this text, I sought to produce a readable text, with a style I hope is simple, direct, and reader-friendly. Even when dealing with complicated economic or financial issues, I tried to make them readily accessible to legal audiences. Hence, this text is neither an encyclopedia nor a traditional hornbook. You will find no stultifying discussions of minutiae (I hope) or lengthy string citations of decades-old cases (or, at least, not very many). My goal is to hit the highpoints—the topics most likely to be covered in a law school course.

Stephen M. Bainbridge

January 2014

ABOUT THE AUTHOR

Stephen Bainbridge is the William D. Warren Distinguished Professor of Law at UCLA School of Law, where he currently teaches Business Associations, Advanced Corporation Law and a seminar on corporate governance. In past years, he has also taught Corporate Finance, Securities Regulation, Mergers and Acquisitions, and Unincorporated Business Associations. Professor Bainbridge previously taught at the University of Illinois Law School (1988–1996). He has also taught at Harvard Law School as the Joseph Flom Visiting Professor of Law and Business (2000–2001), at La Trobe University in Melbourne (2005 and 2007) and at Aoyama Gakuin University in Tokyo (1999).

Professor Bainbridge is a prolific scholar, whose work covers a variety of subjects, but with a strong emphasis on the law and economics of public corporations. He has written over 75 law review articles which have appeared in such leading journals as the Harvard Law Review, Virginia Law Review, Northwestern University Law Review, Cornell Law Review, Stanford Law Review and Vanderbilt Law Review. Bainbridge's most recent books include: Corporate Governance After the Financial Crisis (2012); Business Associations: Cases and Materials on Agency, Partnerships, and Corporations (8th ed. 2012) (with Klein and Ramseyer); Agency, Partnerships, and Limited Liability Entities: Cases and Materials on Unincorporated Business Associations (3d ed. 2012) (with Klein and Ramseyer); Mergers and Acquisitions (3d ed. 2012); The New Corporate Governance in Theory and Practice (2008).

In 2008, Bainbridge received the UCLA School of Law's Rutter Award for Excellence in Teaching. In 1990, the graduating class of the University of Illinois College of Law voted him "Professor of the Year."

In 2008, 2011, and 2012, Professor Bainbridge was named by the National Association of Corporate Directors' Directorship magazine to its list of the 100 most influential people in the field of corporate governance.

TABLE OF CONTENTS

INSIDER TRADING LAW AND POLICY

Chapter 1

INTRODUCTION

The term insider trading is something of a misnomer. It conjures up images of corporate directors or officers using secret information to buy stock from (or sell it to) unsuspecting investors. To be sure, the modern federal insider trading prohibition proscribes a corporation's officers and directors from trading on the basis of material nonpublic information about their firm, but it also casts a far broader net. Consider the following people who have been convicted of illegal insider trading over the years:

- A partner in a law firm representing the acquiring company in a hostile takeover bid who traded in target company stock.

- A Wall Street Journal columnist who traded prior to publication of his column in the stock of companies he wrote about.

- A psychiatrist who traded on the basis of information learned from a patient.

- A financial printer who traded in the stock of companies about which he was preparing disclosure documents.

As you can see, the insider trading laws thus capture a wide range of individuals who trade in a corporation's stock on the basis of material information unknown by the investing public at large.

Insider trading is covered by a number of legal regimes, of which no less than 5 are important for our purposes:

- The disclose or abstain rule under § 10(b) of the Securities Exchange Act of 1934 (Exchange Act) and Securities and Exchange Commission (SEC) Rule 10b–5 thereunder is principally concerned with classic insiders such as corporate officers and directors.[1] It provides that § 10(b)

---

[1] The Securities and Exchange Commission (Commission or SEC) is an independent agency created by Congress in the Exchange Act to enforce the various federal securities laws. Congress gave the SEC power to supplement the securities statutes with various rules and regulations, among which are rules 10b–5 and 14e–3 governing insider trading. Congress also gave the SEC power to investigate alleged violations of the securities laws and to bring civil actions against suspected violators. The SEC's Division of Enforcement handles most insider trading actions, which is the litigation arm of the SEC. See generally Joel Seligman, The Transformation of Wall Street: A History of the Securities and Exchange Commission and Modern Corporate Finance (2d ed. 2003) (describing organization of the SEC and its functions). The SEC may only bring civil actions, but if "the SEC suspects someone of criminal violations ... it has discretion to prepare a formal referral to the Department of Justice," which "has sole jurisdiction to institute criminal proceedings under the Exchange Act." Brian J. Carr, Note, Culpable Intent Required for All

1

and Rule 10b–5 are violated when a corporate insider trades the corporation's stock on the basis of material nonpublic information with shareholders of the corporation without disclosing such information prior to the transaction.

- The misappropriation theory under § 10(b) and Rule 10b–5 deals mainly with persons outside the company in whose stock they traded. It provides that § 10(b) and Rule 10b–5 are violated when a corporate outsider trades in breach of a duty to disclose owed not to the persons with whom the outsider trades, but rather to the source of the information.

- SEC Rule 14e–3 under Exchange Act § 14(e) is limited to insider trading in connection with a tender offer. It prohibits specified insiders and other affiliates of both the bidder and the target from divulging confidential information about a tender offer. It also, subject to narrow exceptions set forth in the Rule, prohibits any person who possesses material information relating to a tender offer by another person from trading in the target company's stock once the bidder has commenced a tender offer or has taken substantial steps towards commencement of the offer.

- Section 16(b) of the Exchange Act prohibits corporate directors, officers, and shareholders owning more than 10% of the firm's stock from earning "short swing profits" by buying and selling stock in a six month period.

- State corporate law principally targets corporate officers and directors who buy stock from shareholders of their company in face-to-face transactions.

All five regulatory schemes are discussed in the chapters that follow, but our attention will focus mainly on the federal prohibition under SEC Rule 10b–5.

At the beginning of the 1900s, state corporate law was the only legal regime regulating insider trading. At that time, as is still true in some states, corporate law allowed insider trading. Federal securities law, especially Rule 10b–5, however, has largely superseded the state common law of insider trading. To be sure, the state rules are still on the books and are still used in a few cases that fall through the cracks of the federal regulatory scheme, but federal law offers regulators and plaintiffs so many procedural and substantive advantages that it has become the dominant legal regime in this area. The most important feature of federal law,

---

Criminal Insider Trading Convictions After United States v. O'Hagan, 40 B.C. L. Rev. 1187, 1191 (1999).

however, may be that it put a cop on the beat. State law relied on firms and shareholders to detect and prosecute insider trading. Under federal law, the SEC and the Justice Department can prosecute inside traders, which has substantially increased the likelihood it will be detected and successfully prosecuted.

A truly significant distinguishing feature of the federal insider trading prohibition has been change. Although the prohibition is only about four decades old, it has seen more shifts in doctrine than most corporate law rules have seen in the last century. Exploring this rich history is a useful exercise—in many respects you cannot understand today's issues without the historical background—but is also is fraught with danger: you must draw clear distinctions between what was the law and what is the law.

One point requiring particular attention is the evolution of new theories on which insider trading liability can be based. We shall see two very important cases in which the Supreme Court restricted the scope of the traditional disclose or abstain rule. In response to those cases, the SEC and the lower courts developed two new theories on which liability could be imposed. As we move through this material, pay close attention to which theory is being discussed at any given moment and consider how that theory differs from the others.

A. A Quick Overview

Under current federal law, there are three basic theories under which trading on inside information becomes unlawful.[2] The disclose or abstain rule and the misappropriation theory were created by the courts under Section 10(b) of the Exchange Act and Rule 10b–5 thereunder. Pursuant to its rule-making authority under Exchange Act Section 14(e), the SEC adopted Rule 14e–3 to proscribe insider trading involving information relating to tender offers.

1. The Disclose or abstain rule

The modern federal insider prohibition began taking form in *SEC v. Texas Gulf Sulphur Co.*[3] The prohibition, as laid out in that opinion, rested on a policy of equality of access to information. Accordingly, under *Texas Gulf Sulphur* and its progeny, virtually anyone who possessed material nonpublic information was required either to disclose it before trading or abstain from trading in the

---

[2] Although insider trading originally was governed in the United States by state corporate law, and those state laws remain on the books, federal law has long since supplanted state law in this area. See infra Chapter 2. Insider trading may also violate other federal statutes, such as the mail and wire fraud laws, which are beyond the scope of this text.

[3] 401 F.2d 833 (2d Cir. 1968), cert. denied, 394 U.S. 976 (1969).

affected company's securities. If the would-be trader's fiduciary duties precluded him from disclosing the information prior to trading, abstention was the only option.

In *Chiarella v. United States*,[4] and *Dirks v. SEC*,[5] the United States Supreme Court rejected the equal access policy. Instead, the Court made clear that liability could be imposed only if the defendant was subject to a duty to disclose prior to trading. Inside traders thus were no longer liable merely because they had more information than other investors in the market place. Instead, a duty to disclose only arose where the inside traders breached a pre-existing fiduciary duty owed to the person with whom they traded.[6]

Creation of this fiduciary duty element substantially narrowed the scope of the disclose or abstain rule. But the rule remains quite expansive in a number of respects. In particular, it is not limited to true insiders, such as officers, directors, and controlling shareholders, but picks up corporate outsiders in two important ways. Even in these situations, however, liability for insider trading under the disclose or abstain rule can only be found where the trader—insider or outsider—violates a fiduciary duty owed to the issuer or the person on the other side of the transaction.

The rule can pick up a wide variety of nominal outsiders whose relationship with the issuer is sufficiently close to the issuer of the affected securities to justify treating them as "constructive insiders," for example, but only in rather narrow circumstances. The outsider must obtain material nonpublic information from the issuer. The issuer must expect the outsider to keep the disclosed information confidential. Finally, the relationship must at least imply such a duty. If these conditions are met, the putative outsider will be deemed a "constructive insider" and subject to the disclose or abstain rule in full measure.[7] If these conditions are not met, however, the disclose or abstain rule simply does not apply. The critical issue thus remains the nature of the relationship between the parties.

The rule also picks up outsiders who receive inside information from either true insiders or constructive insiders. There are a number of restrictions on tippee liability, however. Most important for present purposes, the tippee's liability is derivative of the tipper's, "arising from his role as a participant after the fact in the insider's breach of a fiduciary duty."[8] As a result, the mere fact of a

---

[4] 445 U.S. 222 (1980).

[5] 463 U.S. 646 (1983).

[6] *Chiarella*, 445 U.S. at 232; *Dirks*, 463 U.S. at 653–55.

[7] See *Dirks*, 463 U.S. at 655 n.14.

[8] Id. at 659.

tip is not sufficient to result in liability. What is proscribed is not merely a breach of confidentiality by the insider, but rather a breach of the duty of loyalty imposed on all fiduciaries to avoid personally profiting from information entrusted to them.[9] Thus, looking at objective criteria, the courts must determine whether the insider personally will benefit, directly or indirectly, from his disclosure. So once again, a breach of fiduciary duty is essential for liability to be imposed: a tippee can be held liable only when the tipper has breached a fiduciary duty by disclosing information to the tippee, and the tippee knows or has reason to know of the breach of duty.

Chiarella created a variety of significant gaps in the insider trading prohibition's coverage. Rule 14e–3 and the misappropriation theory were created to fill some of those gaps.

2. Rule 14e–3

Rule 14e–3 prohibits insiders of the bidder and target from divulging confidential information about a tender offer to persons who are likely to violate the rule by trading on the basis of that information. The rule also, with certain narrow and well-defined exceptions, prohibits any person who possesses material information relating to a tender offer by another person from trading in target company securities if the bidder has commenced or has taken substantial steps towards commencement of the bid.

Note that the Rule's scope is very limited. One prong of the Rule (the prohibition on trading while in possession of material nonpublic information) is not triggered until the offeror has taken substantial steps towards making the offer. More important, both prongs of the rule are limited to information relating to a tender offer. As a result, most types of inside information remain subject to the duty-based analysis of Chiarella and its progeny.

3. Misappropriation

Like the traditional disclose or abstain rule, the misappropriation theory requires a breach of fiduciary duty before trading on inside information becomes unlawful. It is not unlawful, for example, for an outsider to trade on the basis of inadvertently overheard information.[10] The fiduciary relationship in question, however, is a quite different one. Under the misappropriation theory, the defendant need not owe a fiduciary duty to the investor with whom he trades. Nor does he have to owe a fiduciary duty to the issuer of the securities that were traded. Instead, the

---

[9] See id. at 662–64.

[10] SEC v. Switzer, 590 F. Supp. 756, 766 (W.D. Okla. 1984).

misappropriation theory applies when the inside trader violates a
fiduciary duty owed to the source of the information. The Supreme
Court validated the misappropriation theory in *U.S. v. O'Hagan*.[11]

B. The Policy Debate

Insider trading is one of the most common violations of the
federal securities laws. It is certainly the violation that has most
clearly captured the public's imagination. Indeed, what other
corporate or securities law doctrine provided the plot line of a major
motion picture, as insider trading did in Oliver Stone's Wall Street
(1987)? Yet, insider trading also remains one of the most
controversial aspects of securities law. Courts and regulators
typically justify the prohibition on fairness or other equity grounds.
Is insider trading clearly unfair, however? People who trade with an
insider who has access to nonpublic information probably feel they
were cheated. According to one poll, however, well over half of all
Americans would trade on inside information if given the chance.
Whether insider trading is unfair thus depends on the eye of the
beholder.

Many leading corporate law scholars contend that the legality
of insider trading should turn not on fairness considerations, but
rather on issues of economic efficiency. Some of these commentators
believe that the prohibition cannot be justified on efficiency
grounds, while others have offered various economic justifications
for the prohibition.

Although virtually no one seriously believes that the federal
insider trading prohibition is likely to be repealed any time soon,
the academic policy debate nevertheless rewards study.
Understanding the policy issues at stake can help inform the way in
which unresolved aspects of the prohibition are settled. For law
students, a review of the policy debate also has considerable
instrumental value. The insider trading debate cannot be
understood without considering the so-called "law and economics"
school of jurisprudence. Many corporate law teachers are
practitioners of law and economics, while even those who are not
often feel compelled to introduce their students to this mode of legal
reasoning. Insider trading is one of the widely-used vehicles for
introducing law and economics to corporate law students.
Accordingly, we shall devote some attention to developing the
economic tools necessary to understanding the debate, as well as
the policy debate itself.

---

[11] 521 U.S. 642 (1997).

C. Some Important Concepts

1.   Profit

In everyday speech, the word "profit" connotes having more money at the end of a transaction than when you started. In the world of insider trading, however, it is also possible to profit by avoiding a loss. Courts have treated the use of inside information to avoid a loss as legally indistinguishable from the use of inside information to make a profit in the more conventional sense.[12] Suppose you are an insider of a corporation and learn that your company has just lost a major contract. You know that when the news becomes public, the company's stock price will decline. In order to avoid that loss, you sell the company shares you own. You sell those shares at $10 per share; when the news becomes public the price declines to $5. You can be prosecuted for insider trading even though you did not make an economic profit and the $5 per share loss you avoided will become the basis on which civil fines may be calculated.

2.   Inside versus market information

All sorts of information can effect the price of a company's stock. Suppose you receive two hot tips. One is from an insider of Acme Company, who tells you that Acme is about to announce a major new contract, which is expected to significantly increase Acme's earnings. The other is from a law school classmate who is a lawyer for Ajax Corporation, who tells you that Ajax is about to make a hostile takeover bid for Acme. Recognizing that both tips are good news for Acme's stock, you buy 1000 shares. You are found out and charged with illegal insider trading.

These examples capture the distinction between inside and market information. Market information is commonly defined as information about events or developments that affect the market for a company's securities, but not the company's assets or earnings. It typically emanates from noncorporate sources and deals primarily with information affecting the trading markets for the corporation's securities.[13] Inside information typically comes from internal corporate sources and involves events or developments affecting the

---

[12] See, e.g., S.E.C. v. Antar, 97 F. Supp.2d 576 (D. N.J. 2000) (holding that "the defendants must be ordered to disgorge any profits made and any losses avoided from their trading of ... stock while in possession of material, nonpublic information").

[13] See U.S. v. Chiarella, 588 F.2d 1358, 1365 n.8 (2d Cir. 1978), rev'd on other grounds, 445 U.S. 222 (1980) ("'Market information' refers to information that affects the price of a company's securities without affecting the firm's earning power or assets. ... Examples include information that an investment adviser will shortly issue a 'buy' recommendation or that a large stockholder is seeking to unload his shares or that a tender offer will soon be made for the company's stock.").

issuer's assets or earnings.[14] The tip about Ajax's takeover bid thus involved market information, while the tip about the new contract involved inside information.

Although this distinction can be helpful, and is often drawn in the literature and cases, it is not dispositive as a legal matter. Assuming the other prerequisites for insider trading liability are satisfied, you can go to jail just as easily for trading on market information as inside information.

3.   Different rules for buying versus selling shares?

As we shall see, much of insider trading law depends on the defendant having a fiduciary duty to the persons with whom the insider traded shares. This presents a question of whether different rules apply when a director sells shares to an outsider rather than buying them from an existing shareholder of the company. A director who buys shares is trading with someone who is already a shareholder of the corporation and, as such, someone to whom the director has fiduciary obligations. A director who sells shares, however, likely is dealing with a stranger, someone not yet a shareholder and, as such, not yet someone to whom the director owes any duties. Assuming *arguendo* that the director's fiduciary duties to shareholders proscribe buying shares from them on the basis of undisclosed material information, the logic of that rule does not necessarily extend to cases in which the director sells to an outsider.

On the other hand, a rule that bans insider trading when a director buys shares from a current shareholder but not when the director sells shares to an outsider seems an absurd elevation of form over substance. As famed Judge Learned Hand explained in *Gratz v. Claughton*[15]:

> For many years a grave omission in our corporation law had been its indifference to dealings of directors or other corporate officers in the shares of their companies. When they bought shares, they came literally within the conventional prohibitions of the law of trusts; yet the decisions were strangely slack in so deciding. When they sold shares, it could indeed be argued that they were not dealing with a beneficiary, but with one whom his purchase made a beneficiary. That should not, however, have obscured the fact that the director or officer assumed a fiduciary relation to the buyer by the very sale; for it would be a sorry distinction to allow him to use the advantage of his

---

[14] Victor Brudney, Insiders, Outsiders, and Informational Advantages Under the Federal Securities Laws, 93 Harv. L. Rev. 322, 329 (1979).

[15] 187 F.2d 46 (2d Cir. 1951).

position to induce the buyer into the position of a beneficiary, although he was forbidden to do so, once the buyer had become one. Certainly this is true, when the buyer knows he is buying of a director or officer, for he expects to become the seller's *cestui que* trust. If the buyer does not know, he is entitled to assume that if his seller in fact is already a director or officer, he will remain so after the sale.[16]

Gratz arose under federal rather than state law and involved a suit under Securities and Exchange Act § 16(b)'s short-swing profit rule rather than the core federal insider trading prohibition under Rule 10b–5. Its relevance for insider trading cases under other provisions of federal law thus long was in doubt. In *Chiarella v. U.S.*,[17] however, the Supreme Court approvingly cited *Gratz* in an insider trading case arising under Rule 10b–5.[18] Although *Chiarella*'s endorsement was mere dicta, as are most of the other relevant precedents, the proposition is now well accepted as a matter of federal law.[19]

---

[16] Id. at 49.

[17] 445 U.S. 222 (U.S. 1980).

[18] Id. at 227 n.8.

[19] As the SEC put it in the seminal *Cady, Roberts* case, "[w]e cannot accept [the] contention that an insider's responsibility is limited to existing shareholders and that he has no special duties when sales of securities are made to non-stockholders." In re Cady, Roberts & Co., 40 S.E.C. 907, 913 (1961). See also U.S. v. Chestman, 947 F.2d 551, 566 n.2 (2d Cir.1991) ("The insider's fiduciary duties, it should be noted, run to a buyer (a shareholder-to-be) and to a seller (a pre-existing shareholder) of securities, even though the buyer technically does not have a fiduciary relationship with the insider prior to the trade."), cert. denied, 503 U.S. 1004 (1992); American Law Institute, Principles of Corporate Governance: Analysis and Recommendations § 5.04 cmt. d (1992) ("A person who becomes a shareholder as a result of a purchase of securities from a director or senior executive will be deemed a shareholder for purposes of asserting a right under [the ALI's proposed state law rule], if the director or senior executive failed to disclose material inside information in making the sale.").

Chapter 2

STATE CORPORATE LAW

Although we now take it for granted that regulating insider trading is a job for the SEC under federal law, it was not always so. Until the 1960s, insider trading was a matter of state corporate law. Since then, of course, the federal prohibition has largely eclipsed state law in this area,[1] but the older state rules are still worth studying. The historical evolution of the insider trading prohibition is not only relevant to understanding current doctrine, but also is highly relevant to understanding the on-going policy debate over the merits of insider trading regulation.[2] This chapter therefore begins with a review of the state common law of insider trading. It then turns to the statutory origins of the federal prohibition, such as they are, leaving the judicial development of current federal doctrine for the next chapter.

A. The State Common Law of Insider Trading

Our overview of the state common law of insider trading is both historical and functional. We'll look first at the three different insider trading rules states adopted in the early 1900s. It turns out that these rules were largely limited to face-to-face transactions, however, so we will then look at how states regulated insider trading in the context of stock market transactions. Completing those two tasks will carry us through the 1930s, when Congress adopted the federal securities laws, but we will defer development of federal law in order to look at how state corporate law treats insider trading today.

1. Three rules for face-to-face transactions

Prior to 1900 it was treatise law that "[t]he doctrine that officers and directors [of corporations] are trustees of the

---

[1] See Treadway Cos., Inc. v. Care Corp., 638 F.2d 357, 375 n.35 (2d Cir. 1980) (stating that "a director's common law liability for trading on inside information has been largely mooted by the advent of a federal cause of action"). But while federal law now dominates insider trading, it has not preempted state law even where state law is more permissive than state law. See Scrushy v. Tucker, 70 So.3d 289, 307–09 (Ala. 2011) (holding that state law insider trading claims were not preempted by federal law); Pfeiffer v. Toll, 989 A.2d 683, 701 (Del. Ch. 2010) (holding that federal law "leaves ample space for a Delaware corporate remedy"). As the late Supreme Court Justice (and former SEC Chairman) William Douglas observed, a state is not required to discourage insider trading just because the federal government has chosen to do so. Lehman Bros. v. Schein, 416 U.S. 386, 389 (1974).

[2] In addition, this author has argued elsewhere that insider trading is a species of federal common law that should look to state corporate law for its substantive content. See Stephen M. Bainbridge, Incorporating State Law Fiduciary Duties into the Federal Insider Trading Prohibition, 52 Wash. & Lee L. Rev. 1189 (1995).

stockholders . . . does not extend to their private dealings with stockholders or others, though in such dealings they take advantage of knowledge gained through their official position."[3] Under this so-called "majority" or "no duty" rule, liability was imposed solely for actual fraud, such as misrepresentation or fraudulent concealment of a material fact. As one court explained, liability arose only where the defendant said or did something "to divert or prevent, and which did divert or prevent, the plaintiff from looking into, or making inquiry, or further inquiries, as to the affairs or condition of the company and its prospects for dividends. . . ."[4]

The first tentative step towards the modern prohibition came in *Oliver v. Oliver*,[5] in which the Georgia Supreme Court announced the so-called "minority" or "duty to disclose" rule. Under *Oliver*, directors who obtained inside information by virtue of their position held the information in trust for the shareholders. Accordingly, directors had a duty to disclose all material information to shareholders before trading with them.

In *Strong v. Repide*,[6] the U.S. Supreme Court offered a third approach to the insider-trading problem. The court acknowledged the majority rule, but declined to follow it. Instead, the court held that, under the particular factual circumstances of the case at bar, "the law would indeed be impotent if the sale could not be set aside or the defendant cast in damages for his fraud."[7] Thus was born the so-called "special facts" or "special circumstances" rule, which holds that although directors generally owe no duty to disclose material facts when trading with shareholders, such a duty can arise in—as the name suggests—"special circumstances."[8] What facts were sufficiently "special" for a court to invoke the rule? In *Strong v. Repide,* the court identified the defendant's concealment of his identity and the defendant's failure to disclose significant facts having a dramatic impact on the stock price as special circumstances.[9] A defendant found liable under either the special

---

[3] H. L. Wilgus, Purchase of Shares of a Corporation by a Director from a Shareholder, 8 Mich. L. Rev. 267 (1910).

[4] Carpenter v. Danforth, 52 Barb. 581, 589 (N.Y.Sup.Ct.1868).

[5] 45 S.E. 232 (Ga. 1903).

[6] 213 U.S. 419 (1909).

[7] Id. at 433.

[8] See Brophy v. Cities Service Co., 70 A.2d 5, 8 (Del.Ch. 1949) (holding that, "in the absence of special circumstances, corporate officers and directors may purchase and sell its capital stock at will"). Although there is some debate as to whether the minority and special circumstances rules were based on the common law tort of fraud or corporate law fiduciary duties, the latter seems to be majority view. See William K.S. Wang & Marc I. Steinberg, Insider Trading 1027 (3d ed. 2010).

[9] In Buckley v. Buckley, 202 N.W. 955 (Mich. 1925), however, the Michigan Supreme Court opined that the special circumstances necessary to impose liability on the insider were "an assured sale, merger, or other fact or condition enhancing the

circumstances or minority rule was subject either to rescission of the transaction or a constructive trust on his profit.[10]

As state law evolved in the early 1900s, both the special circumstances and minority rules rapidly gained adherents. Every court faced with the issue during this period felt obliged to discuss all three rules. Many courts abandoned the majority rule in favor of the newer alternatives.[11] When courts did adhere to the majority rule, they typically went out of their way to demonstrate that the case at bar in fact did not involve any special facts. Even more strikingly, during this period no court deciding the issue as a matter of first impression adopted the old majority rule.[12] As a result, by the late 1930s, a headcount of cases indicated that the special circumstances rule prevailed in a plurality of states, the older no duty rule no longer commanded a majority, and the "minority" or duty to disclose rule had been adopted in a substantial number—albeit, still a minority—of states.[13]

2.   Stock market transactions

Both the special circumstances and minority rules were more limited in scope than may appear at first blush. Most of the cases in which plaintiffs succeeded involved some form of active fraud, not just a failure to disclose. More important, all of these cases involved face-to-face transactions.[14] The vast majority of stock transactions,

---

value of the stock, known by the officer or officers, not known by the stockholder, and not to be ascertained by an inspection of the books." Id. at 956. Some commentators suggest that *Buckley* stands for the proposition that the insider's failure to disclose any fact "not known by the stockholder, and not to be ascertained by an inspection of the books" constitutes the requisite special circumstances. Accordingly, they argue, "*Buckley*'s language seems to require disclosure whenever a director or officer has material information not known to the transacting shareholder." Wang & Steinberg, supra note 8, at 1041. "In many special facts jurisdictions, therefore, the result is virtually the same as in minority rule jurisdictions. . . ." Id. On the other hand, however, one could read *Buckley*'s reference to "an assured sale [or] merger" to mean that special circumstances involve not just material information but highly material information. A merger that is assured to take place, after all, is "the most important event that can occur in a small corporation's life, to wit, its death. . . ." Basic, Inc. v. Levinson, 485 U.S. 224, 238 (1988).

[10] Wang & Steinberg, supra note 8, at 1043.

[11] Id. at 1031.

[12] A 1921 updating of the 1910 Wilgus article identified 13 cases dealing with the duty to disclose inside information. Eight of these cases imposed liability for failure to disclose. Six cases, following the *Strong* special circumstances rule, found special facts justifying liability. The other two cases followed the fiduciary duty approach of Oliver v. Oliver, 118 Ga. 362, 45 S.E. 232 (1903). Of the five cases finding no liability, three cases said they would follow the older rule, but went out of their way to demonstrate that there were no special circumstances. The other two cases refused to adopt the older rule, but found no special circumstances justifying imposing a duty of disclosure. Harold R. Smith, Purchase of Shares of a Corporation by a Director from a Shareholder, 19 Mich. L. Rev. 698, 712–13 (1921).

[13] I. Beverly Lake, The Use for Personal Profit of Knowledge Gained While a Director, 9 Miss. L.J. 427, 448–49 (1937).

[14] Michael Conant, Duties of Disclosure of Corporate Insiders Who Purchase Shares, 46 Cornell L.Q. 53, 54–57 (1960). Another important limitation on both the minority and special circumstances rules was that they applied only to officers,

both then and now, take place on impersonal stock exchanges. In order to be economically significant, an insider trading prohibition must apply to such transactions as well as face-to-face ones.

The leading state case in this area, still found in most corporation law casebooks, is *Goodwin v. Agassiz*.[15] Ignoring some factual complexities unnecessary to understanding the opinion, what happened here is a classic insider-trading story: Defendants were directors and senior officers of a mining corporation. A geologist working for the company advanced a theory suggesting there might be substantial copper deposits in northern Michigan. The company thought the theory had merit and began securing mineral rights on the relevant tracts of land. Meanwhile, the defendants began buying shares on the market. Plaintiff was a former stockholder who had sold his shares on the stock market. The defendants apparently had bought the shares, although neither side knew the identity of the other party to the transaction until much later. When the true facts became known, plaintiff sued the directors, arguing that he would not have sold if the geologist's theory had been disclosed. The court rejected plaintiff's claim, concluding that defendants had no duty to disclose the theory before trading.

Goodwin is commonly thought to stand for the proposition that directors and officers trading on an impersonal stock exchange owe no duty of disclosure to the persons with whom they trade. Although that reading is correct as a bottom line matter, it ignores some potentially important doctrinal complications. The Massachusetts Supreme Judicial court's analysis begins with a nod to the old majority rule, opining that directors generally do not "occupy the position of trustee toward individual stockholders in the corporation."[16] The court went on, however, to note that "circumstances may exist . . . [such] that an equitable responsibility arises to communicate facts,"[17] which sounds like the special circumstances rule. Indeed, the court signaled that Massachusetts would apply the special circumstances rule to face-to-face transactions, explaining that "where a director personally seeks out a stockholder for the purpose of buying his shares without making disclosure of material facts within his peculiar knowledge and not

---

directors, and controlling shareholders. Outsiders and low-level employees were subject to either rule. Wang & Steinberg, supra note 8, at 1032. In addition, although the paucity of cases makes it difficult to draw a firm conclusion, there is some support for the view that the rules applied only when insiders dealt with existing shareholders. Transactions in which insiders sold shares to outsiders in arms-length transactions may not have violated the rules. Id. at 1032–33.

[15] 186 N.E. 659 (Mass. 1933).

[16] Id. at 660.

[17] Id. at 661.

within reach of the stockholder, the transaction will be closely scrutinized and relief may be granted in appropriate instances."[18]

Was the court thus applying the special circumstances rule to stock market transactions? Perhaps. The court took pains to carefully analyze the nature of the information in question, concluding that it was "at most a hope," and was careful to say that there was no affirmative duty to disclose under the circumstances at bar. At the same time, however, the dispositive special circumstance clearly was the stock market context.[19] As to transactions effected on an impersonal exchange, no duty to disclose would be imposed.

Given that federal law later imposed just such a duty, it is instructive to examine carefully the court's explanation for its holding:

> Purchases and sales of stock dealt in on the stock exchange are commonly impersonal affairs. An honest director would be in a difficult situation if he could neither buy nor sell on the stock exchange shares of stock in his corporation without first seeking out the other actual ultimate party to the transaction and disclosing to him everything which a court or jury might later find that he then knew affecting the real or speculative value of such shares. Business of that nature is a matter to be governed by practical rules. Fiduciary obligations of directors ought not to be made so onerous that men of experience and ability will be deterred from accepting such office. Law in its sanctions is not coextensive with morality. It cannot undertake to put all parties to every contract on an equality as to knowledge, experience, skill and shrewdness. It cannot undertake to relieve against hard bargains made between competent parties without fraud.[20]

The insider trading prohibition's defenders find much that is contestable in the court's rationale. Two observations suffice for present purposes: First, notice the strongly normative (and strongly laissez faire) tone of the quoted passage. Why can't the law undertake to ensure that all parties to stock market transaction have at least roughly equal access to information? This question turns out to be one of insider trading jurisprudence's recurring issues. Second, consider the "difficult situation" the court claims an

---

[18] Id.

[19] See Adelson v. Adelson, 806 N.E.2d 108, 120 (Mass. App. 2004) (citing *Goodwin* for the proposition that, "in the absence of special circumstances, directors have no special duty to individual stockholders when purchasing their stock, irrespective of whether the stock was traded on the exchange or purchased . . . in a personal sale").

[20] *Goodwin*, 186 N.E. at 661.

insider trading prohibition would create for "honest directors."[21] Even at its most expansive, the federal insider trading prohibition never required directors to seek out individually those with whom they trade and personally make disclosure of "everything" they know about the company.[22] A workable insider trading prohibition simply requires directors to disclose publicly all material facts in their possession before trading or, if they are not able to do so, to refrain from trading. Corporate policies could be developed to limit director and officer trading to windows of time in which there is unlikely to be significant undisclosed information, such as those following dissemination of periodic corporate disclosures. Such policies are an inconvenience for all concerned, to be sure, but hardly enough to keep able people from serving as directors of publicly traded corporations. Not surprisingly, this aspect of the court's rationale has gotten short shrift from later courts.

B. State Common Law Today

About the same time as *Goodwin* was decided, the New Deal Congresses began adopting the federal securities laws. Although those laws did not preempt state corporate law, federal regulation has essentially superseded them insofar as insider trading is concerned. State law is not just a historical footnote, however. Some cases still fall though the federal cracks, being left for state law to decide. Private party plaintiffs still sometimes include a state law-based count in their complaints. Most important, we will see that state law ought to provide the basic analytical framework within which the federal regime operates. Having said that, however, it must be admitted that the ever-increasing focus of regulators and litigators on federal law aborted the evolution of state common law in this area. With one important exception, discussed below, we are still more or less where we were in the late 1930s.

Although both the special circumstances and minority rules continued to pick up adherents during the decades after *Goodwin* was decided,[23] a number of states continue to adhere to the no duty

---

[21] Id. at 661.

[22] SEC v. Texas Gulf Sulphur Co., 401 F.2d 833, 848 (2d Cir. 1968), cert. denied, 394 U.S. 976 (1969) ("An insider is not, of course, always foreclosed from investing in his own company merely because he may be more familiar with company operations than are outside investors. An insider's duty to disclose information or his duty to abstain from dealing in his company's securities arises only in 'those situations which are essentially extraordinary in nature and which are reasonably certain to have a substantial effect on the market price of the security if (the extraordinary situation is) disclosed.' ").

[23] See, e.g., Broffe v. Horton, 172 F.2d 489 (2d Cir.1949) (diversity case); Childs v. RIC Group, Inc., 331 F. Supp. 1078, 1081 (N.D.Ga.1970), aff'd, 447 F.2d 1407 (5th Cir.1971) (diversity case); Hobart v. Hobart Estate Co., 159 P.2d 958 (Cal.1945). An early line of federal cases arising under Rule 10b–5 applied the special circumstances and, more often, the fiduciary duty rules to face-to-face insider trading

rule.[24] Insofar as stock market transactions are concerned, moreover, *Goodwin* apparently remains the prevailing view.[25] The leading cases are of considerable antiquity, however, so one can easily imagine lawyers arguing that the old no duty precedents should not be followed today. As they might point out, the American Law Institute's Principles of Corporate Governance opine that a duty to disclose exists in both face-to-face and stock market transactions,[26] albeit as yet without much case law support.

C. Derivative Liability for Insider Trading under State Corporate Law

Although the Massachusetts court in *Goodwin* rejected the argument that directors "occupy the position of trustee towards individual stockholders,"[27] it also recognized that directors are fiduciaries of the corporate enterprise. Its holding barring shareholders from seeking direct relief thus did not prohibit corporate actions against inside traders. In turn, this suggested the possibility that shareholders could bring derivative suits on behalf of the corporation against inside traders.[28]

---

transactions. See, e.g., Kohler v. Kohler Co., 319 F.2d 634 (7th Cir.1963); Speed v. Transamerica Corp., 99 F. Supp. 808 (D.Del.1951).

[24] See, e.g., Goodman v. Poland, 395 F. Supp. 660, 678–80 (D.Md. 1975); Fleetwood Corp. v. Mirich, 404 N.E.2d 38, 46 (Ind.App.1980); Yerke v. Batman, 376 N.E.2d 1211, 1214 (Ind.App.1978).

[25] Harry S. Gerla, Issuers Raising Capital Directly from Investors: What Disclosure Does Rule 10b–5 Require?, 28 J. Corp. L. 111, 120–21 (2002) ("No state court had recognized, under state corporate law, a fiduciary duty of disclosure between corporate insiders and shareholders in anonymous stock market transactions.").

[26] American Law Institute, Principles of Corporate Governance: Analysis and Recommendations § 5.04 (1992). The Reporter's Note to § 5.04 explains that:

> Section 5.04 adopts the view that a director or senior executive owes a duty to disclose material facts not otherwise publicly available to persons with whom the director or senior executive effects transactions in the corporation's securities. In so doing, the emphasis is placed on the public availability of material information rather than on the obligation of the director or senior executive to disclose "special facts," whether or not the information is publicly available. If the person with whom the director or senior executive deals is a shareholder, or as a result of the transaction becomes a shareholder, that person may directly enforce this duty if he or she can show harm.

Id. at § 5.04 Rptr's Note 14 (citation omitted).

[27] *Goodwin*, 186 N.E. at 660.

[28] A "direct" shareholder suit is brought to enforce causes of action belonging to the shareholders in their individual capacity. It is typically premised on an injury directly affecting the shareholders and must be brought by the shareholders in their own name. See, e.g., Barth v. Barth, 659 N.E.2d 559, 560 (Ind. 1995) (noting "the well-established general rule is that shareholders of a corporation may not maintain actions at law in their own names to redress an injury to the corporation even if the value of their stock is impaired as a result of the injury"). In contrast, a "derivative" suit is one brought by the shareholder on behalf of the corporation. The cause of action belongs to the corporation as an entity and arises out of an injury done to the corporation as an entity. The shareholder is merely acting as the firm's representative. See Tooley v. Donaldson, Lufkin, & Jenrette, Inc., 845 A.2d 1031 (Del. 2004) (holding that a derivative suit rather than a direct suit should be brought when the injury was suffered by the corporate entity rather than the shareholders

All of the cases we have been discussing thus far were brought as direct actions; i.e., cases in which the plaintiff shareholder sued in his own name seeking compensation for the injury done to him by the insider with whom he traded. In derivative litigation, by contrast, the cause of action belongs to the corporation and any recovery typically goes into the corporate treasury rather than directly to the shareholders.[29] One would normally expect the corporation's board or officers to prosecute such suits. Corporate law recognizes, however, that a corporation's managers sometimes may be reluctant to enforce the corporation's rights. This seems especially likely when the prospective defendant is a fellow director or officer. The derivative suit evolved to deal with such situations, providing a procedural device for shareholders to enforce rights belonging to the corporation.[30]

In *Diamond v. Oreamuno*,[31] the leading insider trading derivative case, defendants Oreamuno and Gonzalez were respectively the Chairman of the Board and President of Management Assistance, Inc. ("MAI"). MAI was in the computer leasing business. It sub-contracted maintenance of leased systems to IBM. As a result of an increase in IBM's charges, MAI's earnings fell precipitously. Before these facts were made public, Oreamuno and Gonzalez sold off 56,500 shares of MAI stock at the then-prevailing price of $28 per share. Once the information was made public, MAI's stock price fell to $11 per share. A shareholder sued derivatively, seeking an order that defendants disgorge their allegedly ill-gotten gains to the corporation. The court held that a derivative suit was proper in this context and, moreover, that insider trading by corporate officers and directors violated their fiduciary duties to the corporation.[32]

---

and any recovery would be paid to the corporate treasury rather than to the shareholders).

[29] See, e.g., Glenn v. Hoteltron Systems, Inc., 547 N.Y.S.2d 816 (1989) (explaining that while corporate recovery is the norm, individual shareholder recovery is appropriate in derivative proceedings when necessary to prevent a wrongdoer from benefiting by a corporate recovery).

[30] See Cohen v. Beneficial Indus. Loan Corp., 337 U.S. 541, 548 (1949) ("This [derivative suit] remedy, born of stockholder helplessness, was long the chief regulator of corporate management and has afforded no small incentive to avoid at least grosser forms of betrayal of stockholders' interests.").

[31] 248 N.E.2d 910 (N.Y. 1969).

[32] There is a procedural oddity inherent in *Diamond*'s willingness to permit derivative suits against inside traders. As is generally the case in corporate law, New York only allows shareholders to bring a derivative suit if they meet the so-called contemporaneous ownership test. To meet that test, the shareholder must hold stock both at the time the wrong was committed and when suit was filed. N.Y. Bus. Corp. L. § 626. In cases like *Diamond*, in which outsiders bought the selling insiders' shares, the purchasers were not shareholders until after the wrong was committed. In the flip category of cases, those in which insiders buy from existing shareholders, the sellers (if they sold all their shares) are no longer shareholders. The effect of the continuing shareholder rule should be obvious: no shareholder in the class most would regard as the inside trader's principal victims can serve as a named plaintiff

Diamond has been a law professor favorite ever since it was decided. A plethora of law review articles have been written on it, mostly in a favorable vein. *Diamond* also still shows up in most corporation law casebooks. In the real world, however, *Diamond* has proven quite controversial. A number of leading opinions in other jurisdictions have squarely rejected its holdings.[33]

Why has *Diamond* proven so controversial? No one contends that officers or directors never can be held liable for using information learned in their corporate capacities for personal profit. An officer who uses information learned on the job to compete with his corporate employer, or to usurp a corporate opportunity, for example, readily can be held liable for doing so. Insider trading differs in an important way from these cases, however. Recall that derivative litigation is intended to redress an injury to the corporate entity. Where an employee uses inside information to compete with her corporate employer, the injury to the employer is obvious. In *Diamond*, however, the employees did not use their knowledge to compete with the firm, but rather to trade in its securities. The injury, if any, to the corporation is far less obvious in such cases. Unlike most types of tangible property, more than one person can use information without necessarily lowering its value. If an officer who has just negotiated a major contract for her corporation thereafter buys some of the firm's stock, for example, it is far from obvious that her trading necessarily reduced the contract's value to the firm.

The *Diamond* court relied on two purportedly analogous precedents to justify allowing a derivative cause of action against inside traders; namely, the Delaware Chancery court's decision in *Brophy v. Cities Service Co.*[34] and the law of agency. On close examination, however, neither provides very much support for Diamond.

In *Brophy*, the defendant insider traded on the basis of information about a stock repurchase program the corporation was about to undertake. In a very real sense, the insider was competing with the corporation, which both agency law and corporate law clearly proscribe. While the *Brophy* court did not require a showing of corporate injury, the insider's conduct in fact directly threatened the corporation's interests. If his purchases caused a rise in the stock price, the corporation would be injured by having to pay more

---

in a *Diamond*-type suit. Where insiders buy, moreover, the allegedly injured selling shareholders cannot even share in any benefit that might flow from a successful derivative suit.

[33] See, e.g., Freeman v. Decio, 584 F.2d 186 (7th Cir.1978) (Indiana law); Schein v. Chasen, 313 So.2d 739, 746 (Fla.1975).

[34] 70 A.2d 5 (Del. Ch. 1949).

for its own purchases. In contrast, the *Diamond* insiders' conduct involved neither competition with the corporation nor a direct threat of harm to it. The information in question related to a historical fact. As such, it simply was not information MAI could use. Indeed, the only imaginable use to which MAI could put this information would be to itself buy or sell its own securities before announcing the decline in earnings. Under the federal securities laws, however, MAI could not lawfully make such trades.[35]

The *Diamond* court made two moves to evade this problem. First, it asserted that proof of injury was not legally necessary, which seems inconsistent with the notion that a derivative suit is a vehicle for redressing injuries done to the corporation. Second, the court inferred that MAI might have suffered some harm because of the defendants' conduct, even though the complaint failed to allege any such harm. In particular, the court surmised that the defendants' conduct might have injured MAI's reputation. As we shall see in Chapter 13, however, this is not a very likely source of corporate injury. Accordingly, it is quite easy to distinguish *Brophy* from *Diamond*.[36]

Agency law proves an equally problematic justification for the *Diamond* result. According to the Restatement (Second) of Agency, which was the current edition and thus the guiding reference when *Diamond* was decided, the principal-agent relationship is a fiduciary one with respect to matters within the scope of the agency relationship. More to the point for present purposes, § 388 of the Agency Restatement imposes a duty on agents to account for profits made in connection with transactions conducted on the principal's behalf.[37] The comments to that section further expand this duty's scope, requiring the agent to account for any profits made by the use of confidential information even if the principal is not harmed by the agent's use of the information. Section 395 provides that an agent may not use for personal gain any information "given him by the principal or acquired by him during the course of or on account of his agency."[38]

---

[35] As we'll see in the next section, however, the Delaware Supreme Court has reaffirmed that proof of injury to the corporation is not required in order for a shareholder derivative suit to be proper under Delaware law. At least in this regard, Delaware law is consistent with *Diamond*.

[36] But see Thomas v. Roblin Industries, Inc., 520 F.2d 1393, 1397 (3rd Cir. 1975) ("We read both *Diamond* and *Brophy* to stand for the same fundamental proposition: as a matter of common law, a fiduciary of a corporation who trades for his own benefit on the basis of confidential information acquired through his fiduciary position breaches his duty to the corporation and may be held accountable to that corporation for any gains without regard to whether the corporation suffered damages as a result of the transaction.").

[37] Restatement (Second) of Agency § 388 (1958).

[38] Id. at § 395.

One can plausibly argue, however, that the apparent bar on insider trading created by agency law is not as strict as it first appears. The broad prohibition of self-dealing in confidential information appears solely in the comments to §§ 388 and 395. In contrast, the black letter text of § 388 speaks only of profits made "in connection with transactions conducted by [the agent] on behalf of the principal."[39] One must stretch the phrases "in connection with" and "on behalf of" pretty far in order to reach insider-trading profits. Similarly, § 395, which speaks directly to the issue of self-dealing in confidential information, only prohibits the use of confidential information for personal gain "in competition with or to the injury of the principal."[40] Arguably, agency law thus requires an injury to the principal before insider-trading liability can be imposed.

Freeman v. Decio,[41] the leading case rejecting *Diamond*'s approach, supports this argument. In *Freeman*, the court noted both *Diamond* and the comments to §§ 388 and 395, but nonetheless held that corporate officers and directors could not be held liable for insider trading as a matter of state corporate law without a showing that the corporation was injured by their conduct. *Freeman* conceded that if all confidential information relating to the firm were a corporate asset, plaintiffs would not need to show an injury to the corporation in order for the insider's trades to constitute a breach of duty. The court said, however, such a view puts the cart before the horse. One should first ask whether there was any potential loss to the corporation before deciding whether to treat the information in question as a firm asset. The court further concluded that most instances of insider trading did not pose any cognizable risk of injury to the firm. According to the court, any harm caused by insider trading was borne mainly by the investors with whom the insider trades, rather than the firm. Unlike *Brophy*, moreover, there was no competition with the firm or loss of a corporate opportunity, because there was no profitable use to which the corporation could have lawfully put this information.[42]

---

[39] Id. at § 388.

[40] Id. at § 395.

[41] 584 F.2d 186 (7th Cir.1978). The Florida Supreme Court likewise rejected "the innovative ruling of the New York Court of Appeals in *Diamond*, [instead] . . . adher[ing] to previous precedent established by the courts in this state that actual damage to the corporation must be alleged in the complaint to substantiate a stockholders' derivative action." Schein v. Chasen, 313 So.2d 739, 746 (Fla.1975) (citations omitted).

[42] The drafters of the ALI *Principles of Corporate Governance* adopted the *Diamond* position:

When a claim against a director or senior executive is based on use of undisclosed information when trading in the corporation's securities, some courts have found a breach of the duty of fair dealing only if there has been a showing of harm to the corporation. Other authorities have taken the position

Which of these cases was correctly decided as a matter of public policy? Unfortunately, we are not yet ready to decide between *Diamond* and *Freeman*. The basic issue that divides them is whether all confidential information relating to the firm is a corporate asset. Put another way, did MAI have a protected property right in all such information? Answering that question is a task best deferred until Chapter 13 below, in which we'll look at the allocation of property rights in information.

Having said that, there are other policy grounds for believing that *Diamond* was wrongly decided. In particular, by allowing state law-based derivative claims, *Diamond* raises the prospect of duplicative liability for defendants:

> In the years since the *Diamond* decision the class action suit under Rule 10b–5 has developed into an effective remedy for insider trading. In addition, under Section 16(b) of the Exchange Act ... a corporation may recover "short-swing profits" realized by insiders trading in the corporation's stock. Under these circumstances a common law claim to recover profits from insiders presents an actual, and needless, risk of double liability.[43]

Because the absence of a federal insider trading prohibition at the time was a major part of the New York court's justification for the result in *Diamond*, the subsequent emergence of just such a prohibition undercuts much of the rationale for the decision.

---

that even in the absence of significant harm to the corporation a director or senior executive may not utilize corporate position or corporate property or non-public corporate information to advance the director's or senior executive's pecuniary interest. Section 5.04 adopts the latter view, but places limitations on the right of the corporation to sue under such circumstances.

American Law Institute, supra note 26, at § 5.04 cmt. a. The limitations to which the drafters refer include the following:

§ 5.04 does not authorize the corporation to seek damages on behalf of shareholders who may have a claim based on harm suffered by them. Furthermore, to the extent that shareholders assert harm to themselves in violation of § 5.04 as a result of insider trading, the primary right to recovery would be in the shareholders, and if the shareholders recovered, under § 5.04(c) the corporation would not also be entitled to obtain recovery on the same facts for a violation of § 5.04 on a theory of unjust enrichment.

Id. at § 5.04 cmt. d(2)(a).

[43] Frankel v. Slotkin, 795 F. Supp. 76, 80 (E.D.N.Y. 1992). See also American Law Institute, supra note 26, at § 5.04 cmt. d(2)(a) ("Because § 5.04 is not intended to detract from federal or state securities laws and may conceivably give rise to claims by both the corporation and aggrieved shareholders, the court should take appropriate steps to limit the possibility of multiple recovery against the director or senior executive on varying theories of liability under state and federal law, unless specific separate damages can be shown.").

1. Derivative liability for insider trading under Delaware law

As noted above, in justifying its decision in *Diamond*, the New York Court of Appeals relied heavily on the Delaware Supreme Court's 1949 decision in *Brophy v. City Service Co.*[44] Given Delaware's status as the leading state corporate law jurisdiction, it's useful to ask whether *Brophy* remains good law in Delaware.

The Delaware Supreme Court, in fact, has reaffirmed *Brophy*'s validity at least twice since 2004.[45] In *Kahn v. Kolberg Kravis Roberts & Co.*,[46] the court explained that "for a plaintiff to prevail on a Brophy claim":

> The plaintiff must show that: "1) the corporate fiduciary possessed material, nonpublic company information; and 2) the corporate fiduciary used that information improperly by making trades because she was motivated, in whole or in part, by the substance of that information."[47]

In doing so, the court also specifically rejected the argument that "the purpose of *Brophy* is to 'remedy harm to the corporation.' "[48] As a result, a shareholder derivative suit premised on a *Brophy* claim is proper even if the plaintiff is unable to show that the defendant's trading harmed the corporation. If plaintiff is able to prove the two elements of a *Brophy* claim, the defendant properly may be compelled to disgorge his profits to the corporation so as to prevent what the court called "unjust enrichment based on the misuse of confidential corporate information."[49]

---

[44] 70 A.2d 5 (Del. Ch. 1949).

[45] Kahn v. Kolberg Kravis Roberts & Co., L.P., 23 A.3d 831 (Del. 2011); In re Oracle Corp., 867 A.2d 904 (Del.Ch.2004), aff'd, 872 A.2d 960 (Del.2005).

[46] 23 A.3d 831 (Del. 2011).

[47] Id. at 838 (quoting *Oracle*, 867 A.2d at 934).

[48] Id. at 840. In doing so, the Delaware Supreme Court rejected a trend in Chancery Court cases to the contrary, going so far as to expressly abrogate the leading Chancery Court holding that harm was an essential element of the *Brophy* claim. Id. (abrogating Pfeiffer v. Toll, 989 A.2d 683 (Del. Ch. 2010)). In retrospect, the Delaware Supreme Court's rejection of a proof of harm requirement was not surprising. In *Pfeiffer*, the Chancery Court had required proof of both actual and proximate causation for a *Brophy* claim to lie. That requirement was difficult to square with the Supreme Court's decision in Cede & Co. v. Technicolor, Inc., 634 A.2d 345 (Del. 1993), which held that "the measure of any recoverable loss . . . under an entire fairness standard of review is not necessarily limited to the difference between the price offered and the 'true' value as determined under appraisal proceedings." Id. at 371. As the Chancery Court subsequently observed in O'Reilly v. Transworld Healthcare, Inc., 745 A.2d 902 (Del.Ch. 1999), "[a]n action for a breach of fiduciary duty arising out of disclosure violations in connection with a request for stockholder action does not include the elements of reliance, causation and actual quantifiable monetary damages." Id. at 917. In light of those precedents, *Pfeiffer*'s incorporation of those elements into the *Brophy* claim was highly questionable.

[49] *Kahn*, 23 A.3d at 840.

As for the argument that state corporate law remedies were unnecessary and potentially duplicative in light of the development of the federal insider trading prohibition, the Delaware Supreme Court dismissed it almost out of hand:

> Just as the *Brophy* court relied on the seminal decision in *Guth v. Loft*, we also rely on the *Guth* court's rationale in this case
>
> . . .
>
>> The rule, inveterate and uncompromising in its rigidity, does not rest upon the narrow ground of injury or damage to the corporation resulting from a betrayal of confidence, but upon a broader foundation of a wise public policy that, for the purpose of removing all temptation, extinguishes all possibility of profit flowing from a breach of the confidence imposed by the fiduciary relation.
>>
>> Given *Guth*'s eloquent articulation of Delaware's public policy and the fact that "Delaware law dictates that the scope of recovery for a breach of the duty of loyalty is not to be determined narrowly," we find no reasonable public policy ground to restrict the scope of disgorgement remedy in *Brophy* cases—irrespective of arguably parallel remedies grounded in federal securities law.[50]

Kahn thus may presage a revival of the long dormant *Brophy* claim as a core principle of Delaware corporate law and a regular feature in derivative litigation.

---

[50] Id. (footnotes omitted).

Chapter 3

THE FEDERAL INSIDER TRADING PROHIBITION: STATUTORY BACKGROUND

The modern federal insider trading prohibition has its statutory basis in the federal securities laws, principally the Exchange Act. As with the other New Deal-era securities laws, the Exchange Act was a response to the 1929 stock market crash and the subsequent depression. Congress hoped these laws would ameliorate the economic crisis caused by the crash. Towards that end, all of the various statutes shared two basic purposes: protecting investors engaged in securities transactions and assuring public confidence in the integrity of the securities markets.[1] The basic question thus presented is whether insider trading implicates those concerns.

A. Did Congress Intend to Outlaw Insider Trading in 1934?

From the beginning, disclosure was Congress' favorite tool for regulating securities. As the Supreme Court later stated, the federal securities statutes' fundamental aim was "to substitute a philosophy of full disclosure for the philosophy of caveat emptor and thus achieve a high standard of business ethics in the securities industry."[2] Accordingly, prohibitions of fraud and manipulation in connection with the purchase or sale of securities buttressed the Exchange Act's disclosure requirements.

Does insider trading violate the disclosure obligations created by the Exchange Act? If not, is it otherwise captured by the Act's prohibition of fraud and manipulation? The Supreme Court, among others, thinks so: "A significant purpose of the Exchange Act was to eliminate the idea that use of inside information for personal advantage was a normal emolument of corporate office."[3] Careful examination of the statutory text and the relevant legislative

---

[1] See Ernst & Ernst v. Hochfelder, 425 U.S. 185, 195, 96 S.Ct. 1375, 1382, 47 L.Ed.2d 668, 677 (1976) (explaining that the securities laws were designed "to protect investors against fraud and to promote ethical standards of honesty and fair dealing"); Sargent v. Genesco, Inc., 492 F.2d 750, 760 (5th Cir. 1974) ("The basic intent of section 10(b) and rule 10b–5 and indeed, of the Exchange Act, is to protect investors and instill confidence in the securities markets by penalizing unfair dealings.").

[2] SEC v. Capital Gains Research Bureau, Inc., 375 U.S. 180, 186 (1963).

[3] Dirks v. SEC, 463 U.S. 646, 653 n. 10 (1983).

25

history, however, suggests that regulating insider trading was not one of the Exchange Act's original purposes.[4]

The core of the modern federal insider trading prohibition derives its statutory authority from § 10(b) of the Exchange Act, which provides in pertinent part that:

> It shall be unlawful for any person, directly or indirectly, by the use of any means or instrumentality of interstate commerce or of the mails, or of any facility of any national securities exchange . . .
>
> (b) To use or employ, in connection with the purchase or sale of any security registered on a national securities exchange or any security not so registered, any manipulative or deceptive device or contrivance in contravention of such rules and regulations as the SEC may prescribe as necessary or appropriate in the public interest or for the protection of investors.[5]

Notice two things about the statutory text. First, it does not actually make anything illegal. Put more formally, § 10(b) is not self-executing. It grants authority to the SEC to prohibit "any manipulative or deceptive device or contrivance" and then makes the use of such proscribed devices illegal. Until the SEC exercises its rulemaking authority, however, the statute does nothing of substance.

Second, note the absence of the word "insider." Nothing in § 10(b) explicitly proscribes insider trading. To be sure, § 10(b) often is described as a "catchall" intended to capture various types of securities fraud not expressly covered by more specific provisions of the Exchange Act.[6] What the SEC catches under § 10(b), however, must not only be fraud, but also within the scope of the authority delegated to it by Congress.[7] Section 10(b) received little attention during the hearings on the Exchange Act and apparently was seen simply as a grant of authority to the SEC to prohibit manipulative devices not covered by § 9. As Thomas Corcoran, a prominent member of President Roosevelt's administration and leader of the Exchange Act's supporters put it, § 10(b) was intended to prohibit the invention of "any other cunning devices" besides those

---

[4] See generally Stephen M. Bainbridge, Incorporating State Law Fiduciary Duties into the Federal Insider Trading Prohibition, 52 Wash & Lee L. Rev. 1189, 1228–1237 (1995); Michael P. Dooley, Enforcement of Insider Trading Restrictions, 66 Va. L. Rev. 1, 55–69 (1980); Frank H. Easterbrook, Insider Trading Secret Agents, Evidentiary Privileges, and the Production of Information, 1981 Sup. Ct. Rev. 309, 317–20.

[5] 15 U.S.C.S. § 78j(b) (2013).

[6] Chiarella v. U.S., 445 U.S. 222, 234–35 (1980).

[7] Ernst & Ernst v. Hochfelder, 425 U.S. 185, 212–14 (1976).

prohibited by other sections.[8] Only a single passage, albeit an oft-cited one, in the Exchange Act's voluminous legislative history directly indicates insider trading was one of those cunning devices: "Among the most vicious practices unearthed at the hearings ... was the flagrant betrayal of their fiduciary duties by directors and officers of corporations who used their positions of trust and the confidential information which came to them in such positions, to aid them in their market activities."[9] In context, however, this passage does not deal with insider trading as we understand the term today, but rather with manipulation of stock prices by pools of insiders and speculators through cross sales, wash sales, and similar "cunning" methods.[10] Nothing else in the legislative history suggests that Congress intended § 10(b) to create a sweeping prohibition of insider trading.

To the extent the 1934 Congress addressed insider trading, it did so not through § 10(b), but rather through § 16(b), which permits the issuer of affected securities to recover insider short-swing profits. As we will see in Chapter 14, § 16(b) imposes quite limited restrictions on insider trading. It does not reach transactions occurring more than six months apart, nor does it apply to persons other than those named in the statute or to transactions in securities not registered under § 12. Indeed, some have argued that § 16(b) was not even intended to deal with insider trading, but rather with manipulation.[11] In any event, given that Congress could have struck at insider trading both more directly and forcefully, and given that Congress chose not to do so, § 16(b) offers no statutory justification for the more sweeping prohibition under § 10(b).

B. Did the SEC Intend Rule 10b–5 to Outlaw Insider Trading in 1942?

If Congress had intended in 1934 that the SEC use § 10(b) to craft a sweeping prohibition on insider trading, moreover, the SEC was quite dilatory in doing so. Rule 10b–5, the foundation on which the modern insider trading prohibition rests, was not promulgated until 1942, eight years after the Exchange Act passed Congress. The Rule provides:

> It shall be unlawful for any person, directly or indirectly, by the use of any means or instrumentality of interstate

---

[8] Stock Exchange Regulation: Hearing on H.R. 7852 and H.R. 8720 Before the House Comm. on Interstate and Foreign Commerce, 73d Cong., 2d Sess. 115 (1934).

[9] S. Rep. No. 1455, 73d Cong., 2d Sess. 55 (1934).

[10] Dooley, supra note 4, at 56 n. 235.

[11] Id. at 56–58.

commerce, or of the mails or of any facility of any national securities exchange,

(a) To employ any device, scheme, or artifice to defraud,

(b) To make any untrue statement of a material fact or to omit to state a material fact necessary in order to make the statements made, in the light of the circumstances under which they were made, not misleading, or

(c) To engage in any act, practice, or course of business which operates or would operate as a fraud or deceit upon any person,

in connection with the purchase or sale of any security.[12]

The rule's three subsections outlaw three types of conduct in connection with the purchase or sale of a security: the use of any device, scheme or artifice to defraud; material misstatements and omissions; and any act, practice or course of business that operates as a fraud. As a technical matter, conduct "involving primarily a failure to disclose" falls under "the first and third subsections of Rule 10b–5," while an affirmative misrepresentation (broadly defined so as to include a failure to state a fact necessary to make statements made not misleading) falls under the second subsection.[13] Because most modern insider trading cases involve exclusively impersonal stock market transactions rather than face-to-face transactions, and thus implicate omissions rather than misrepresentations, it is the first and third sections of the Rule that normally are implicated in insider trading cases today.[14]

In practice, of course, courts tend to lump the clauses together, such that differences between them rarely matter very much.[15] The distinction between omissions and misrepresentations, however, does come into play in insider trading cases in one critical respect. This is so because not all omissions give rise to liability. Instead, liability for omissions arises only if the defendant had a duty to speak. As we shall see, this requirement has been a central feature

---

[12] 17 C.F.R. § 240.10b–5 (2013).

[13] Finkel v. Docutel/Olivetti Corp., 817 F.2d 356, 360 (5th Cir.1987).

[14] Both the statute and the rule plainly require a jurisdictional nexus; i.e., there must be a use of a means or instrumentality of interstate commerce, the mails, or any facility of a national securities exchange in order for the statute to be applicable. In most cases, this requirement is easily satisfied. Basically, if the defendant made a phone call or sent a letter in connection with the fraud, § 10(b) can apply. Section 10(b) will also apply if the defendant takes either of those steps indirectly; for example, if the defendant orders his broker to sell shares, and the broker uses the phone or the mails, the statute is triggered. Given that the vast majority of modern insider trading occurs on national securities exchanges or Nasdaq, of course, the jurisdictional nexus typically is a merely pleading technicality in these cases.

[15] 1 Alan R. Bromberg & Lewis D. Lowenfels, Securities Fraud & Commodities Fraud § 2.6 (2012).

of the Supreme Court's insider trading jurisprudence, because of the necessity to find a duty to disclose applicable to the alleged inside trader.[16]

Note that, as with § 10(b) itself, the rule on its face does not prohibit (or even speak to) insider trading. Indeed, the SEC for many years allowed Rule 10b–5 to lay dormant with respect to insider trading on public secondary trading markets. Instead, like state common law, the initial Rule 10b–5 insider trading cases were limited to face-to-face and change-of-control transactions. Not until 1961 did the SEC finally conclude that insider trading on an impersonal stock exchange violated Rule 10b–5.[17] Only then did the modern federal insider trading prohibition at last begin to take shape.

C. Insider Trading as Federal Common Law

The modern insider trading prohibition thus is a creature of SEC administrative actions and judicial opinions, only loosely tied to the statutory language and its legislative history. U.S. Supreme Court Chief Justice William Rehnquist famously observed that Rule 10b–5 is "a judicial oak which has grown from little more than a legislative acorn."[18] Nowhere in Rule 10b–5 jurisprudence is this truer than where the insider trading prohibition is concerned, given the tiny (arguably nonexistent) legislative acorn on which it rests. As a former SEC solicitor once admitted, the "[m]odern development of the law of insider trading is a classic example of common law in the federal courts."[19]

---

[16] The distinction between omission and misrepresentation cases comes into play in private party litigation because reliance and transaction causation are presumed in omission cases. In private party litigation under Rule 10b–5, plaintiff generally must prove that he or she reasonably relied upon the defendant's fraudulent words or conduct. In some misrepresentation cases, of course, reliance and transaction causation may be presumed under the so-called "fraud on the market" theory. A rebuttable presumption arises under this theory if plaintiff can prove defendant made material public misrepresentations, the security was traded on an efficient market, and plaintiff traded in the security between the time the misrepresentations were made and the truth was revealed. Basic Inc. v. Levinson, 485 U.S. 224 (1988). Where the fraud on the market presumption is inapplicable or has been rebutted, the reliance must be proven.

Plaintiff also must prove both transaction causation and loss causation. The former is analogous to but for causation in tort law—it is a showing that defendant's words or conduct caused plaintiff to engage in the transaction in question. Loss causation is somewhat analogous to the tort law concept of proximate causation—it involves showing that the defendant's words or conduct caused plaintiff's economic loss. In omission cases, both transaction causation and reliance generally are presumed so long as plaintiff can show defendant had a duty to disclose and failed to do so. Affiliated Ute Citizens v. U.S., 406 U.S. 128 (1972).

[17] 40 S.E.C. 907 (1961).

[18] Blue Chip Stamps v. Manor Drug Stores, 421 U.S. 723, 737 (1975).

[19] Paul Gonson & David E. Butler, In Wake of "Dirks," Courts Debate Definition of "Insider," Legal Times, Apr. 2, 1984, at 16, col. 1.

D. Subsequent Federal Legislative Action

Congress passed legislation affecting the insider trading prohibition twice in the 1980s. The Insider Trading Sanctions Act of 1984[20] was intended to increase the deterrent effect of the insider trading prohibition without changing the substantive common law governing insider trading cases. Towards that end, the Act's principal operative provision created a civil penalty of up to three times the profit gained, or loss avoided, through trading while in possession of material nonpublic information.[21] The Insider Trading and Securities Fraud Enforcement Act of 1988[22] further upped the enforcement ante, while again leaving the substantive law of insider trading to the courts.[23] Defining insider trading thus remains a matter of federal common law.

---

[20] Pub. L. No. 98–376, 98 Stat. 1264 (1984).

[21] See infra Chapter 11.B.1.

[22] Pub. L. No. 100–704, 102 Stat. 4677 (1988).

[23] See infra Chapter 11.B.2.

Chapter 4

COMMON LAW ORIGINS OF THE FEDERAL INSIDER TRADING PROHIBITION

The modern federal insider trading prohibition fairly can be said to have begun with the SEC's enforcement action *In re Cady, Roberts & Co.*[1] Curtiss-Wright Corporation's board of directors decided to reduce the company's quarterly dividend. One of the directors, J. Cheever Cowdin, was also a partner in Cady, Roberts & Co., a stock brokerage firm. Before the news was announced, Cowdin informed one of his partners, Robert M. Gintel, of the impending dividend cut. Gintel then sold several thousand shares of Curtiss-Wright stock held in customer accounts over which he had discretionary trading authority. When the dividend cut was announced, Curtiss-Wright's stock price fell several dollars per share. Gintel's customers thus avoided substantial losses.

Cady, Roberts involved what is now known as tipping: an insider (the tipper) who knows confidential information does not himself trade, but rather informs (tips) someone else (the tippee) who does trade. It also involved trading on an impersonal stock exchange, instead of a face-to-face transaction. As the SEC acknowledged, this made *Cady, Roberts* a case of first impression.[2] Prior 10b–5 cases in which inside information was used for personal gain had involved issues of tortious fraudulent concealment little different from the sorts of cases with which the state common law had dealt.[3] Notwithstanding that limitation, the SEC held that Gintel had violated Rule 10b–5. In so doing, it articulated what became known as the "disclose or abstain" rule; namely, that an insider in possession of material nonpublic information must disclose such information before trading or, if disclosure is impossible or improper, abstain from trading.[4]

It was not immediately clear what precedential value *Cady, Roberts* would have.[5] It was an administrative ruling by the SEC,

---

[1] 40 S.E.C. 907 (1961).

[2] Id.

[3] See, e.g., Speed v. Transamerica Corp., 99 F. Supp. 808 (D. Del. 1951) (omissions in connection with what amounted to a tender offer); Kardon v. Nat'l Gypsum Co., 73 F. Supp. 798 (E.D. Pa. 1947) (sale of control negotiated face to face); In re Ward La France Truck Corp., 13 S.E.C. 373 (1943) (same).

[4] *Cady, Roberts*, 40 S.E.C. at 911.

[5] See, e.g., Recent Decisions, 48 Va. L. Rev. 398, 403–04 (1962) (arguing that "in view of the limited resources of the Commission, the unfortunate existence of more positive and reprehensible forms of fraud, and the inherent problems

not a judicial opinion. It involved a regulated industry closely supervised by the SEC. There was the long line of precedent, represented by *Goodwin v. Agassiz*,[6] to the contrary.[7] In short order, however, the basic *Cady, Roberts* principles became the law of the land.

A. *Texas Gulf Sulphur*

In March of 1959, agents of Texas Gulf Sulphur Co. found evidence of an ore deposit near Timmons, Ontario.[8] In October 1963, Texas Gulf Sulphur began ground surveys of the area. In early November, a drilling rig took core samples from depths of several hundred feet. Visual examination of the samples suggested commercially significant deposits of copper and zinc. Texas Gulf Sulphur's president ordered the exploration group to maintain strict confidentiality, even to the point of withholding the news from other Texas Gulf Sulphur directors and employees. In early December, a chemical assay confirmed the presence of copper, zinc, and silver. At the subsequent trial, several expert witnesses testified that they had never heard of any other initial exploratory drill hole showing comparable results. Over the next several months, Texas Gulf Sulphur acquired the rights to the land under which this remarkable ore deposit lay. In March and early April 1964, further drilling confirmed that Texas Gulf Sulphur had made a significant ore discovery. After denying several rumors about the find, Texas Gulf Sulphur finally announced its discovery in a press conference on April 16, 1964.[9]

Throughout the fall of 1963 and spring of 1964, a number of Texas Gulf Sulphur insiders bought stock and/or options on company stock. Others tipped off outsiders. Still others accepted stock options authorized by the company's board of directors without informing the directors of the discovery. Between November 1963 and March 1964, the insiders were able to buy at prices that were slowly rising, albeit with fluctuations, from just under $18 per share to $25 per share. As rumors began circulating in late March and early April, the price jumped to about $30 per share. On April 16th, the stock opened at $31, but quickly jumped to $37 per share. By May 15, 1964, Texas Gulf Sulphur's stock was

---

concerning proof and evidence adhering to any controversy involving a breach of duty of disclosure, there is little prospect of excessive litigation evolving pursuant to [*Cady, Roberts*]").

6   186 N.E. 659 (Mass. 1933).

7   See Chapter 2.A.2.

8   SEC v. Texas Gulf Sulphur Co., 401 F.2d 833 (2d Cir.1968), cert. denied, 394 U.S. 976 (1969).

9   See generally Kenneth G. Patrick, Perpetual Jeopardy: The Texas Gulf Sulphur Affair (1972) (providing an extensive analysis of the case and its background).

trading at over $58 per share—a 222% rise over the previous November's price. Any joy the insiders may taken from their profits was short-lived, however, as the SEC sued them for violating Rule 10b–5.

Texas Gulf Sulphur is the first of the truly seminal insider trading cases. It is still in most of the case books, in large part because it presents such a stark and classic fact pattern. In examining *Texas Gulf Sulphur*, however, it is critical to distinguish between what the law was and what the law is. Although much of what was said in that opinion is still valid, the core insider trading holding is no longer good law.

B. The Disclose or Abstain Rule

In *Texas Gulf Sulphur*, the Second Circuit Court of Appeals held that an insider possessing material nonpublic information the insider must either disclose such information before trading or abstain from trading until the information has been disclosed.[10] Thus was born what is now known as the "disclose or abstain" rule (a.k.a. the "classical" rule).[11]

The name is something of a misnomer, of course. The court presumably phrased the rule in terms of disclosure because this was an omissions case under Rule 10b–5. Recall that in such cases the defendant must owe a duty of disclosure to some investor in order for liability to arise. As illustrated by the facts of *Texas Gulf Sulphur* itself, however, disclosure will rarely be a practical option. During the relevant period, Texas Gulf Sulphur had no affirmative duty to disclose the ore strike. Instead, as the Second Circuit correctly noted, the timing of disclosure is a matter for the business judgment of corporate managers, at least in the absence of any affirmative disclosure requirements imposed by the stock exchanges or the SEC.[12] In this case, moreover, delaying disclosure served a valuable corporate purpose. Confidentiality prevented competitors from buying up the mineral rights and kept down the price landowners would charge for them. The company therefore had no

---

[10] See *Texas Gulf Sulphur*, 401 F.2d at 848 (quoting In re Cady, Roberts, 40 SEC 907, 912 (1961), for the proposition that "anyone who, trading for his own account in the securities of a corporation has 'access, directly or indirectly, to information intended to be available only for a corporate purpose and not for the personal benefit of anyone' may not take 'advantage of such information knowing it is unavailable to those with whom he is dealing,' i.e., the investing public").

[11] See Laventhall v. Gen. Dynamics Corp., 704 F.2d 407, 410 (8th Cir.1983) (holding that "corporate insiders must either disclose material inside information known to them or refrain from trading in the shares of the corporation").

[12] See *Texas Gulf Sulphur*, 401 F.2d at 851 n.12 ("We do not suggest that material facts must be disclosed immediately; the timing of disclosure is a matter for the business judgment of the corporate officers entrusted with the management of the corporation within the affirmative disclosure requirements promulgated by the exchanges and by the SEC.").

duty to disclose the discovery, at least up until the time that the land acquisition program was completed.[13]

Given that the corporation had no duty to disclose, and had decided not to disclose the information, the insiders' fiduciary duties to the corporation would preclude them disclosing it for personal gain. In this case, the company's president had specifically instructed insiders in the know to keep the information confidential, but such an instruction was not technically necessary. Agency law precludes a firm's agents from disclosing confidential information that belongs to their corporate principal,[14] as all information relating to the ore strike clearly did.

Disclosure by an insider who wishes to trade thus is only feasible if there is no legitimate corporate purpose for maintaining secrecy. These situations, however, presumably will be relatively rare—it is hard to imagine many business developments that can be disclosed immediately without working some harm to the corporation. In most cases, the disclose or abstain rule really does not provide the insider with a disclosure option; instead, the duty typically will be one of complete abstention.[15]

C. The Equal Access Policy

The policy foundation on which the Second Circuit erected the disclose or abstain rule was equality of access to information. The court contended that the federal insider trading prohibition was intended to assure that "all investors trading on impersonal exchanges have relatively equal access to material information."[16] Put another way, the majority thought Congress intended "that all members of the investing public should be subject to identical market risks."[17]

The equality of access principle admittedly has some intuitive appeal. As we shall see, the SEC consistently has tried to maintain it as the basis of insider trading liability. Many commentators still endorse it on fairness grounds. The implications of the equal access

---

[13] See id. ("Here, a valuable corporate purpose was served by delaying the publication of the K–55–1 discovery.").

[14] See Restatement (Second) of Agency § (1958) (stating that "an agent is subject to a duty to the principal not to use or to communicate information confidentially given him by the principal or acquired by him during the course of or on account of his agency").

[15] See Thomas Lee Hazen, Identifying the Duty Prohibiting Outsider Trading on Material Nonpublic Information, 61 Hastings L.J. 881, 891 (2010) ("Although the disclose or abstain rule is phrased in the alternative, rarely, if ever, is disclosure a viable alternative. Accordingly, the rule boils down to a duty to abstain from trading until the company or other rightful owner of the information makes a decision to disclose it and the information has been digested by the market.").

[16] SEC v. Texas Gulf Sulphur Co., 401 F.2d 833, 848 (2d Cir.1968), cert. denied, 394 U.S. 976 (1969).

[17] Id. at 852.

principle become troubling when we start dealing with attenuated circumstances, however, especially with respect to market information. Suppose a representative of Texas Gulf Sulphur had approached a landowner in the Timmons area to negotiate purchasing the mineral rights to the land. Texas Gulf Sulphur's agent does not disclose the ore strike, but the landowner turns out to be pretty smart. She knows Texas Gulf Sulphur has been drilling in the area and has heard rumors that it has been buying up a lot of mineral rights. She puts two and two together, reaches the obvious conclusion, and buys some Texas Gulf Sulphur stock. Under a literal reading of *Texas Gulf Sulphur*, has our landowner committed illegal insider trading?

The surprising answer is "probably." The *Texas Gulf Sulphur* court stated that the insider trading prohibition applies to "anyone in possession of material inside information," because Congress intended § 10(b) to assure that "all investors trading on impersonal exchanges have relatively equal access to material information."[18] The court further stated that the prohibition applies to anyone who has "access, directly or indirectly" to confidential information (here is the sticking point) if he or she knows that the information is unavailable to the investing public. The only issue thus perhaps would be a factual one turning on the landowner's state of mind; namely, did she know she was dealing with confidential information. If so, the equal access policy would seem to justify imposing a duty on her. Indeed, as the Second Circuit explained in a later case, *Texas Gulf Sulphur* established the proposition that "[a]nyone . . . who regularly receives material nonpublic information may not use that information to trade in securities without incurring an affirmative duty to disclose," whether he or she is a "corporate insider or not."[19] Only the qualifier "regularly" would exempt our farmer.

In effect, *Texas Gulf Sulphur* thus created "a general duty between all participants in market transactions to forgo actions based on material non-public information."[20] Many questioned

---

[18] SEC v. Texas Gulf Sulphur Co., 401 F.2d 833, 847 (2d Cir.), cert. denied, 394 U.S. 976 (1968). To be sure, the farmer in the hypothetical is relying on market information rather than inside information, but we have seen that one can be penalized for trading on the basis of the former just as one can for trading on the latter, see Chapter 1.C.2. In addition, the farmer might argue that she is not "obligated to confer upon outside investors the benefit of [her] superior financial or other expert analysis by disclosing [her] educated guesses or predictions." *Texas Gulf Sulphur*, 401 F.2d at 848. On the other hand, if the information is material, she may be obliged to disclose the "basic facts so that outsiders may draw upon their own evaluative expertise in reaching their own investment decisions with knowledge equal to that of the insiders." Id. at 849.

[19] U.S. v. Chiarella, 588 F.2d 1358, 1365 (2d Cir. 1978), rev'd, 445 U.S. 222 (1980).

[20] Chiarella v. U.S., 445 U.S. 222, 233 (1980).

whether the insider trading prohibition should stretch quite that far. As the prohibition continued to develop, some significant shrinking in fact took place, but that is a story for the next chapter.

D. A Note on Corporate Liability for Misrepresentations

Among many other legal rules established in *Texas Gulf Sulphur* is the principle of corporate liability for misrepresentations or omissions committed by agents of the corporation. Although the Supreme Court has confirmed the implied right of action under Rule 10b–5, it has limited private party standing to persons who actually buy or sell a security.[21] This may seem trivial or obvious, but it is not. Suppose the executives of a company wanted to drive down the price of the firm's stock so that they could buy it for themselves. They put out false bad news about the company. You were considering buying stock in the company but were dissuaded by the bad news put out by the executives. If you later try to sue, arguing that but for the executives' misconduct you would have bought some of the company's stock, the Supreme Court's standing rules will bar you from bringing suit.

Although one must have either purchased or sold a security in order to have standing to sue under Rule 10b–5, one need not have purchased or sold in order to be a proper party defendant. In *Texas Gulf Sulphur*, the defendant corporation issued a misleading press release. Because the corporation had neither bought nor sold any securities during the relevant period, it argued it could not be held liable under Rule 10b–5. The court rejected this argument, observing that Rule 10b–5 on its face prohibits fraud "in connection with the purchase or sale of any security." The court interpreted this language as requiring "only that the device employed, whatever it might be, be of a sort that would cause reasonable investors to rely thereon, and, in connection therewith, so relying, cause them to purchase or sell a corporation's securities."[22]

Interestingly, however, Professors Jonathan Macey and Geoffrey Miller have used *Texas Gulf Sulphur* as an example of why the law should sometimes permit companies to engage in "strategic misrepresentations":

> Texas Gulf Sulphur had secretly discovered huge deposits of copper, zinc, and silver in the Timmins field in Canada. In order to profit from this discovery, Texas Gulf Sulphur had to acquire the mineral rights to the land containing the minerals.

---

[21] Blue Chip Stamps v. Manor Drug Stores, 421 U.S. 723 (1975).

[22] SEC v. Texas Gulf Sulphur Co., 401 F.2d 833 (2d Cir.1968), cert. denied, 394 U.S. 976 (1969).

Had the firm not kept the information confidential, it would have lost some, if not all, of the value of its discovery, because the landowners could have captured these gains by simply raising the price of the mineral rights, mining the minerals themselves, or selling the mineral rights to competing firms. Insider trading based on this confidential information posed a particular threat to Texas Gulf Sulphur shareholders due to the possibility that market professionals would correctly interpret the significance of such trading, thereby compromising Texas Gulf Sulphur's acquisition program. When Texas Gulf Sulphur discovered that some of its officers and directors had been involved in insider trading, the need to protect shareholders' interests by denying any rumors about the discovery became even more acute.[23]

Although those denials would be false, and thus would subject Texas Gulf Sulphur to liability under current law, Professors Macey and Miller contend companies should be allowed to mislead in situations such as the one faced by Texas Gulf Sulphur so as to protect the greater interests of shareholders.[24]

---

[23] Jonathan R. Macey & Geoffrey P. Miller, Good Finance, Bad Economics: An Analysis of the Fraud-on-the-Market Theory, 42 Stan. L. Rev. 1059, 1071 (1990).

[24] See id. (stating that "we would permit insiders to make such strategic misrepresentations even in situations . . . where there is trading by insiders. Indeed, it seems clear that in these circumstances, the advantages to shareholders from strategic misrepresentation are even greater than in other cases.").

Chapter 5

THE SUPREME COURT CREATES THE MODERN FEDERAL INSIDER TRADING PROHIBITION

Although *Strong v. Repide*[1] gave the Supreme Court an early start on insider trading, the prohibition developed without further assistance from the court for over seven decades. In the 1980s, however, the Supreme Court issued two decisions—*Chiarella v. U.S.*[2] and *Dirks v. SEC*[3]—that significantly cut back on the scope of *Texas Gulf Sulphur*'s disclose or abstain rule.

A. *Chiarella v. U.S.*

Vincent Chiarella was an employee of Pandick Press, a financial printer that prepared tender offer disclosure materials, among other documents. In preparing those materials Pandick used codes to conceal the names of the companies involved, but Chiarella broke the codes. He purchased target company shares before the bid was announced, then sold the shares for considerable profits after announcement of the bid.

Chiarella was one of the first of a series of high profile takeover-related insider trading cases during the 1980s. Obviously, one can significantly increase takeover profits if one knows in advance that a takeover will be forthcoming. If you know of an impending bid prior to its announcement, you can buy up stock at the low pre-announcement price and sell or tender at the higher post-announcement price. The earlier one knows of the bid, of course, the greater the spread between your purchase and sale prices and the greater the resulting profit. By using options, rather than actually buying target stock, you can further increase your profits, because options permit one to control larger blocks of stock for the same investment. During the 1980s, a number of Wall Street takeover players—among whom Dennis Levine, Ivan Boesky, and Michael Milken are the best known—allegedly added millions of illegally gained insider trading dollars to the already vast fortunes they realized from more legitimate takeover activity.[4]

---

[1] 213 U.S. 419 (1909).

[2] 445 U.S. 222 (1980).

[3] 463 U.S. 646 (1983).

[4] The volatile mix of takeovers and insider trading is entertainingly depicted in Oliver Stone's movie Wall Street (1987). For a fascinating popular history of the 1980s insider trading scandals, see James B. Stewart, Den of Thieves (1991). For a

39

Relative to some of those who followed him into federal court, Vincent Chiarella was small fry. But his case produced the first landmark Supreme Court insider trading ruling since *Strong v. Repide*.

Chiarella was convicted in a U.S. District Court of violating Rule 10b–5 by trading on the basis of material nonpublic information. The Second Circuit affirmed his conviction, applying the same equality of access to the information-based disclose or abstain rule it had created in *Texas Gulf Sulphur*.[5] Under the equal access-based standard, Chiarella clearly loses; he had greater access to information than those with whom he traded. But notice that Chiarella was not an employee, officer, or director of any of the companies in whose stock he traded. He worked solely for Pandick Press, which in turn was not an agent of any of those companies. Pandick worked for acquiring companies; it did not work for the takeover targets in whose stock Chiarella traded.

Chiarella's conviction thus demonstrated how far the federal insider trading prohibition had departed from its state common law predecessors. Recall that state common law had required, where it imposed liability at all, a fiduciary relationship between buyer and seller. The mere fact that one party had more information than the other was not grounds for setting aside the transaction or imposing damages. Yet, it was for that reason alone that the Second Circuit upheld Chiarella's conviction.[6]

1.   The majority opinion

In a majority opinion written by Justice Lewis Powell, the Supreme Court reversed Chiarella's conviction.[7] In doing so, the court squarely rejected the notion that § 10(b) was intended to assure all investors equal access to information. The Court said it could not affirm Chiarella's conviction without recognizing a

---

spirited defense of Milken, see Daniel R. Fischel, Payback: The Conspiracy to Destroy Michael Milken and his Financial Revolution (1995).

[5] See U.S. v. Chiarella, 588 F.2d 1358 (2d Cir. 1978) ("The draftsmen of our nation's securities laws, rejecting the philosophy of caveat emptor, created a system providing equal access to the information necessary for reasoned and intelligent investment decisions."), rev'd, 445 U.S. 222 (1980); see generally supra Chapter 4.B.

[6] See Chiarella, 588 F.2d at 1362 (opining that the U.S. securities laws "created a system providing equal access to information necessary for reasoned and intelligent investment decisions"); see also id. at 1365 ("Anyone corporate insider or not who regularly receives material nonpublic information may not use that information to trade in securities without incurring an affirmative duty to disclose.").

[7] Chiarella v. U.S., 445 U.S. 222 (1980). For detailed analyses of the *Chiarella* decision from various perspectives, see David C. Bayne, The Insider's Natural Law Duty: *Chiarella* and the "Fiduciary" Fallacy, 19 J. Corp. L. 681 (1994); Frank H. Easterbrook, Insider Trading, Secret Agents, Evidentiary Privileges and the Production of Information, 1981 Sup. Ct. Rev. 309; Donald C. Langevoort, Words From On High About Rule 10b–5: *Chiarella*'s History, Central Bank's Future, 20 Del. J. Corp. L. 865 (1995); Donald C. Langevoort, Insider Trading and the Fiduciary Principle: A Post-*Chiarella* Restatement, 70 Calif. L. Rev. 1 (1982).

general duty between all participants in market transactions to forego trades based on material, nonpublic information, and it refused to impose such a duty.

The *Chiarella* decision thus made clear that the disclose or abstain rule is not triggered merely because the trader possesses material nonpublic information. When a Rule 10b–5 action is based upon nondisclosure, there can be no fraud absent a duty to speak, and no such duty arises from the mere possession of nonpublic information. Instead, the disclose or abstain theory of liability for insider trading was now premised on the inside trader being subject to a duty to disclose to the party on the other side of the transaction that arose from a relationship of trust and confidence between the parties thereto:

> [T]he element required to make silence fraudulent—a duty to disclose—is absent in this case. No duty could arise from petitioner's relationship with the sellers of the target company's securities, for petitioner had no prior dealings with them. He was not their agent, he was not a fiduciary, he was not a person in whom the sellers had placed their trust and confidence. He was, in fact, a complete stranger who dealt with the sellers only through impersonal market transactions.
>
> We cannot affirm petitioner's conviction without recognizing a general duty between all participants in market transactions to forgo actions based on material, nonpublic information. Formulation of such a broad duty, which departs radically from the established doctrine that duty arises from a specific relationship between two parties, should not be undertaken absent some explicit evidence of congressional intent.[8]

Chiarella radically limited the scope of the insider trading prohibition as it had been defined in *Texas Gulf Sulphur*. Consider the landowner hypothetical discussed in the last chapter: Under an equal access to information-based standard, she is liable for insider trading because she had material information unavailable to those with whom she traded. Under *Chiarella*, however, she cannot be held liable. She is neither the agent nor other type of fiduciary of

---

[8] *Chiarella*, 445 U.S. at 232–33 (citation omitted). The court made short work of the recurrent question of whether the insider trading prohibition applies when investors are selling at arms-length to unaffiliated persons or applies just when they are buying from shareholders. The Court did so by favorably noting that the SEC, in *Cady, Roberts*, had "embraced the reasoning of Judge Learned Hand [in Gratz v. Claughton, 187 F.2d 46, 49 (2d Cir.), cert. denied, 341 U.S. 920 (1951).] that 'the director or officer assumed a fiduciary relation to the buyer by the very sale; for it would be a sorry distinction to allow him to use the advantage of his position to induce the buyer into the position of a beneficiary although he was forbidden to do so once the buyer had become one.'" *Chiarella*, 445 U.S. at 227 n.8. Fairly read, the opinion implies that the Supreme Court had likewise embraced that reasoning.

Texas Gulf Sulphur shareholders and, presumably, has no other special relationship of trust and confidence with them. Accordingly, she is free to trade on the basis of what she knows without fear of liability. The policy conundrum now flipped, of course. After *Texas Gulf Sulphur*, the question was how large a net should the prohibition cast. After *Chiarella*, the question was how broad should be the scope of immunity created by the new fiduciary relationship requirement, a question we will take up in the next several Chapters.

2.   The other opinions

In a separate opinion joined by Justice Thurgood Marshall, Justice Harry Blackmun dissented on grounds that neither the statutory text nor the legislative history supported the majority's requirement that there be a breach of a duty arising out of a fiduciary or similar relationship of trust and confidence. Instead, Justice Blackmun argued, the securities laws were intended to broadly ensure fairness in the market place. Accordingly, Justice Blackmun preferred a rule banning use of nonpublic information not lawfully available to the market generally.[9]

Chief Justice Burger dissented on grounds that "a person who has misappropriated nonpublic information has an absolute duty to disclose that information or to refrain from trading."[10] Put another way, Chief Justice Burger thought that illegal insider trading occurred whenever someone trading in the stock market had obtained an informational advantage through unlawful means. His opinion thus foreshadowed, albeit imperfectly, the misappropriation theory as it later evolved.[11] The majority opinion declined "decide whether this theory has merit" because Burger's standard "was not submitted to the jury" in its instructions.[12] As the Court explained, because it "cannot affirm a criminal conviction on the basis of a theory not presented to the jury, [the Court would] not speculate upon whether such a duty exists, whether it has been breached, or whether such a breach constitutes a violation of § 10(b)."[13]

Justice Brennan concurred with the majority's result. In his separate opinion, he explained that he agreed with the Chief Justice that the use of misappropriated information was unlawful. In this specific case, however, the jury had not been instructed "that one element of the offense was the improper conversion or

---

[9] Id. at 246–47 (Blackmun, J., dissenting).

[10] Id. at 240 (Burger, C.J., dissenting).

[11] See infra Chapter 7.C.

[12] *Chiarella*, 445 U.S. at 234.

[13] Id. at 236–37.

misappropriation of that nonpublic information."[14] In the absence of such an instruction, Brennan agreed with the majority, the misappropriation theory could not be used to sustain Chiarella's conviction. Justice Stevens also concurred on similar grounds, albeit without explicitly endorsing a misappropriation theory.[15]

B. *Dirks v. SEC*

In the 1960s and early 1970s, Equity Funding Corporation of America appeared to be a hugely successful financial services conglomerate selling insurance, mutual funds, and other investments to retail customers. In fact, however, since at least 1964, at least 100 Equity Funding senior employees had engaged in one of the massive accounting frauds in U.S. history. Among other things, for example, they set up a computer dedicated exclusively to documenting fictional insurance policies that were then recorded on the company's balance sheet as assets and whose purported premia were recorded on the company's income statement.

Raymond Dirks was a securities analyst who played a critical role in uncovering the massive Equity Funding fraud. Dirks first began investigating Equity Funding after receiving allegations from Ronald Secrist, a former officer of Equity Funding, that the corporation was engaged in widespread fraudulent corporate practices. Dirks passed the results of his investigation to the SEC and the Wall Street Journal, but also discussed his findings with various clients. A number of those clients sold their holdings of Equity Funding securities before any public disclosure of the fraud, thereby avoiding substantial losses. After the fraud was made public and Equity Funding went into receivership, the SEC began an investigation of Dirk's role in exposing the fraud. One might think Dirks deserved a medal (one suspects Mr. Dirks definitely felt that way), but one would be wrong.[16] The SEC censured Dirks for violating the federal insider trading prohibition by repeating the allegations of fraud to his clients.

Under the *Texas Gulf Sulphur* equal access to information standard, tipping of the sort at issue in *Dirks* presented no conceptual problems. The tippee had access to information unavailable to those with whom he traded and, as such, is liable. After *Chiarella*, however, the tipping problem was more complex. Neither Dirks nor any of his customers were agents, officers, or

---

[14] *Chiarella*, 445 U.S. at 239 (Brennan, J., concurring).

[15] Id. at 238 (Stevens, J., concurring).

[16] The extent to which Dirks should be credited with exposing the Equity Funding fraud is a matter of debate. Arguably, it was not until state insurance regulators from California and Illinois conducted a surprise audit of an Equity Funding subsidiary that the fraud actually came to light. See Dirks v. SEC, 463 U.S. 646, 669 n.2 (1983) (Blackmun, J., dissenting).

directors of Equity Funding. Likewise, none of them had any other form of special relationship of trust and confidence with those with whom they traded.

In reversing Dirk's censure, the Supreme Court expressly reaffirmed its rejection of the equal access standard and its requirement of a breach of fiduciary duty in order for liability to be imposed. Again writing for the majority, Justice Powell explained that:

> We were explicit in *Chiarella* in saying that there can be no duty to disclose where the person who has traded on inside information "was not [the corporation's] agent, . . . was not a fiduciary, [or] was not a person in whom the sellers [of the securities] had placed their trust and confidence." Not to require such a fiduciary relationship, we recognized, would "depar[t] radically from the established doctrine that duty arises from a specific relationship between two parties" and would amount to "recognizing a general duty between all participants in market transactions to forgo actions based on material, nonpublic information."[17]

Recognizing that this formulation posed problems for tipping cases, the court held that a tippee's liability is derivative of that of the tipper, "arising from [the tippee's] role as a participant after the fact in the insider's breach of a fiduciary duty." A tippee therefore can be held liable only when the tipper breached a fiduciary duty by disclosing information to the tippee, and the tippee knows or has reason to know of the breach of duty.[18]

On the *Dirks* facts, this formulation precluded imposition of liability. To be sure, Secrist was an employee and, hence, a fiduciary of Equity Funding. But the mere fact that an insider tips nonpublic information is not enough under *Dirks*. What *Dirks* effectively proscribes is not merely a breach of confidentiality by the insider, but rather the breach of a fiduciary duty of loyalty to refrain from profiting on information entrusted to the tipper.[19]

---

[17] Dirks v. SEC, 463 U.S. 646, 654–55 (1983) (citations omitted).

[18] Justice Blackmun dissented in an opinion joined by Justices Brennan and Marshall. See Dirks v. SEC, 463 U.S. 646, 677 (1983) (Blackmun, J., dissenting) ("The court justifies Secrist's and Dirks' action because the general benefit derived from the violation of Secrist's duty to shareholders outweighed the harm caused to those shareholders, . . . in other words, because the end justified the means. Under this view, the benefit conferred on society by Secrist's and Dirks' activities may be paid for with the losses caused to shareholders trading with Dirks' clients.").

[19] Technically, of course, Rule 10b–5 liability is grounded not on a breach of fiduciary duty but on violation of a disclosure obligation. Under *Dirks*, the tippee has a duty of disclosure to those with whom he trades where the tipper breaches a fiduciary duty by making the tip. Hence, the tippee does not succeed to any fiduciary duty. Instead, it is the tippee's duty of disclosure that is said to be derivative of the tipper's breach of duty.

Looking at objective criteria, courts must determine whether the insider-tipper personally benefited, directly or indirectly, from his disclosure. Secrist tipped off Dirks in order to bring Equity Funding's misconduct to light, not for any personal gain. Absent the requisite personal benefit, liability could not be imposed.[20]

C. Powell's Motivation

By virtue of having been assigned both *Chiarella* and *Dirks*, Justice Powell had the opportunity to define the basic outline of the modern insider trading prohibition. Subsequent courts have had to work within the limits he established. The question of what motivated Powell's approach to these cases thus takes on considerable import. Professor Adam Pritchard has made a detailed study not only of the opinions but also of the background materials available in the late Justice Powell's papers.[21] Pritchard concludes that:

> These opinions reflect Powell's unease with the SEC's efforts to expand Rule 10b–5 through aggressive interpretation. Powell thought "that the SEC should have gone to Congress long ago. Rather, it has elected to write expansive Rules (e.g., Rule 10b–5, drafted by Louis Loss one morning), and then undertake to extend the vague language of the Rule to the edge of rationality." Powell saw Rule 10b–5's jurisprudence as a species of "federal common law." The courts needed to develop workable rules. This common law perspective gave wide latitude for policy. Powell worried that prohibitions against insider trading could chill incentives for analysts and other market professionals to uncover information about publicly traded companies.[22]

Powell's concern for market professionals was brought back to the fore of insider trading litigation by the rash of prosecutions in the early part of this decade of hedge fund managers and the so-called expert networks on which those managers relied for information. Expert networks were developed in the last decade to act as matchmakers between experts in various fields and financial market professionals. If a hedge fund manager wanted to consult with a physician about the likely effectiveness of a new drug or medical device before investing in the firm that had produced it, the expert witness would arrange for the manager to meet with the

---

[20] The Eleventh Circuit has held that the personal benefit requirement applies to tipping cases brought under the misappropriation theory of liability, rejecting an SEC argument to the contrary. SEC v. Yun, 327 F.3d 1263 (11th Cir. 2003).

[21] A.C. Pritchard, Justice Lewis F. Powell, Jr., and the Counterrevolution in the Federal Securities Laws, 52 Duke L.J. 841 (2003).

[22] Id. at 930–31.

right expert. The consultant would get a handsome fee and the network would get a finder's fee. All too often, however, the expert turned out to be an insider of the company in question who passed inside information to the hedge fund manager.

In *Dirks*, however, Justice Powell had based his ruling in large part on a concern that overly zealous enforcement of insider trading bans can have a highly detrimental effect on market efficiency:

> Imposing a duty to disclose or abstain solely because a person knowingly receives material nonpublic information from an insider and trades on it could have an inhibiting influence on the role of market analysts, which the SEC itself recognizes is necessary to the preservation of a healthy market. It is commonplace for analysts to "ferret out and analyze information," 21 S.E.C. Docket at 1406, and this often is done by meeting with and questioning corporate officers and others who are insiders. And information that the analysts obtain normally may be the basis for judgments as to the market worth of a corporation's securities. The analyst's judgment in this respect is made available in market letters or otherwise to clients of the firm. It is the nature of this type of information, and indeed of the markets themselves, that such information cannot be made simultaneously available to all of the corporation's stockholders or the public generally.[23]

In a footnote to that passage, Powell further explained that the SEC itself "expressly recognized that '[t]he value to the entire market of [analysts'] efforts cannot be gainsaid; market efficiency in pricing is significantly enhanced by [their] initiatives to ferret out and analyze information, and thus the analyst's work redounds to the benefit of all investors.' "[24]

Notice that Powell expressly endorsed allowing market analysts to "meet[ ] with and question[ ] corporate officers and others who are insiders. . . ." Facilitating such meetings is precisely what expert networks do. To be sure, that doesn't give the networks a license to facilitate tipping by insiders. But it is nevertheless fair to wonder whether the targeting of expert networks was overdone and thereby chilled legitimate market analysis. If so, such targeting may have done more damage to market efficiency than any of the alleged insider trading activity.

Pritchard explains that Powell also was concerned with the impact of insider trading regulation on the efficient functioning of capital markets:

---

[23] Dirks v. SEC, 463 U.S. 646, 658–59 (1983).

[24] Id. at 658 n.17.

He saw the SEC's efforts to impose a "parity of information" rule as undermining "incentives to perform market research in order to discover undervalued stocks and thereby bring about a more efficient allocation of resources." Powell agreed with a student author in the Harvard Law Review: "[t]he courts must also recognize . . . the importance of preserving incentives for legitimate economic effort, such as gathering new information or perceptively analyzing generally available facts."[25]

As we will see in Chapter 13.A.1 the question of how insider trading affects efficient pricing of securities in the capital markets is a key part of the policy debate over whether and, if so, how insider trading should be regulated.

---

[25] Pritchard, supra note 21, at 931.

Chapter 6

THE DISCLOSE OR ABSTAIN RULE TODAY

Taken together, *Chiarella* and *Dirks* replaced the *Texas Gulf Sulphur* insider trading regime with a much narrower one. In this chapter, we explore the elements of the modern post-*Chiarella* disclose or abstain rule.

A. The Requisite Fiduciary Relationship and the Class of Potential Defendants

1. The fiduciary duty requirement

In both *Chiarella* and *Dirks*, the Supreme Court frequently spoke of the need to show the existence of a "fiduciary relationship" as a predicate to liability.[1] As Justice Frankfurter observed, however, albeit in a different context, "to say that a man is a fiduciary only begins analysis; it gives direction to further inquiry. To whom is he a fiduciary? What obligations does he owe as a fiduciary? In what respect has he failed to discharge those obligations?"[2] Only one passage in Justice Powell's *Dirks* opinion suggests an answer to those questions and it does so in a most unsatisfactory way:

> In the seminal case of *In re Cady, Roberts & Co.*, the SEC recognized that the common law in some jurisdictions imposes on "corporate 'insiders,' particularly officers, directors, or controlling shareholders" an "affirmative duty of disclosure . . . when dealing in securities." The SEC found that . . . breach of this common law duty also establish[ed] the elements of a Rule 10b–5 violation. . . .[3]

While Justice Powell's opinion acknowledged that this common-law duty exists only in "some jurisdictions," he went on—without any explanation or citation of authority—to extrapolate therefrom a rule that all "insiders [are] forbidden by their fiduciary relationship from personally using undisclosed corporate information to their advantage."[4] Given that such a rule exists only in "some jurisdictions," the requisite fiduciary obligation apparently

---

[1] See, e.g., Dirks v. SEC, 463 U.S. 646, 654 (1983); Chiarella v. U.S., 445 U.S. 222, 232 (1980).

[2] SEC v. Chenery Corp., 318 U.S. 80, 85–86 (1943).

[3] *Dirks*, 463 U.S. at 653.

[4] Id. at 659.

arises out of federal—not state—law. A federal source for the fiduciary relationship element also is suggested by Justice Powell's contention "that '[a] significant purpose of the Exchange Act was to eliminate the idea that use of inside information for personal advantage was a normal emolument of corporate office.' "[5] His repeated references to a *"Cady, Roberts* duty" may also point towards a federal source for the requisite duty. There is at least the implication that *Cady, Roberts* created a federal duty prohibiting insider trading, which has become part of the overall bundle of fiduciary duties to which insiders are subject.

This understanding of *Dirks* was implicitly confirmed by the Supreme Court's more recent decision in *U.S. v. O'Hagan*.[6] The majority reaffirmed the *Chiarella/Dirks* requirement of a fiduciary relationship, broadly holding that the "relationship of trust and confidence" between insiders and shareholders "gives rise to a duty to disclose" or to abstain.[7] Again, given that many states impose no such duty on corporate officers and directors, one might reasonably assume that the duty of which the court spoke is federal in origin.

Accordingly, in applying the modern disclose or abstain rule, one must first determine whether a fiduciary relationship exists between the inside trader and those with whom he is about to trade. Presumably one looks to federal law to make that determination, although we shall see that this proves quite problematic.[8] If the requisite fiduciary relationship is present, the disclose or abstain obligation attaches.

As Justice Frankfurter's comment suggests, however, any given fiduciary relationship carries with it a number of obligations. The nature of those obligations, moreover, varies from one type of fiduciary relationship to another. A corporate director may enter into various types of contracts with the corporation, for example, that would be barred in the case of a trustee dealing with trust assets. The question thus arises as to which of the various duties to which corporate insiders are subject is the relevant one in this context. Unfortunately, the Supreme Court once again was not very

---

[5] Id. at 662 (quoting In re Cady, Roberts & Co., 40 S.E.C. 907, 912 n.15 (1961)).

[6] 521 U.S. 642 (1997). Although *O'Hagan* arose under the so-called misappropriation theory, rather than the disclose or abstain rule, this aspect of the opinion appears to be of general applicability.

[7] Id. at 652.

[8] See Chapter 7.B.1. But see S.E.C. v. Cochran, 214 F.3d 1261 (10th Cir. 2000) (holding that "a duty to disclose under § 10(b) may be present if either a federal statute (other than § 10(b) itself) or state statutory or common law recognizes a fiduciary or similar relationship of trust and confidence giving rise to such a duty between the defendant and the plaintiff. We express no view as to whether there might be additional sources for such a duty, such as professional rules of conduct or federal common law.").

precise on this score. Its opinions speak mainly of a duty to disclose before trading, but left the issue uncertain.

Some courts phrased the inquiry in terms of a duty of confidentiality—asking whether the inside trader had violated a duty to keep the information in question confidential.[9] Using a duty of confidentiality as the requisite fiduciary duty, however, makes little sense in the insider trading context. Unlike most types of tangible property, more than one person can use the same piece of information at the same time. An insider's use of information, moreover, does not necessarily lower its value to its corporate owner. When an executive that has just negotiated a major contract for his employer thereafter inside trades in the employer's stock, for example, the value of the contract to the employer has not been lowered nor, absent some act of disclosure, has the executive violated his duty of confidentiality. Using nonpublic information for personal gain thus is not inconsistent with a duty of confidentiality, unless one's trades somehow reveal the information.

Alternatively, one might conclude that the fiduciary duty requirement requires a breach by the inside trader of a duty to refrain from self-dealing in nonpublic information. This conclusion finds some support in *Dirks*. Justice Powell, for example, described the elements of an insider trading violation as: "(i) the existence of a relationship affording access to inside information intended to be available only for a corporate purpose, and (ii) the unfairness of allowing a corporate insider to take advantage of that information by trading without disclosure."[10] Another passage likewise described insider trading liability as arising from "the 'inherent unfairness involved where one takes advantage' of 'information intended to be available only for a corporate purpose and not for the personal benefit of anyone.'"[11] Yet another noted that insiders are "forbidden by their fiduciary relationship from using undisclosed

---

[9] See, e.g., U.S. v. Libera, 989 F.2d 596 (2d Cir.1993), cert. denied, 510 U.S. 976 (1993); U.S. v. Carpenter, 791 F.2d 1024, 1034 (2d Cir.1986), aff'd on other grounds, 484 U.S. 19 (1987).

This phrasing is especially common in cases arising under the misappropriation theory. See SEC Rule 10b5–2(b)(1) (stating that the requisite "duty of trust or confidence" exists whenever "a person agrees to maintain information in confidence."); see also S.E.C. v. Yun, 327 F.3d 1263, 1272–73 (11th. Cir. 2003) (holding that "a spouse who trades in breach of a reasonable and legitimate expectation of confidentiality held by the other spouse sufficiently subjects the former to insider trading liability. . . . Of course, a breach of an agreement to maintain business confidences would also suffice."); SEC v. Kirch, 2003 WL 21459647 (N.D.Ill.2003) (holding "that the 'duty of loyalty and confidentiality' owed by the outsider . . . to the person . . . who shared confidential information with him or her . . . is not limited to fiduciary relationships in the limited sense that requires such factors as control and dominance on the part of the fiduciary. Instead that 'duty of loyalty and confidentiality' can be (and is) created by precisely the type of [confidentiality] policy and expectations that are present . . . here. . . .").

[10] Dirks v. SEC, 463 U.S. 646, 653 (1983).

[11] Id. at 654.

corporate information for their personal gain."[12] The focus in each instance is on the duty to refrain from self-dealing.

This approach, however, would exacerbate the tension between the Supreme Court's insider trading regime and the rest of its Rule 10b–5 jurisprudence. In *Santa Fe Industries, Inc. v. Green*,[13] the Supreme Court held that Rule 10b–5 is concerned with disclosure and fraud, not with fiduciary duties.[14] The court did so in large measure out of a concern that the contrary decision would result in federalizing much of state corporate law and thereby overriding well-established state policies of corporate regulation. While its holding is not squarely on point, the rationale of *Santa Fe* seems directly applicable to the insider trading prohibition. The court held, for example, that Rule 10b–5 did not reach claims "in which the essence of the complaint is that shareholders were treated

---

[12] Id. at 659.

[13] 430 U.S. 462 (1977). In that case, the plaintiffs were minority shareholders of a Santa Fe subsidiary who were dissatisfied with the consideration they were paid for their stock in a short-form merger Santa Fe had effected with the subsidiary. Although plaintiffs had state law remedies, such as the statutory appraisal proceeding, they opted to sue under Rule 10b–5. Plaintiffs claimed that the merger violated Rule 10b–5 because it was effected without prior notice to the minority shareholders and was done without any legitimate business purpose. They also claimed that their shares had been undervalued. Both claims raised, quite directly, the question of what conduct is covered by the rule. The Supreme Court held that plaintiffs had not stated a cause of action under Rule 10b–5.

Drawing on the plain text and legislative history of the rule, the court concluded that a 10b–5 cause of action arises only out of deception or manipulation. Deception requires a misrepresentation or omission. Because the plaintiffs received full disclosure, there was no misrepresentation or omission. In addition, neither of plaintiffs' claims went to disclosure violations; rather, both went to the substance of the transaction. Plaintiffs were not claiming that Santa Fe lied to them, but that the transaction was unfair. In other words, they were claiming that a breach of fiduciary duty gives rise to a cause of action under 10b–5. The Supreme Court held that a mere breach of duty will not give rise to liability under 10b–5.

Manipulation is conduct intended to mislead investors by artificially affecting market activity. In other words, defendant must engage in conduct that creates artificial changes in the price of a security or volume of trading in a security. Again, Santa Fe was mainly being charged with a breach of the state law fiduciary duties a majority shareholder owes to minority shareholders. Nothing Santa Fe did constituted unlawful manipulation.

In addition to its textual arguments, the Supreme Court also relied on policy considerations grounded in federalism. The court clearly was concerned that allowing plaintiffs to go forward in this case would federalize much of state corporate law, in many cases overriding well-established state policies of corporate regulation. In the court's view, if the Santa Fe plaintiffs were allowed to sue, every breach of fiduciary duty case would give rise to a federal claim under Rule 10b–5. The court refused to give the Rule 10b–5 such an expansive reach, instead holding that it did not reach "transactions which constitute no more than internal corporate mismanagement." Id. at 479. *Santa Fe* was a critical holding in Rule 10b–5's evolution, putting the substantive fairness of a transaction outside the rule's scope. The rule henceforth was limited to disclosure violations. *Santa Fe* also implied a second—and potentially even more significant—constraint on the rule in suggesting that misconduct covered by state corporate law should be left to state law. For a more detailed treatment of the relationship between *Santa Fe* and the Supreme Court's insider trading jurisprudence, see Stephen M. Bainbridge, Incorporating State Law Fiduciary Duties into the Federal Insider Trading Prohibition, 52 Wash & Lee L. Rev. 1189, 1258–61 (1995).

[14] See Chapter 7.B.1.

unfairly by a fiduciary."[15] This is of course the very essence of the complaint made in insider trading cases. The court also held that extension of Rule 10b–5 to breaches of fiduciary duty was unjustified in light of the state law remedies available to plaintiffs. As we have seen, insider trading plaintiffs likewise have state law remedies available to them. Granted, those remedies vary from state to state and are likely to prove unavailing in many cases, but the same was true of the state law appraisal remedy at issue in *Santa Fe.* Finally, the court expressed reluctance "to federalize the substantial portion of the law of corporations that deals with transactions in securities, particularly where established state policies of corporate regulation would be overridden."[16] In view of the state law standards discussed in Chapter 2 above, of course, this is precisely what the federal insider trading prohibition did. Given that *Santa Fe* requires that all other corporate fiduciary duties be left to state law, why should insider trading be singled out for special treatment?

Dirks and *Chiarella* simply ignored the doctrinal tension between their fiduciary duty-based regime and Santa Fe. In *O'Hagan*, Justice Ginsburg's majority opinion sought to solve the problem by describing *Santa Fe* as "underscoring that § 10(b) is not an all-purpose breach of fiduciary duty ban; rather it trains on conduct involving manipulation or deception."[17] Accordingly, she held that federal law focuses on the failure to disclose that one is about to inside trade. She thus explained that a "fiduciary who '[pretends] loyalty to the principal while secretly converting the principal's information for personal gain' . . . 'dupes' or defrauds the principal."[18]

---

[15] Id. at 477.

[16] Id. at 479.

[17] U.S. v. O'Hagan, 521 U.S. 642, 655 (1997).

[18] Id. at 653–54. Justice Ginsburg's approach fails to solve the problem. Granted, insider trading involves deception in the sense that the defendant by definition failed to disclose nonpublic information before trading. Persons subject to the disclose or abstain theory, however, often are also subject to a state law-based fiduciary duty of confidentiality, which precludes them from disclosing the information. As to them, the insider trading prohibition collapses into a requirement to abstain from trading on material nonpublic information. As such, it really is their failure to abstain from trading, rather than their nondisclosure, which is the basis for imposing liability. A former SEC Commissioner more or less admitted as much: "Unlike much securities regulation, the insider trading rules probably do not result in more information coming into the market: The 'abstain or disclose' rule for those entrusted with confidential information usually is observed by abstention." Charles C. Cox & Kevin S. Fogarty, Bases of Insider Trading Law, 49 Ohio St. L.J. 353 (1988). Yet, *Santa Fe* clearly precludes the creation of such duties. The conceptual conflict between the Supreme Court's current insider trading jurisprudence and its more general Rule 10b–5 precedents remains unresolved. See generally Stephen M. Bainbridge, Incorporating State Law Fiduciary Duties into the Federal Insider Trading Prohibition, 52 Wash. & Lee L. Rev. 1189 (1995); Richard W. Painter et al., Don't Ask, Just Tell: Insider Trading after United States v. O'Hagan, 84 Va. L. Rev. 153 (1998); Larry E. Ribstein, Federalism and Insider Trading, 6 Sup. Ct Econ. Rev. 123 (1998).

In other words, the predicate for insider trading liability under the disclose or abstain rule is the breach of a duty of disclosure arising out of a fiduciary relationship or similar relationship of trust and confidence between the insider and the person with whom she trades. As a result, the disclose or abstain rule focuses on insiders and certain outsiders whose affairs are so closely linked with that of the corporation as to make them constructively insiders.

2. Insiders

At common law, the insider trading prohibition focused on corporate officers and directors. As Chapter 14 explains, the short-swing profit insider trading restrictions provided by § 16(b) similarly are likewise limited to officers, directors, and shareholders owning more than 10 percent of the company's stock. One of the many issues resolved in the seminal *Texas Gulf Sulphur* case was whether the prohibition is restricted to that class of persons. Some of the defendants in that case were mere middle managers and even field workers, who were far down the corporate organizational chart from the rarified level occupied by Section 16 insiders. The *Texas Gulf Sulphur* court nevertheless had little difficulty finding that such mid-level corporate employees were insiders for purposes of Rule 10b–5, holding that "directors or management officers are, of course, by this Rule, precluded from [insider] dealing, but the Rule is also applicable to one possessing [nonpublic] information who may not be strictly termed an 'insider' within the meaning of [section] 16(b) of the Act."[19]

Did *Chiarella's* rejection of the equal access test reopen the question of how far down the corporate ladder Rule 10b–5 extended? Recall that the Supreme Court had said Chiarella could not be held liable under Rule 10b–5 because, as to the target companies' shareholders, "he was not their agent, he was not a fiduciary, [and] he was not a person in whom the sellers had placed their trust and confidence."[20] Are all corporate employees—even those at the very bottom of the organization chart—such persons?

As an example, suppose Anna Abel is a geologist employed by Acme Mining Company. She is assigned to do exploratory work, looking for new mines. In the course of her work, Anna discovers a substantial ore deposit. Before informing her bosses of the discovery, Anna buys 10,000 shares of Acme stock.

---

[19] SEC v. Texas Gulf Sulphur Co., 401 F.2d 833, 848 (2d Cir.), cert. denied, 394 U.S. 976 (1969).

[20] Chiarella v. U.S., 445 U.S. 222, 232 (1980).

Anna obviously is not a person in whom Acme's shareholders have placed their trust and confidence—after all, Acme's shareholders likely do not even know of Anna's existence. On the other hand, Anna is an agent of Acme and, as such, will be deemed a fiduciary of Acme's shareholders for purposes of Rule 10b–5.[21] Persons higher up the organization chart, such as officers, directors, and controlling shareholders likewise will be deemed insiders subject to the disclose or abstain rule.[22]

Suppose, however, that Anna had written a memo to her supervisors describing the ore discovery. A janitorial employee of Acme's discovered the memo while cleaning Anna's office and bought a few shares. Although the janitor may be an agent of Acme, he is not a key employee given access to confidential information for a corporate purpose. Even so, the prevailing view is that the janitor will be deemed an insider.[23]

What about former insiders who have quit, been fired, or retired? The prevailing view is that they remain insiders with respect to information acquired before their termination even if they wait to trade until after they have left the firm.[24]

3. Constructive insiders

What about persons who have a close relationship to the issuer but are not employees, directors, or shareholders of the issuer? As an example, suppose Barry Baker is Acme Mining Company's CEO. Barry informs Acme's outside counsel, Carla Charles, that the company has made a major ore discovery and asks her to work on legal issues relating to it. Carla thereupon secretly buys 1,000 shares of Acme stock. Although Carla owes fiduciary duties to Acme by virtue of the lawyer-client relationship, she is not a classic insider. She is more akin to an independent contractor than an employee. Nevertheless, the Supreme Court has made clear that persons such as Carla can be treated as though they are insiders:

> Under certain circumstances, such as where corporate information is revealed legitimately to an underwriter, accountant, lawyer, or consultant working for the corporation,

---

[21] See Restatement (Third) of Agency § 1.01 (2006) ("Agency is [a] fiduciary relationship. . . .").

[22] Moss v. Morgan Stanley Inc., 719 F.2d 5, 10 (2d Cir.1983), cert. denied, 465 U.S. 1025 (1984) (stating that "it is well settled that traditional corporate 'insiders'— directors, officers and persons who have access to confidential information—must preserve the confidentiality of nonpublic information that belongs to and emanates from the corporation").

[23] See, e.g., SEC v. Falbo, 14 F. Supp.2d 508 (S.D.N.Y. 1998) (holding secretary and electrical contractor liable for trading in employer's stock on the basis of material nonpublic information they learned in the course of their employment).

[24] William K.S. Wang & Marc I. Steinberg, Insider Trading 306–07 (3d ed. 2010).

these outsiders may become fiduciaries of the shareholders. The basis for recognizing this fiduciary duty is not simply that such persons acquired nonpublic corporate information, but rather that they have entered into a special confidential relationship in the conduct of the business of the enterprise and are given access to information solely for corporate purposes. . . . For such a duty to be imposed, however, the corporation must expect the outsider to keep the disclosed nonpublic information confidential, and the relationship at least must imply such a duty.[25]

Under this formulation, Carla Charles is a so-called constructive insider. She entered into a confidential relationship with Acme—specifically, a lawyer-client relationship—in the course of the company's business.[26] She was given access to information about the ore strike for a corporate purpose—to work on legal issues relating to the discovery. Even in the absence of any explicit expectation of confidentiality on the corporation's part, courts dealing with inside trading by lawyers in such cases typically have inferred both the requisite expectation and the duty to respect it.

To explore the outer limits of the constructive insider theory, consider the following examples. First, David Delta is Acme Mining Company's chief geologist. As a going away present for his daughter Donna, who is leaving home for college, David tells her about the company's major ore discovery. Donna thereupon secretly buys 100 Acme shares. Second, a few days later David goes out for after work drinks with a close friend, Edward Eagle. David has a few too many adult beverages and, in the course of his drunken ramblings, starts talking about the company's ore strike. Edward, who is unaffiliated with Acme, thereupon secretly buys 10,000 Acme shares.

Although Donna Delta and Eddie Eagle also learned of the ore strike from corporate sources, neither will be deemed constructive

---

[25] Dirks v. SEC, 463 U.S. 646, 655 n. 14 (1983). Note that for a constructive insider to face liability, the *Dirks* formulation seems to require that she trade on the basis of information learned from the issuer. If the alleged constructive insider learned the information from other sources, she has not been "given access to information solely for corporate purposes" and thus should not be subject to the disclose or abstain rule. If so, is the same true of classical insiders? Suppose a CEO learned confidential information about his company from another source from which he inferred that the company's stock would soon drop in price. On the basis of that information, the CEO sold some of the shares of company stock he owned. The SEC takes the position that the CEO would be liable in that situation, but it has been persuasively argued that "the duty to disclose extends only to information received as a result of acting as in the [insider's] fiduciary capacity [vis-à-vis the issuer]." Donald C. Langevoort Insider Trading: Regulation, Enforcement, and Prevention § 3.7 at 3–12 (2012).

[26] See U.S. v. Chestman, 947 F.2d 551, 568 (2nd Cir.1991) (identifying the attorney and client relationship as one of several examples of "hornbook fiduciary relations" for purposes of the insider trading prohibition), cert. denied, 503 U.S. 1004 (1992).

insiders. Neither entered into a confidential relationship with Acme. For an outsider to be treated as a constructive insider, moreover, there must be both an affirmative expectation that the recipient of the information will use the information solely for the benefit of the issuer, and some sort of assent to that duty. Neither Donna nor Eddie agreed to respect the confidentiality of the information, nor did either have any sort of relationship with Acme from which such an agreement might be implied.

Although *Dirks* clearly requires that the recipient of the information in some way agree to keep it confidential, courts have sometimes overlooked that requirement. In *SEC v. Lund*,[27] for example, Lund and another businessman discussed a proposed joint venture between their respective companies. In those discussions, Lund received confidential information about the other's firm. Lund thereafter bought stock in the other's company. The court determined that by virtue of their close personal and professional relationship, and because of the business context of the discussion, Lund was a constructive insider of the issuer. In doing so, however, the court focused almost solely on the issuer's expectation of confidentiality. It failed to inquire into whether Lund had agreed to keep the information confidential.

Lund is usefully contrasted with *Walton v. Morgan Stanley & Co.*[28] Morgan Stanley represented a company considering acquiring Olinkraft Corporation in a friendly merger. During exploratory negotiations Olinkraft gave Morgan confidential information. Morgan's client ultimately decided not to pursue the merger, but Morgan allegedly later passed the acquired information to another client planning a tender offer for Olinkraft. In addition, Morgan's arbitrage department made purchases of Olinkraft stock for its own account. The Second Circuit held that Morgan was not a fiduciary of Olinkraft, because, "[p]ut bluntly, although, according to the complaint, Olinkraft's management placed its confidence in Morgan Stanley not to disclose the information, Morgan owed no duty to observe that confidence."[29] Although *Walton* was decided under state law, it has been cited approvingly in a number of federal insider trading opinions and is generally regarded as a more accurate statement of the law than *Lund*.[30] Indeed, a subsequent

---

[27] 570 F. Supp. 1397 (C.D.Cal.1983). Even under *Lund*, neither Donna nor Eddie should have liability. Unlike Lund, neither of our hypotheticals involved disclosures made in the course of business negotiations. Both involved purely personal relationships.

[28] 623 F.2d 796 (2d Cir.1980).

[29] Id. at 799.

[30] See, e.g., Dirks v. SEC, 463 U.S. 646, 662 n. 22 (1983); U.S. v. Chestman, 947 F.2d 551, 567–58 (2d Cir.1991), cert. denied, 503 U.S. 1004 (1992); Moss v. Morgan Stanley Inc., 719 F.2d 5 (2d Cir.1983), cert. denied, 465 U.S. 1025 (1984).

case from the same district court in which the *Lund* case had been tried effectively acknowledged that *Lund* had been wrongly decided:

> What the Court seems to be saying in *Lund* is that anytime a person is given information by an issuer with an expectation of confidentiality or limited use, he becomes an insider of the issuer. But under *Dirks*, that is not enough; the individual must have expressly or impliedly entered into a fiduciary relationship with the issuer.[31]

Even this statement does not go far enough, however, because it does not acknowledge the additional requirement of an affirmative assumption of the duty of confidentiality.[32]

4.   Is the issuer an insider?

Suppose Ajax Corporation begins a program of repurchasing its own stock. At all relevant times, Ajax possesses—and is trading on the basis of—material nonpublic information about itself. Is Ajax guilty of insider trading? Yes. Many judicial decisions confirm that the issuer is subject to the same disclose or abstain rule that applies to its insiders, such that an issuer who trades in its own securities on the basis of material nonpublic information violates Rule 10b–5.[33] An issuer selling securities avoids this problems—as well as complies with the requirements of the Securities Act of 1933—by making a public offering in which investors receive a prospectus or

---

[31] SEC v. Ingram, 694 F. Supp. 1437, 1440 (C.D.Cal.1988).

[32] See SEC v. Talbot, 430 F. Supp.2d 1029 (C.D. Cal. 2006) (holding that absent an express agreement to maintain the confidentiality of information, the mere reposing of confidential information in another does not give rise to the necessary fiduciary duty).

[33] See, e.g., Shaw v. Digital Equip. Corp., 82 F.3d 1194, 1204 (1st Cir.1996) (stating that, if corporate issuers of stock were not subject to liability under the insiders-trading law, "a corporate issuer selling its own securities would be left free to exploit its informational trading advantage, at the expense of investors, by delaying disclosure of material nonpublic negative news until after completion of the offering"), superseded by statute on other grounds, 15 U.S.C. § 78u–4(b)(1)–(2); McCormick v. Fund American Companies, Inc., 26 F.3d 869, 876 (9th Cir. 1994) ("Numerous authorities have held or otherwise stated that the corporate issuer in possession of material nonpublic information, must, like other insiders in the same situation, disclose that information to its shareholders or refrain from trading with them."); Smith v. Duff & Phelps, Inc., 891 F.2d 1567, 1572–75 (11th Cir.1990) (holding that the issuer has a duty to disclose merger negotiations to an employee who departs voluntarily and cashes in his shares as a condition of termination); Jordan v. Duff & Phelps, Inc., 815 F.2d 429, 435–39 (7th Cir.1987) (same), cert. dismissed, 485 U.S. 901 (1988); Kohler v. Kohler Co., 319 F.2d 634, 638 (7th Cir.1963) (stating that "underlying principles [mandating disclosure of material nonpublic information] apply not only to majority stockholders of corporations and corporate insiders, but equally to corporations themselves"); In re Thornburg Mortg., Inc. Sec. Litig., 824 F. Supp.2d 1214, 1246 (D. N.M. 2011) ("The abstain-or-disclose rule applies both to individual insiders and to corporate issuers that engage in a public offerings of securities."); Green v. Hamilton Int'l Corp., 437 F. Supp. 723, 728 (S.D.N.Y.1977) (opining that "there can be no doubt that the prohibition against 'insider' trading extends to a corporation"); see also Levinson v. Basic, Inc., 786 F.2d 741, 746 (6th Cir.1986) (explaining that "courts have held that a duty to disclose [merger] negotiations arises in situations such as where the corporation is trading in its own stock"), vacated on other grounds, 485 U.S. 224 (1988).

a private placement in which they typically receive an offering memorandum, both of which provide extensive disclosures. An issuer buying securities often will make use of a self-tender offer pursuant to the rules under Exchange Act § 13(e), which include extensive disclosure requirements.[34]

B. Tipping

In considering tipping, two of our earlier examples will be helpful. Recall that David Delta (an Acme insider) told his daughter about the ore discovery (an outsider). She then trades in Acme stock. David is the tipper; daughter Donna is the tippee. Recall that *Dirks* held that tippees could be held liable, provided two conditions are met: (1) the tipper breached a fiduciary duty to the corporation by making the tip and (2) the tippee knew or had reason to know of the breach.

The requirement that the tip constitute a breach of duty on the tipper's part eliminates many cases in which an insider discloses information to an outsider. It would be perfectly proper for Acme's CEO to tell its outside legal counsel about the ore discovery, so long as he does so for the purpose of enabling her to perform legal work on the company's behalf. After all, making disclosures for a legitimate corporate purpose violates no fiduciary obligation.[35]

In addition, not every disclosure made in violation of a fiduciary duty constitutes an illegal tip. Recall the example in which David Delta (Acme general counsel and thus an insider) became intoxicated and in that state accidentally disclosed the ore discovery to a personal friend. David may have been careless in getting drunk, but in the absence of evidence that his claimed drunkenness was a sham intended to evade the tipping rules, he at worst is guilty of violating his duty of care. What *Dirks* proscribes is not a breach of any duty, however, but solely a breach of the duty of loyalty forbidding fiduciaries to personally benefit from the disclosure.

1. Example

An instructive case is *SEC v. Switzer*,[36] which involved Barry Switzer, the well-known former coach of the Oklahoma Sooners and Dallas Cowboys football teams. Phoenix Resources Company was an oil and gas company. One day in 1981, Phoenix's CEO, George Platt, and his wife attended a track meet to watch their son compete. Coach Switzer was also at the meet, watching his son.

---

[34] For an analysis of tipping by the issuer, see Chapter 9.

[35] See Chapter 9 for a more expansive treatment of so-called selective disclosure.

[36] 590 F. Supp. 756 (W.D.Okla.1984).

Platt and Switzer had known each other for some time. Platt had Oklahoma football season tickets and his company had sponsored Switzer's television show. Sometime in the afternoon Switzer laid down on a row of bleachers behind the Platts to sunbathe. Platt, purportedly unaware of Switzer's presence, began telling his wife about a recent business trip to New York. In that conversation, Platt mentioned his desire to dispose of or liquidate Phoenix. Platt further talked about several companies bidding on Phoenix. Platt also mentioned that an announcement of a "possible" liquidation of Phoenix might occur the following Thursday. Switzer overheard this conversation and shortly thereafter bought a substantial number of Phoenix shares and tipped off a number of his friends. Because Switzer was neither an insider nor constructive insider (do you see why?) of Phoenix, the main issue was whether Platt had illegally tipped Switzer.

Per *Dirks*, the critical issue was whether Platt had violated his fiduciary duty by obtaining an improper personal benefit: "Absent some personal gain, there has been no breach of duty to stockholders. And absent a breach by the insider [to his stockholders], there is no derivative breach [by the tippee]."[37] The court found that Platt did not obtain any improper benefit. The court further found that the information was inadvertently (and unbeknownst to Platt) overheard by Switzer. Chatting about business with one's spouse in a public place may be careless, but it is not a breach of one's duty of loyalty. Accordingly, as the court explained, "Rule 10b–5 does not bar trading on the basis of information inadvertently revealed by an insider."[38]

Eddie Eagle (the friend of the drunken insider in our example) will argue that his position is analogous to Switzer's. David Delta did not intentionally disclose the information; nor did he do so for personal gain. Instead, he inadvertently disclosed it while rambling drunkenly. This is a legally sound argument, although query whether a jury is likely to believe it in a real world case.

2.   What constitutes the requisite personal benefit?

In the prior hypothetical in which David gave a tip to his daughter, Donna might try to argue that her father did not personally gain from the tip, but this argument would be unavailing. In *Dirks*, the Supreme Court identified several situations in which the requisite personal benefit can be found. The most obvious is the quid pro quo setting, in which the tipper gets some form of pecuniary gain. Nonpecuniary gain can also qualify,

---

[37] *Dirks*, 463 U.S. at 662.

[38] *Switzer*, 590 F. Supp. at 766.

however. Suppose a corporate CEO discloses information to a wealthy investor not for any legitimate corporate purpose, but solely to enhance his own reputation. *Dirks* would find a personal benefit on those facts. The SEC has consistently taken the position that a tipper who receives sexual favors from the tippee has received the requisite personal benefit.[39] Finally, and most relevantly to our hypothetical, *Dirks* indicated that liability could be imposed where the tip is a gift. David's gift to Donna satisfies the breach element because it is analogous to the situation in which David trades on the basis of the information and then gives his daughter the profits.

The question of what constitutes the requisite personal benefit was posed by well-known economics blogger Megan McArdle in connection with the insider trading case against prominent Wall Street executive Rajat Gupta:

> Rajat Gupta, formerly a director at Proctor and Gamble and Goldman Sachs, has been indicted on multiple counts of passing insider information about the companies he was supposed to be helping to oversee. He is alleged to have delivered this information to Raj Rajaratnam, the hedge-fund manager who just got 11 years for insider trading.
>
> . . . This is a very interesting case, because Gupta is not accused of having directly profited from the tips. He's accused merely of having used them to build his relationship with Rajaratnam.
>
> . . . [I]nsider trading cases usually require proving that the insider who delivered the information did so for some gain. That gain doesn't have to be immediate, or in cash, but it does have to be something that you can point to and say "That's what he got out of it".
>
> "Rajaratnam's goodwill" is slightly more nebulous than I believe usually goes to trial. And that's not just because you have to spend hours in court arguing about whether this is actually valuable. It's also because without a gain, there's less in the way of a paper trail. . . .[40]

---

[39] See, e.g., SEC v. Thayer, [1983–1984 Transfer Binder] Fed. Sec. Litig. Rep. (CCH) ¶ 99,718 (S.D.N.Y. Jan. 5, 1984) (complaint alleged "personal private relationship" to show tipper benefitted from trades by his mistress/tippee); SEC Litig. Rel., Court Enters Final Judgment Against James J. McDermott And Kathryn B. Gannon (Jun. 7, 2005) (noting that McDermott and porn star Gannon "were involved in a relationship" when the tips took place).

[40] Megan McArdle, Can You Be Guilty of Insider Trading Without Personal Gain?, The Atlantic (Oct. 27, 2011), http:// www.theatlantic.com/business/archive/ 2011/10/can-you-be-guilty-of-insider-trading-without-personal-gain/247489.

McArdle was not the only commentator who raised this issue in connection with the Gupta case. University of Chicago law professor Randal Picker opined that:

> According to Wayne State University Law School professor Peter J. Henning in a recent New York Times article, there are complications to each aspect of this case. . . .
>
> Proving Gupta received a personal benefit from his alleged tips to Rajaratnam is likely the hardest aspect of the case for the Department of Justice. In Dirks vs. SEC, the Supreme Court said that to prove insider trading by a tipper, "the test is whether the insider personally will benefit, directly or indirectly, from his disclosure. Absent some personal gain, there has been no breach of duty to stockholders." The indictment itself is surprisingly muted on this aspect, merely stating that Gupta "provided the inside information to Rajaratnam because of Gupta's friendship and business relationships with Rajaratnam. Gupta benefitted and hoped to benefit from his friendship and business relationships with Rajaratnam in various ways, some of which were financial". Gupta's lawyer, in contrast, stated that during the time in question his client lost his entire investment in the Galleon Fund. It will be interesting to see what evidence prosecutors have to demonstrate how exactly Gupta benefitted (especially since the financial relationships between Gupta and Rajaratnam cited in the indictment occurred mostly from 2003 through 2006, well before 2008).[41]

Any analysis of this issue must start by recognizing that Gupta was not charged with insider trading as such. Instead, he was charged with the related offense of tipping information to an outsider who then used it to trade. As a tipper, Gupta could be held liable if the government showed—as it succeeded in doing—that he (a) disclosed material nonpublic information to Rajaratnam (b) in return for a personal benefit (c) expecting Rajaratnam to trade. The question raised by McArdle goes to the second prong; namely, whether Gupta making tips "to build his relationship with Rajaratnam" rises to the requisite personal benefit. In short, it does.

Dirks itself held that the tipper can be held liable when he "receive[s] a direct or indirect personal benefit from the disclosure, such as a pecuniary gain or a reputational benefit that will

---

[41] Stephen M. Bainbridge, "Can You Be Guilty of Insider Trading Without Personal Gain?" Yes, ProfessorBainbridge.com (Nov. 6, 2011) (quoting a no longer available internet blog post by Picker), http://www.professorbainbridge.com/professorbainbridgecom/2011/11/can-you-be-guilty-of-insider-trading-without-personal-gain-yes.html.

translate into future earnings."[42] The court further explained that "The elements of fiduciary duty and exploitation of nonpublic information also exist when an insider makes a gift of confidential information to a trading relative or friend. The tip and trade resemble trading by the insider himself followed by a gift of the profits to the recipient."[43] As the Second Circuit later explained, by this formulation "the Supreme Court has made plain that to prove a § 10(b) violation, the SEC need not show that the tipper expected or received a specific or tangible benefit in exchange for the tip."[44] In that case, the court held that "The close friendship between [tipper] Downe and [tippee] Warde suggests that Downe's tip was 'inten[ded] to benefit' Warde, and therefore allows a jury finding that Downe's tip breached a duty under § 10(b)."[45] If a "close friendship" is not too nebulous, getting on the good side of a major player in the hedge fund industry is a very easy case. The Gupta case thus can be instructively contrasted with *SEC v. Maxwell*,[46] which rejected tipper liability on grounds that the alleged tipper was unlikely to receive any future pecuniary or reputational benefit from giving tips to his barber. As a major hedge fund manager, Rajaratnam was no mere barber.

As Thomson Reuters' Accelus blog explained:

In *S.E.C. v. Sekhri*, the court both distinguished and refined the concept of personal benefit as an element of insider trading:

The first part of Sehgal's argument fails because it is based on an overly narrow interpretation of the rule stated in Dirks. While Sehgal is correct in arguing that the evidence must show that Sekhri sought some personal benefit from disclosing the nonpublic information to Sehgal in order to have breached his fiduciary duty, he ignores the remainder of the Court's statement. . . . While noting that the insider must seek to benefit from disclosing inside information, the Supreme Court noted that "[t]here are objective facts and circumstances that often justify [the] inference" that the insider benefitted from the disclosure. . . . For example, "[t]he elements of fiduciary duty and exploitation of nonpublic information also exist when an insider makes a gift of confidential information to a trading relative or friend." . . . (emphasis added (by Court)). Thus, when Sekhri disclosed insider information to his

---

[42] *Dirks,* 463 U.S. at 663.

[43] Id. at 664.

[44] SEC v. Warde, 151 F.3d 42, 48 (2d Cir. 1998).

[45] Id. at 49.

[46] 341 F. Supp. 2d 941 (S.D. Ohio 2004).

father-in-law, Sehgal, it may be inferred that Sekhri received some personal benefit from the gift of information. Likewise, the burden of proof shifts from the SEC to Sehgal, and Sehgal must prove that his son-in-law derived no benefit from the disclosure in order to negate the inference that Sekhri benefitted from the transaction.

In the case of Gupta and Rajaratnam, the two men, in addition to years-long friendship, had a number of investments together.[47]

Not surprisingly, the jury apparently had no difficulty finding the requisite personal benefit, as it convicted Gupta of multiple counts of illegal tipping.

3. Can the tipper be liable if the tippee is not?

At least in theory, it is possible for a tipper to be liable even if the tippee is not liable. The breach of duty is enough to render the tipper liable, but the tippee must know of the breach in order to be held liable. As the Second Circuit explained in *SEC v. Obus*:[48]

> [T]ipper liability requires that (I) the tipper had a duty to keep material non-public information confidential; (2) the tipper breached that duty by intentionally or recklessly relaying the information to a tippee who could use the information in connection with securities trading; and (3) the tipper received a personal benefit from the tip. Tippee liability requires that (1) the tipper breached a duty by tipping confidential information; (2) the tippee knew or had reason to know that the tippee improperly obtained the information (i.e., that the information was obtained through the tipper's breach); and (3) the tippee, while in knowing possession of the material non-public information, used the information by trading or by tipping for his own benefit.[49]

Tippee liability thus is not an element of the case against tippers.

4. Tipping chains

Suppose, for example, that Tipper tells Tippee #1 who tells Tippee #2 who trades. Can Tippee #2 be held liable? If the preconditions of tipping liability are satisfied, there is nothing in *Dirks* to foreclose such liability. Donald Langevoort, for example, suggests that liability in tipping chain cases should require a three-

---

[47] Thomson Reuters Accelus Staff, Gupta Under Fire: Feds Come at Former Goldman Director with Both Barrels, Business Law Currents (Oct. 27, 2011), http://currents.westlawbusiness.com/Article.aspx?id=3330bda0–eb82–4185–ab83–90d99bb8a52e & cid= & src= & sp=.

[48] 693 F.3d 276 (2d Cir.2012).

[49] Id. at 289.

part showing: "each person in the chain (1) was given the information expressly for the purpose of facilitating trading based on inside information, (2) knew that the information was material and nonpublic, and knew or had reason to know that it came to him as a result of some breach of duty by an insider."[50] He goes on to note, however, that tipping chain cases—"albeit without any substantial judicial discussion of the underlying issue"—generally have imposed liability "simply on a showing that the person came into possession of information that he knew was material and nonpublic and which he knew or had reason to know was obtained via a breach of fiduciary duty by an insider."[51] In *Obus*, for example, the Second Circuit opined that:

> A tipper will be liable if he tips material non-public information, in breach of a fiduciary duty, to someone he knows will likely (1) trade on the information or (2) disseminate the information further for the first tippee's own benefit. The first tippee must both know or have reason to know that the information was obtained and transmitted through a breach and intentionally or recklessly tip the information further for her own benefit. The final tippee must both know or have reason to know that the information was obtained through a breach and trade while in knowing possession of the information.[52]

As this formulation suggests, however, it often will be difficult to prosecute tipping chain cases, because of the potential difficulties inherent in proving the requisite knowledge on the part of remote tippees.

C. Other Elements

It is not enough merely to show that the alleged inside trader falls into one of the proper classes of potential defendants, of course. The insider trading cause of action includes a number of other elements, among which the most important are: (1) the information must be material; (2) the information must be nonpublic; (3) the defendant must have traded while in possession of such information or, perhaps, on the basis of such information. It may also be the case that the defendant must have traded in equity securities, as it is not clear whether trading in debt securities violates the federal insider trading prohibition.

---

[50] Langevoort, supra note 25, § 4.10 at 4–28.1.

[51] Id. at 4–28.2.

[52] *Obus*, 693 F.3d at 288. The court further explained that the tippee could be held liable on the basis of "conscious avoidance," citing SEC v. Musella, 678 F. Supp. 1060, 1063 (S.D.N.Y.1988), for the proposition that *Dirks* was "satisfied where the defendants, tippees at the end of a chain, 'did not ask [about the source of information] because they did not want to know.'" *Obus*, 693 F.3d at 288–89.

1. Materiality

Under Rule 10b–5, only material misrepresentations or omissions are actionable. Materiality is determined by asking whether there is a substantial likelihood that a reasonable investor would consider the information important in deciding how to act. When one is dealing with speculative or contingent facts, of course, this test can be hard to apply. Recall that in *Goodwin v. Agassiz*,[53] for example, the defendants were buying stock based on a theory that land in the area the company worked might have commercially significant copper deposits. At the time the defendants traded, the theory was just that—a theory, which had not been verified. Today that aspect of the case would raise the question of whether the information was material, as defined by the federal securities law.

In *Basic Inc. v. Levinson*,[54] the Supreme Court adopted what it called "a highly fact-dependent probability/magnitude balancing approach" for determining the materiality of contingent facts such as the theory at issue in *Goodwin*. Basic had issued three public denials that it was engaged in merger negotiations with a prospective acquirer. Those statements were false; Basic in fact was secretly negotiating a possible merger with another company. When the merger was finally announced, a class action was brought on behalf of those investors who had sold Basic stock during the period between the false denials and the merger announcement. The plaintiff class allegedly received a lower price for their shares than would have been the case if Basic had told the truth.

The core issue was whether the denials were material. When the denials were made, it had not been certain that the merger would go through. The probability/magnitude balancing test was thus appropriate. As to the probability part of the equation, the court looked to "indicia of interest in the transaction at the highest corporate levels."[55] Evidence such as "board resolutions, instructions to investment bankers, and actual negotiations between principals or their intermediaries may serve as indicia of interest."[56] As to magnitude, the court deemed it quite high, opining that a merger is "the most important event that can occur in a small corporation's life, to wit, its death. . . ."[57] Notice, however, that magnitude appears to have both a relative and an absolute component. A merger of a small company into a large company, for

---

[53] 186 N.E. 659 (Mass. 1933); see Chapter 2.A.2.

[54] 485 U.S. 224 (1988).

[55] Id. at 239.

[56] Id.

[57] Id. at 238.

example, is a big deal for the target, but may be insignificant from the acquirer's perspective.

Although the probability/magnitude language sounds technically sophisticated and precise, in fact it is inherently subjective and indeterminate. You may recall the famous Hand Formula from torts—multiply the probability of injury times the magnitude of the likely resulting injury; if the product is less than the benefits of adequate precautions, liability for allegedly negligent conduct may be imposed.[58] At first glance, the *Basic* test sounds like the Hand formula, but on closer examination, there is no magic product to serve as a threshold above which information becomes material. The court never tells us how high a probability or how large a magnitude is necessary for information to be deemed material. One thus inside trades on the basis of speculative information knowing that a jury, acting with the benefit of hindsight, may reach a different conclusion about how probability and magnitude should be balanced than you did.

In a case like *Texas Gulf Sulphur*, it is just as important to determine when the information in question became material as it is to determine whether the information was material. Consider how the materiality standard would apply at two critical dates: November 12, when the visual assay indicated a potentially significant ore strike, and April 7, when the results of additional test holes confirmed that mining would be commercially viable. To review, materiality is defined by whether there is a substantial likelihood that a reasonable investor would consider the omitted fact important in deciding whether to buy or sell securities.[59] Where a fact is contingent or speculative, moreover, materiality is determined by balancing the indicated probability that the event will occur and the anticipated magnitude of the event in light of the totality of the company's activity.[60]

Under these standards, the ore discovery was certainly material as of April 7. The additional test holes had confirmed that the initial core sample was not an aberration—Texas Gulf Sulphur really had a major find on its hands. After April 7, the critical issue is not whether the strike will pay off, but when. The balancing test thus is not at issue, because we are no longer dealing with a contingent fact. Given the size of the discovery, this was certainly information any reasonable investor would consider significant.

It is less clear that the information known on November 12th would be regarded as material as of that date. Before April there

---

[58] U.S. v. Carroll Towing Co., 159 F.2d 169, 173 (2d Cir.1947).

[59] TSC Industries, Inc. v. Northway, Inc., 426 U.S. 438, 449 (1976).

[60] Basic Inc. v. Levinson, 485 U.S. 224, 238 (1988).

was only one core sample. While that sample was remarkable, only a highly trained geologist would be able to draw conclusions from it. Since it would take a highly sophisticated investor with considerable expertise in mining operations to understand the relevance of the find, perhaps the hypothetical reasonable investor would not consider it important. On the other hand, the *Texas Gulf Sulphur* opinion cited the testimony of a stockbroker who opined that one good test hole was a widely accepted signal to buy mining stock.[61]

One might also consider the response of the company and the insiders. The firm's decision to acquire options on the surrounding land tends to point towards a finding of materiality. According to the court, so did the insiders' own trading conduct, which raises the controversial question of whether the allegedly illegal insider trading behavior can serve as proof that the facts on which the insider traded were material. The problem, of course, is the potential for bootstrapping. If the allegedly illegal trade proves that the information is material, the materiality requirement becomes meaningless because all information in the defendant's possession when he or she traded would be material. Nonetheless, a footnote in the Supreme Court's *Basic* opinion flatly stated that "trading and profit making by insiders can serve as an indication of materiality."[62]

2. Nonpublic information; or when can insiders trade?

In most cases, as we have seen, the disclose or abstain rule collapses into a duty of abstention—disclosure typically is not a feasible alternative, as there usually is a legitimate corporate purpose for keeping the nonpublic information confidential. How long does this abstention obligation run? When can insiders start trading in their company's securities?

The simple answer is that insiders may only trade after the information in question has been made public. The difficulty, of course, is knowing whether or not the information in question has

---

[61] SEC v. Texas Gulf Sulphur Co., 401 F.2d 833, 850–51 (2d Cir.), cert. denied, 394 U.S. 976 (1968). The court explained that:

> Roche, a Canadian broker whose firm specialized in mining securities, characterized the importance to investors of the results of K–55–1. He stated that the completion of "the first drill hole" with "a 600 foot drill core is very very significant . . . anything over 200 feet is considered very significant and 600 feet is just beyond your wildest imagination." He added, however, that it "is a natural thing to buy more stock once they give you the first drill hole." Additional testimony revealed that the prices of stocks of other companies, albeit less diversified, smaller firms, had increased substantially solely on the basis of the discovery of good anomalies or even because of the proximity of their lands to the situs of a potentially major strike.

Id.

[62] *Basic*, 485 U.S. at 240 n.18.

entered the public domain. Because insiders with access to confidential information trade at their own risk, this timing issue is a critical question.

Texas Gulf Sulphur again is instructive. The ore strike was first announced by a press release to the Canadian news media disseminated at 9:40 a.m. on April 16, 1964.[63] A news conference with the American media followed at 10 a.m. on the same day. The news appeared on the Dow Jones ticker tape at 10:54 a.m. that day. Defendant Crawford had telephoned his stockbroker at midnight on the 15th with instructions to buy Texas Gulf Sulphur stock when the Midwest Stock Exchange opened the next morning. Defendant Coates left the April 16th news conference to call his stockbroker shortly before 10:20 a.m. In addition to executing Coates' order, the broker ordered an additional 1500 Texas Gulf Sulphur shares for himself and other customers. Crawford and Coates conceded that they traded while in possession of material information, but claimed that the information had been effectively disseminated to the public (and thus had lost its nonpublic character) before their trades were executed.

The court disagreed, holding that before insiders may act upon material information, the information must have been disclosed in a manner that ensures its availability to the investing public.[64] Merely waiting until a press release has been read to reporters, as Coates did, is not enough. The information must have been widely disseminated and public investors must have an opportunity to act on it. At a minimum, the court opined, insiders therefore must wait until the news could reasonably be expected to appear over the Dow Jones broad tape—the news service that transmits investment news to brokers and investment professionals.[65]

Although appearance of the information on the broad tape serves as a widely used rule of thumb, the court noted "in passing that, where the news is of a sort which is not readily translatable into investment action, insiders may not take advantage of their advance opportunity to evaluate the information by acting immediately upon dissemination."[66] Instead, in such cases, it might

---

[63] SEC v. Texas Gulf Sulphur Co., 401 F.2d 833, 850–51 (2d Cir.), cert. denied, 394 U.S. 976 (1968).

[64] See id. at 854 ("Before insiders may act upon material information, such information must have been effectively disclosed in a manner sufficient to insure its availability to the investing public.").

[65] See id. (holding that "at the minimum Coates should have waited until the news could reasonably have been expected to appear over the media of widest circulation, the Dow Jones broad tape"). The broad tape was a wider version of the famous ticker tape that provided continuous reports of major news developments and other financial information. Today it appears on a website rather than the older paper tape.

[66] Id. at 854 n.18.

be advisable to require insiders to allow "a 'reasonable waiting period' during which outsiders may absorb and evaluate disclosures."[67] As a result, various other rules of thumb have beep proposed, ranging from "waiting for the morning newspaper to carry the information" to "fifteen minutes after the [broad] tape runs."[68]

Unlike other aspects of *Texas Gulf Sulphur*, this rule is still good law today. It also makes good policy sense. The efficient capital markets hypothesis, about which more will be said in Chapter 13, tells us that all currently available public information about a corporation is reflected in the market price of its securities. However, the hypothesis depends on the ability of investment professionals to adjust their selling and offering prices to reflect that information. By requiring that insiders wait at least until the news has gone out over the Dow Jones wire, the court assured that brokers would have the information before trading; in other words, the price should have already started rising (or falling, as the case may be) to reflect the new information.

3. Scienter

One can easily mislead investors without intending to do so. Even an honest mistake might cause some to be misled. As such, it is not apparent that liability for securities fraud should be premised on intent. Tort law encourages drivers to drive more safely, because they can be held liable for negligent accidents. Tort law also encourages manufacturers to put out safer products by imposing strict liability for defective products. Should securities law be any less rigorous in encouraging accurate disclosure?

Liability in fact can be imposed for unintentional misrepresentations under some securities law provisions. Sections 11 and 12(a)(2) of the 1933 Securities Act, for example, require no evidence from plaintiff with respect to the defendant's state of mind.[69] Instead, state of mind is an affirmative defense under these provisions.[70] In order to make out the state of mind defense, moreover, defendants must show that they were non-negligent.[71]

Under Rule 10b–5, however, the Supreme Court has held that plaintiff's prima facie case must include proof defendant acted with

---

[67] Id.

[68] Billard v. Rockwell International Corp., 526 F. Supp. 218, 220 (S.D.N.Y. 1981).

[69] See Herman & MacLean v. Huddleston, 459 U.S. 375, 382 (1983) ("If a plaintiff purchased a security issued pursuant to a registration statement, he need only show a material misstatement or omission to establish his prima facie case.").

[70] Ernst & Ernst v. Hochfelder, 425 U.S. 185, 208 (1976).

[71] Id.

scienter, which the court defined as a mental state embracing intent to deceive, manipulate or defraud. Although this formulation clearly precludes Rule 10b–5 liability for those who are merely negligent,[72] the Supreme Court left open the issue of whether recklessness alone met the scienter requirement.[73] Subsequent lower court decisions, however, uniformly have held that recklessness suffices.[74]

In insider trading cases, there are a variety of ways of proving that the defendant acted with the requisite scienter. A departure from the defendant's normal trading activities, such as unusually large trades, for example, can justify an inference of scienter.[75] Efforts by the defendant to conceal her trading activities also can justify drawing such an inference.[76] Timing can also justify such an inference, such as where the defendant is shown to have traded immediately after receiving a telephone call from an alleged tipper.[77] In tipping cases, the scienter requirement can be satisfied by a showing that the "tippee knew or had reason to know that confidential information was initially obtained and transmitted improperly" and "the tippee intentionally or recklessly traded while in knowing possession of that information."[78]

4. Possession v. use

The SEC long has argued that trading while in knowing possession of material nonpublic information satisfies Rule 10b–5's scienter requirement.[79] To evaluate that argument, let's explore a hypothetical based on the facts of *Diamond v. Oreamuno*,[80] discussed in Chapter 2.C above. Insiders of MAI sold their holdings

---

[72] Aaron v. SEC, 446 U.S. 680 (1980); Ernst & Ernst v. Hochfelder, 425 U.S. 185 (1976).

[73] *Ernst & Ernst*, 425 U.S. at 194 n. 12.

[74] See Joseph A. Grundfest & A.C. Pritchard, Statutes with Multiple Personality Disorders: The Value of Ambiguity in Statutory Design and Interpretation, 54 Stan. L. Rev. 627, 651 (2002) ("Since [Ernst & Ernst v. Hochfelder, 425 U.S. 185, 197 (1976),] every court of appeals that has addressed the issue has held that recklessness satisfies the scienter requirement of Section 10(b).").

[75] In re Silicon Graphics, Inc. Securities Litigation, 183 F.3d 970, 986 (9th Cir. 1999) ("Although 'unusual' or 'suspicious' stock sales by corporate insiders may constitute circumstantial evidence of scienter, insider trading is suspicious only when it is 'dramatically out of line with prior trading practices at times calculated to maximize the personal benefit from undisclosed inside information.'"; citations and footnote omitted).

[76] Wang & Steinberg, supra note 24, at 190.

[77] Id. at 193.

[78] SEC v. Obus, 693 F.3d 276, 287–88 (2d Cir. 2012).

[79] See SEC v. MacDonald, 699 F.2d 47, 50 (1st Cir. 1983) (holding that the scienter "requirement is satisfied if at the time defendant purchased stock he had actual knowledge of undisclosed material information; knew it was undisclosed, and knew it was material, i.e., that a reasonable investor would consider the information important in making an investment decision").

[80] 248 N.E.2d 910 (N.Y. 1969).

of firm stock while in possession of bad news that was both material and nonpublic. As such, they avoided significant losses that would have resulted from the drop in MAI's stock price that occurred when the bad news was made public. Suppose one of the defendants claimed the bad news had not caused his sale; instead, he argues that he would have sold his MAI stock regardless of whether he thought the stock would be going up or down in the future. Perhaps he needed money to pay catastrophic medical bills, for example. Alternatively, perhaps he had a pattern of disposing of MAI stock at regular intervals. Many senior corporate executives receive a substantial portion of their compensation in the form of stock grants or options, which they periodically liquidate to realize their cash value. In either case, our hypothetical defendant would have traded while in possession of material nonpublic information, but not on the basis of such information. Can he be held liable?

In *U.S. v. Teicher*,[81] the Second Circuit answered that question affirmatively, albeit in a passage that appears to be dictum. An attorney tipped stock market speculators about transactions involving clients of his firm. On appeal, defendants objected to a jury instruction pursuant to which they could be found guilty of securities fraud based upon the mere possession of fraudulently obtained material nonpublic information without regard to whether that information was the actual cause of their transactions. The Second Circuit held that any error in the instruction was harmless, but went on to opine in favor of a knowing possession test. The court interpreted *Chiarella* as comporting with "the oft-quoted maxim that one with a fiduciary or similar duty to hold material nonpublic information in confidence must either 'disclose or abstain' with regard to trading."[82] The court also favored the possession standard because it "recognizes that one who trades while knowingly possessing material inside information has an informational advantage over other traders."[83]

In *S.E.C. v. Adler*,[84] the Eleventh Circuit rejected *Teicher* in favor of a use standard. Under *Adler*, "when an insider trades while in possession of material nonpublic information, a strong inference arises that such information was used by the insider in trading. The insider can attempt to rebut the inference by adducing evidence that there was no causal connection between the information and

---

[81] 987 F.2d 112 (2d Cir.1993).

[82] Id. at 120.

[83] Id.

[84] 137 F.3d 1325 (11th Cir. 1998). The Ninth Circuit subsequently agreed with *Adler* that proof of use, not mere possession, is required. The Ninth Circuit further held that in criminal cases no presumption of use should be drawn from the fact of possession—the government must affirmatively proof use of nonpublic information. U.S. v. Smith, 155 F.3d 1051 (9th Cir. 1998).

the trade—i.e., that the information was not used."[85] Although defendant Pegram apparently possessed material nonpublic information at the time he traded, he introduced strong evidence that he had a plan to sell company stock and that that plan predated his acquisition of the information in question. If proven at trial, evidence of such a pre-existing plan would rebut the inference of use and justify an acquittal on grounds that he lacked the requisite scienter. Similarly, the court opined, evidence that the allegedly illegal trades were consistent with trading also would rebut the inference of use.

The choice between *Adler* and *Teicher* is difficult. On the one hand, in adopting the Insider Trading Sanctions Act of 1984,[86] Congress imposed treble money civil fines on those who illegally trade "while in possession" of material nonpublic information. In addition, a use standard significantly complicates the government's burden in insider trading cases, because motivation is always harder to establish than possession, although the inference of use permitted by Adler substantially alleviates this concern.

On the other hand, a number of decisions have acknowledged that a pre-existing plan and/or prior trading pattern can be introduced as an affirmative defense in insider trading cases, as such evidence tends to disprove that defendant acted with the requisite scienter. In contrast, *Teicher*'s mere possession test is inconsistent with Rule 10b–5's scienter requirement, which requires fraudulent intent (or, at least, recklessness). In addition, dictum in each of the Supreme Court's insider trading opinions also appears to endorse the use standard. Indeed, contrary to the *Teicher* court's claim, *Chiarella* simply did not address the distinction between a knowing possession and a use standard. Finally, the *Teicher* court's reliance on the trader's informational advantage is inconsistent with *Chiarella*'s rejection of the equal access test.

In 2000, the SEC tried to resolve this issue by adopting Rule 10b5–1, which states that Rule 10b–5's prohibition of insider trading is violated whenever someone trades "on the basis of" material nonpublic information.[87] Because one is deemed, subject to certain affirmative defenses, to have traded "on the basis of" material nonpublic information if one was aware of such information at the time of the trade, Rule 10b5–1 formally rejects the *Adler* position.[88] In practice, however, the difference between *Adler* and Rule 10b5–1 may prove insignificant. On the one hand,

---

[85] Id. at 1337.

[86] The Act is described in detail in § Chapter 11.A.

[87] Exchange Act Rel. No. 43,154 (Aug. 15, 2000).

[88] 17 C.F.R. § 240.10b5–1(a).

Adler created a presumption of use when the insider was aware of material nonpublic information. Conversely, as noted, Rule 10b5–1 provides affirmative defenses for insiders who trade pursuant to a pre-existing plan, contract, or instructions. As a result, the two approaches should lead to comparable outcomes in many cases.

Even though Rule10b5–1 thus can be squared with *Adler*, the SEC clearly intended the Rule to resurrect the mere possession test to the fullest extent possible. Did the SEC have authority to do so in the face of contrary judicial holdings? There is some evidence that supports the SEC's position. In adopting the Insider Trading Sanctions Act of 1984, for example, Congress imposed treble money civil fines on those who illegally trade "while in possession" of material nonpublic information.

The bulk of the evidence, however, raises serious doubts as to the validity of Rule 10b5–1. The SEC cannot adopt rules that go beyond the scope of the statutes authorizing them.[89] The Supreme Court has consistently held that Section 10(b) of the Exchange Act, which provides the authority under which Rule 10b–5 was adopted, prohibits only fraud and manipulation.[90] In turn, as we have seen, fraud requires proof that the defendant intended to deceive (i.e., scienter). Indeed, the Supreme Court explained in *Dirks* that "[i]t is not enough that an insider's conduct results in harm to investors; rather a violation [of Rule 10b–5] may be found only where there is 'intentional or willful conduct designed to deceive or defraud investors.' "[91] Yet, as the Ninth Circuit pointed out in *Smith*, "a knowing-possession standard would ... go a long way toward making insider trading a strict liability crime."[92] Second, as the Ninth Circuit also noted, "the Supreme Court has consistently suggested, albeit in dictum, that Rule 10b–5 requires that the government prove causation in insider trading prosecutions."[93] In other words, the government must prove that the defendant used the inside information in making the relevant trading decisions. Rule 10b5–1's failure to impose such a requirement on the government thus leaves it vulnerable to challenge.

There are three affirmative defenses available under Rule 10b5–1, under each of which:

---

[89] See Business Roundtable v. SEC, 905 F.2d 406, 408 (D.C. Cir. 1990).

[90] See, e.g., Santa Fe Industries, Inc. v. Green, 430 U.S. 462, 473 (1977) ("The language of § 10(b) gives no indication that Congress meant to prohibit any conduct not involving manipulation or deception.").

[91] Dirks v. SEC, 463 U.S. at 646, 663 n. 23 (1983).

[92] U.S. v. Smith, 155 F.3d 1051, 1068 n.25 (9th Cir.1998).

[93] Id. at 1067.

[A] person's purchase or sale is not "on the basis of" material nonpublic information if the person making the purchase or sale demonstrates that:

(A) Before becoming aware of the information, the person had:

(1) Entered into a binding contract to purchase or sell the security,

(2) Instructed another person to purchase or sell the security for the instructing person's account, or

(3) Adopted a written plan for trading securities. . . .[94]

These affirmative defenses are available only if the contract, instruction, or plan meets the following conditions:

(1) Specified the amount of securities to be purchased or sold and the price at which and the date on which the securities were to be purchased or sold;

(2) Included a written formula or algorithm, or computer program, for determining the amount of securities to be purchased or sold and the price at which and the date on which the securities were to be purchased or sold; or

(3) Did not permit the person to exercise any subsequent influence over how, when, or whether to effect purchases or sales; provided, in addition, that any other person who, pursuant to the contract, instruction, or plan, did exercise such influence must not have been aware of the material nonpublic information when doing so. . . .[95]

The purchase or sale must be made pursuant to the plan, which includes a requirement that the plan not have been changed so as to permit the transaction.[96] Finally, the plan must have been established "in good faith and not as part of a plan or scheme to evade the prohibitions of this section."[97] While the foregoing affirmative defenses are available to both individuals and entities, an additional affirmative defense is available solely to entities:

A person other than a natural person also may demonstrate that a purchase or sale of securities is not "on the basis of" material nonpublic information if the person demonstrates that:

---

[94] 17 C.F.R. § 240.10b5–1(c)(1)(i).

[95] Id. at § 240.10b5–1(c)(1)(i)(B).

[96] Id. at § 240.10b5–1(c)(1)(i)(C).

[97] Id. at § 240.10b5–1(c)(1)(ii).

(i) The individual making the investment decision on behalf of the person to purchase or sell the securities was not aware of the information; and

(ii) The person had implemented reasonable policies and procedures, taking into consideration the nature of the person's business, to ensure that individuals making investment decisions would not violate the laws prohibiting trading on the basis of material nonpublic information. These policies and procedures may include those that restrict any purchase, sale, and causing any purchase or sale of any security as to which the person has material nonpublic information, or those that prevent such individuals from becoming aware of such information.[98]

There is growing evidence that many executives are abusing Rule 10b5–1 by establishing or amending trading plans while in possession of material nonpublic information on the basis of which they proceeded to trade while using the plan for cover.[99]

In one high-profile example, the SEC filed a civil complaint on June 4, 2009, against the former CEO of Countrywide Financial, Angelo Mozilo, and other former Countrywide executives, alleging that they used Rule 10b5–1 plans to trade illegally on inside information (to the tune of nearly $140 million, in Mr. Mozilo's case). Although all of these sales occurred through Rule 10b5–1 plans, the SEC alleges— citing internal correspondence such as an e-mail stating that the company was "flying blind"—that Mr. Mozilo had material nonpublic information about Countrywide's deteriorating mortgage business when he instituted his trading plans. The SEC also took particular note of the fact that he implemented no fewer than four separate plans during a three-month period, and that sales under the plans began soon after their adoption.[100]

Securities attorney Manuel Rivera suggests the following best practices so as to minimize the risk that a corporation's insiders will abuse their Rule 10b5–1 plan:

Getting the board involved and pre-clearing plans, amendments, and terminations. The Council of Institutional Investors recommended that public company boards of

---

[98] Id. at § 240.10b5–1(c)(2).

[99] See Linda Chatman Thomsen, Dir., Div. of Enforcement, SEC, Opening Remarks Before the 15th Annual NASPP Conference (Oct. 10, 2007), http://www. sec.gov/news/speech/2007/spch101007lct.htm (explaining that the SEC is closely monitoring 10b5–1 plans to determine whether they are being abused).

[100]   David Lamarre, Keeping Current: Securities, 19–DEC Bus. L. Today 20, 20 (2009).

directors be explicitly responsible for oversight of Rule 10b5–1 plans. The board, or an appropriate board committee such as the nominating and corporate governance committee or compensation committee, could be vested with responsibility for overseeing Rule 10b5–1 plans for corporate insiders. Board oversight could increase vigilance concerning inappropriate practices and encourage best practices in the adoption, amendment, or termination of Rule 10b5–1 plans. In addition, new Rule 10b5–1 plans, plan amendments and plan terminations should be pre-cleared by a designated internal compliance officer.

Permitting plan adoption or modification only at designated times. To avoid suspicions of actions while in possession of material non-public information, Rule 10b5–1 plans should be adopted and modified only at times when the corporate insider can buy or sell securities under the company's insider-trading policy, such as during an open trading window or soon after an earnings announcement (when material non-public information will be communicated to the public).

Creating a template for plans entered into by company insiders. The company should select one broker to handle all Rule 10b5–1 plans of company insiders and require that company insiders establish and administer their plans through this broker. The designated broker should not handle other securities transactions for the company insider, to avoid undue influence over the broker. In addition, the company should obtain the broker's standard form of Rule 10b5–1 plan and amend the form in order to codify standard terms that are consistent with the company's policy decisions concerning these plans. For example, the standard plan of a broker may provide for a waiting period of two weeks between adoption of a plan and execution of a trade, but if, as discussed below, the company determines to require a longer gap period, the broker's form would be customized to provide this. In addition, if warranted, the company may require all insiders to adopt Rule 10b5–1 plans. For example, if the company makes restricted stock unit awards to insiders, the company could require the insiders to adopt plans providing that upon delivery of stock upon satisfaction of vesting conditions, a sufficient number of the vested shares will be sold to satisfy the associated tax withholding obligation. Some proxy advisory firms, such as ISS, believe that corporate executives should be prohibited from trading company stock outside of a Rule 10b5–1 plan.

Implementing a waiting period before the initial trade. Because a short period between adoption or adoption of a Rule 10b5–1 plan and the first trade execution under the plan may signal that an insider possessed material non-public information at the time his decision concerning adoption or amendment of the plan occurred, it is advisable to implement a meaningful waiting period before initial trading activity can occur. A common period used for this purpose is thirty days, and some companies require longer periods.

Adopt disclosure best practices. Although the SEC does not require current disclosure of the adoption of Rule 10b5–1 plans on Form 8–K, some companies make voluntary disclosures of corporate insider plans. Since trades by directors and executive officers must be reported on Form 4 and require a Form 144 filing, making the market aware of the existence of these plans and their terms upon adoption may reduce the perception of unplanned insider selling. Disclosure best practices espoused by ISS include a requirement that the adoption, amendment, or termination of a Rule 10b5–1 plan be disclosed on an accelerated basis—within two business days—by filing a Form 8–K, and requiring Form 4 reports concerning trade executions to mention that the transactions were pursuant to a Rule 10b5–1 plan.

Discourage overlapping plans, frequent plan modifications, and terminations. Corporate policies should discourage company insiders from adopting multiple Rule 10b5–1 plans with overlapping execution terms, since this can be viewed as an attempt to use timing to take advantage of material non-public information. Generally, plans should have a term of at least a year, since short-term plans are more likely to be scrutinized as having been motivated by inside knowledge. Similarly, modification of existing plans should occur only when the insider does not possess material non-public information, otherwise the purpose of the plan would be defeated. In addition, if corporate insiders terminate plans, this could be interpreted as an abusive practice in that it may raise questions about whether the plan was adopted in good faith. Companies should consider adopting policies that discourage insiders from amending or terminating Rule 10b5–1 plans. One recommendation is that companies require board approval to amend or terminate a plan, such approval to be granted only under extraordinary circumstances. In addition, some companies bar corporate insiders from adopting new Rule 10b5–1 plans for six months or a year after a plan termination, to deter insiders from adopting plans or terminating them other than in good faith.[101]

5. Trading in debt securities

One of the areas in which the Supreme Court's failure to specify the source and nature of the fiduciary obligation underlying the disclose or abstain rule has proven especially problematic is insider trading in debt securities. Yet, the prohibition's application to debt securities has received surprisingly little judicial attention. One court has held that insider trading in convertible debentures violates Rule 10b–5,[102] but this case is distinguishable from those involving nonconvertible debt securities. Because they are convertible into common stock at the option of the holder, both the market price and interest rate paid on such instruments are affected by the market price of the underlying common stock. Federal securities law recognizes the close relationship of convertibles to common stock by defining the former as equity securities.[103] As such, the status of insider trading in nonconvertible debt remains unresolved. A strong argument can be made, however, that the prohibition should not extend to trading in nonconvertible debt.

In most states, neither the corporation nor its officers and directors have fiduciary duties to debtholders. Instead, debtholders' rights are limited to the express terms of the contract and an implied covenant of good faith.[104] Cases in a few jurisdictions purport to recognize fiduciary duties running to holders of debt securities, but the duties imposed in these cases are more accurately characterized as the same implied covenant of good faith found in most other jurisdictions.[105]

The distinction between this implied covenant and a fiduciary duty is an important one for our purposes. An implied covenant of good faith arises from the express terms of a contract and is used to fulfill the parties' mutual intent. In contrast, a fiduciary duty has little to do with the parties' intent. Instead, courts use fiduciary duties to protect the interests of the duty's beneficiary. Accordingly,

---

[101] Manuel G. Rivera, Staying Ahead of the Curve in Complying With Current and Anticipated Securities Regulations, 2013 WL 2136544 at *13–15.

[102] In re Worlds of Wonder Sec. Litig., 1990 WL 260675 (N.D.Cal. 1990).

[103] 17 C.F.R. § 230.405 ("The term equity security means any stock or similar security . . . or any security convertible, with or without consideration into such a security. . . .").

[104] See, e.g., Metropolitan Life Ins. Co. v. RJR Nabisco, Inc., 716 F. Supp. 1504 (S.D.N.Y.1989); Katz v. Oak Indus., 508 A.2d 873 (Del.Ch.1986).

[105] See, e.g., Broad v. Rockwell Int'l Corp., 642 F.2d 929 (5th Cir.), cert. denied, 454 U.S. 965 (1981); Gardner & Florence Call Cowles Found. v. Empire, Inc., 589 F. Supp. 669 (S.D.N.Y.1984), vacated, 754 F.2d 478 (2d Cir.1985); Fox v. MGM Grand Hotels, Inc., 187 Cal.Rptr. 141 (Cal.Ct.App.1982).

a fiduciary duty requires the party subject to the duty to put the interests of the beneficiary of the duty ahead of his own, while an implied duty of good faith merely requires both parties to respect their bargain.

A two-step move thus will be required if courts are to impose liability under the disclose or abstain rule on those who inside trade in debt securities. First, the clear holdings of *Chiarella* and *Dirks* must be set aside so that the requisite relationship can be expanded to include purely contractual arrangements and the requisite duty expanded to include mere contractual covenants. Second, the implied covenant of good faith must be interpreted as barring self-dealing in nonpublic information by corporate agents. In that regard, consider the leading *Met Life* decision, which indicates that a covenant of good faith will be implied only when necessary to ensure that neither side deprives the other side of the fruits of the agreement.[106] The fruits of the agreement are limited to regular payment of interest and ultimate repayment of principal. Because insider trading rarely affects either of these fruits, it does not violate the covenant of good faith.

Insofar as public policy is concerned, the argument for creating fiduciary duties—federal or state—running to bondholders is extremely weak. Bond issuances are repeat transactions. Where parties expect to have repeated transactions, the risk of self-dealing by one party is constrained by the threat that the other party will punish the cheating party in future transactions. The issuer's management has a strong self-interest in the corporation's cost of capital (i.e., avoiding takeovers, maximizing personal wealth, avoiding firm failure). Management therefore will be slow to do anything that unnecessarily increases their cost of capital. But if they abuse their current bondholders, that will come back to haunt them the next time they want to use the bond market to raise capital. If investors care about protection from insider trading, management therefore will provide it by contract.

In addition, negotiations between the issuer and the underwriters that market the debt securities will produce efficient levels of protection. Because the bond market is dominated by a small number of institutional investors, the relationship between underwriters and bondholders is another example of the repeat transaction phenomenon. Underwriters will not sully their reputations with bondholders for the sake of one issuer. Moreover, in a firm commitment underwriting, the underwriters buy the securities from the issuer. If the indenture does not provide

---

[106]   Metropolitan Life Ins. Co. v. RJR Nabisco, Inc., 716 F. Supp. 1504, 1517 (S.D.N.Y.1989).

adequate levels of protection, the underwriters will be unable to sell the bonds. Again, if debtholders care about insider trading, the contract will prohibit it.

The disclose or abstain theory thus should not prohibit insiders from trading in debt securities on the basis of material nonpublic information. Having said that, however, various alternative theories of liability may come into play in this context. In particular, the misappropriation theory might apply. Suppose a corporate officer traded in the firm's debt securities using material nonpublic information belonging to the corporation. As the argument would go, even though the officer owes no fiduciary duties to the bondholders, he owes fiduciary duties to the corporation. The violation of those duties might suffice for liability under the misappropriation theory. The misappropriation theory clearly would not reach trading by an issuer in its own debt securities.[107]

D. New Theories Emerge to Fill the Post-*Chiarella* Gaps

Chiarella created a variety of significant gaps in the insider trading prohibition's coverage. Suppose Ajax Inc. is planning a takeover bid for Acme Corporation. Anne Associate is an outside attorney whose law firm represents Ajax. In the course of representing Ajax, Anne learns about the planned takeover bid. Anne thereupon purchases 1000 Acme shares. When Ajax's bid is announced, the price of Acme stock rises and Anne sells at a considerable profit.

Under the classic disclose or abstain rule, Anne has not violated the insider trading prohibition. Whatever duties she owed Ajax, she owed no duty to the shareholders of Acme. Like Vincent Chiarella, she is a stranger to them. Accordingly, the requisite breach of fiduciary duty is not present in her transaction.

Just as there had been nothing historically or doctrinally inevitable about *Texas Gulf Sulphur*'s imposition of the equal access standard, however, there equally was nothing inevitable on either score about the Supreme Court's rejection of that standard. The equal access standard was consistent with a trend towards affirmative disclosure obligations and away from *caveat emptor* that was sweeping across a broad swath of the common law. In rejecting this trend, Justice Powell arguably shifted the focus of insider trading liability from deceit to agency, a point that becomes

---

[107] See Salovaara v. Jackson Nat'l Life Ins., 66 F. Supp. 2d 593, 601 (D.N.J. 1999) (declining to "to extend *O'Hagan* to a civil case involving a transaction [by an issuer] for high yield debt securities"), aff'd on other grounds, 246 F. 3d 289 (3d Cir. 2001).

especially significant later in our analysis,[108] but nothing in the text of the statute or the rule explicitly mandated that shift. The way was thus left open for the SEC and the lower courts to evade the *Chiarella/Dirks* framework by developing new theories of liability, which is precisely what happened.

In response to the narrowing of the insider trading prohibition's scope it had suffered at Justice Powell's hands, the SEC developed two new theories of liability—the misappropriation theory and Rule 14e–3—that recaptured much, but not all, of the ground it lost in *Chiarella* and *Dirks*. Both theories were subsequently upheld by the Supreme Court in *U.S. v. O'Hagan*.[109] Evaluating an insider trading case thus now requires one to consider three distinct theories of liability (not counting § 16(b)). Subsequent chapters take them up in turn.

---

[108]   A. C. Pritchard, *United States v. O'Hagan*: Agency Law and Justice Powell's Legacy for the Law of Insider Trading, 78 Bos. Univ. L. Rev. 13 (1998).

[109]521 U.S. 642 (1997).

Chapter 7

THE MISAPPROPRIATION THEORY

The misappropriation theory's origins are commonly—but incorrectly—traced to Chief Justice Burger's *Chiarella* dissent. Burger contended that the way in which the inside trader acquires the nonpublic information on which he trades could itself be a material circumstance that must be disclosed to the market before trading. Accordingly, he argued, "a person who has misappropriated nonpublic information has an absolute duty [to the persons with whom he trades] to disclose that information or to refrain from trading."[1] The majority did not address the merits of this theory, instead rejecting it solely on the ground that such a theory had not been presented to the jury and therefore could not sustain a criminal conviction.[2]

The way was thus left open for the SEC to urge and the lower courts to adopt the misappropriation theory as an alternative basis of insider trading liability. In *U.S. v. Newman*,[3] for example, employees of an investment bank misappropriated confidential information concerning proposed mergers involving clients of the firm. As had been true of Vincent Chiarella, the *Newman* defendants' employer worked for prospective acquiring companies, while the trading took place in target company securities. As such, the *Newman* defendants owed no fiduciary duties to the investors with whom they traded. In this instance, moreover, neither the investment bank nor in its clients traded in the target companies' shares contemporaneously with the defendants. In upholding the *Newman* defendant's convictions, the Second Circuit did not follow Chief Justice Burger's *Chiarella* dissent. Instead, the court held that by misappropriating confidential information for personal gain, the defendants had defrauded their employer and its clients and that that fraud sufficed to impose insider trading liability on the defendants.

Like the traditional disclose or abstain rule, the misappropriation theory requires a breach of a duty of disclosure arising out of a fiduciary relationship before trading on inside

---

[1] Chiarella v. U.S., 445 U.S. 222, 240 (1980) (Burger, C.J., dissenting).

[2] Id. at 236–37 ("Because we cannot affirm a criminal conviction on the basis of a theory not presented to the jury, . . . we will not speculate upon whether [the misappropriation theory] exists, whether it has been breached, or whether such a breach constitutes a violation of § 10(b).").

[3] 664 F.2d 12 (2d Cir. 1981), cert. denied, 464 U.S. 863 (1983).

information becomes unlawful.[4] As the *Newman* holding indicates, however, the fiduciary relationship in question is a quite different one. Under the misappropriation theory, the defendant need not owe any duties to the investor with whom he trades. Likewise, he need not have a fiduciary relationship with the issuer of the securities that were traded. Instead, the misappropriation theory applies when the inside trader has a fiduciary relationship with the source of the information.[5] In *Newman*, for example, the defendants' duties ran to their employer and, in turn, to the prospective acquirers that had hired the investment bank to represent them. If the misappropriation theory had been available against Chiarella, for example, his conviction could have been upheld even though he owed no duties to those with whom he had traded. Instead, the breach of the duty he owed to Pandick Press would have sufficed.

The Supreme Court first took up the misappropriation theory in *Carpenter v. U.S.*,[6] in which a Wall Street Journal reporter and his confederates misappropriated information belonging to the Journal. The Supreme Court upheld the resulting convictions under the mail and wire fraud statutes, holding that confidential business information is property protected by those statutes from being taken by trick, deceit, or chicanery. As to the defendants' securities fraud convictions, however, the court split 4–4. Following the long-standing tradition governing evenly divided Supreme Court decisions, the lower court ruling was affirmed without opinion, but that ruling had no precedential or stare decisis value.

The way was thus left open for lower courts to reject the misappropriation theory, which the Fourth and Eighth Circuits subsequently did in, respectively, *U.S. v. Bryan*[7] and *U.S. v. O'Hagan*.[8] These courts held that Rule 10b–5 imposed liability only where there has been deception upon the purchaser or seller of securities, or upon some other person intimately linked with or affected by a securities transaction. Because the misappropriation theory involves no such deception, but rather simply a breach of fiduciary duty owed to the source of the information, the theory could not stand. The Supreme Court took cert in *O'Hagan* to resolve

---

[4] See S.E.C. v. Switzer, 590 F. Supp. 756, 766 (W.D.Okla. 1984) (holding that it is not unlawful to trade on the basis of inadvertently overheard information).

[5] S.E.C. v. Dorozhko, 606 F. Supp.2d 321, 332 (S.D.N.Y. 2008), rev'd on other grounds, 574 F.3d 42 (2d Cir. 2009) ("The misappropriation theory holds that § 10(b) may be violated by persons who do not owe a fiduciary duty to other market participants, but nevertheless do owe a fiduciary or similar duty to the source of their information.").

[6] 484 U.S. 19 (1987).

[7] 58 F.3d 933 (4th Cir.1995).

[8] 92 F.3d 612 (8th Cir.1996), rev'd, 521 U.S. 642 (1997).

the resulting split between these circuits and the prior Second Circuit holdings validating the misappropriation theory.

A. *O'Hagan* Facts

James O'Hagan was a partner in the Minneapolis law firm of Dorsey & Whitney. In July 1988, Grand Metropolitan PLC (Grand Met), retained Dorsey & Whitney in connection with its planned takeover of Pillsbury Company. Although O'Hagan was not one of the lawyers on the Grand Met project, he learned of their intentions and began buying Pillsbury stock and call options on Pillsbury stock. When Grand Met announced its tender offer in October, the price of Pillsbury stock nearly doubled, allowing O'Hagan to reap a profit of more than $4.3 million.

O'Hagan was charged with violating 1934 Act § 10(b) and Rule 10b–5 by trading on misappropriated nonpublic information. As with *Chiarella* and the *Newman* defendants, O'Hagan could not be held liable under the disclose or abstain rule as a constructive insider because he worked for the bidder but traded in target company stock. He was neither a classic insider nor a constructive insider of the issuer of the securities in which he traded.[9]

B. The Issues

Both § 10(b) and Rule 10b–5 sweep broadly, capturing "any" fraudulent or manipulative conduct "in connection with" the purchase or sale of "any" security. Despite the almost breathtaking expanse of regulatory authority Congress thereby delegated to the Commission, the Supreme Court has warned against expanding the concept of securities fraud beyond that which the words of the statute will reasonably bear. From a textualist perspective, the validity of the misappropriation theory thus depends upon whether (1) the deceit, if any, worked by the misappropriator on the source of the information constitutes deception as the term is used in § 10(b) and Rule 10b–5 and (2) any such deceit is deemed to have occurred "in connection with" the purchase or sale of a security.

---

[9] O'Hagan was also indicted for violations of Rule 14e–3, which proscribes insider trading in connection with tender offers, and the federal mail fraud and money laundering statutes. The Eighth Circuit overturned O'Hagan's convictions under those provisions. As to Rule 14e–3, the court held that the SEC lacked authority to adopt a prohibition of insider trading that does not require a breach of fiduciary duty. *O'Hagan*, 92 F.3d at 622–27. As to O'Hagan's mail fraud and money laundering convictions, the Eighth Circuit also reversed them on grounds that the indictment was structured so as to premise the charges under those provisions on the primary securities fraud violations. Id. at 627–28. Accordingly, in view of the court's reversal of the securities fraud convictions, the latter counts could not stand either. The Supreme Court reversed on all points, reinstating O'Hagan's convictions under all of the statutory violations charged in the indictment. U.S. v. O'Hagan, 521 U.S. 642 (1997). The court's Rule 14e–3 holding is discussed infra Chapter 10.

1.   Deceit on the source of the information; herein of *Santa Fe*

In *Bryan*, the Fourth Circuit defined fraud—as the term is used in § 10(b) and Rule 10b–5—"as the making of a material misrepresentation or the nondisclosure of material information in violation of a duty to disclose."[10] So defined, fraud is present in a misappropriation case only in a technical and highly formalistic sense. Although a misappropriator arguably deceives the source of the information, any such deception is quite inconsequential. The source of the information presumably is injured, if at all, not by the deception, but by the conversion of the information by the misappropriator for his own profit. Hence, it is theft—and any concomitant breach of fiduciary duty—by the misappropriator that is truly objectionable. Any deception on the source of the information is purely incidental to the theft. Accordingly, the Fourth Circuit held, the misappropriation theory runs afoul of the Supreme Court's holding in *Santa Fe* that a mere breach of duty cannot give rise to Rule 10b–5 liability.[11] As the court explained, "the misappropriation theory [improperly] transforms § 10(b) from a rule intended to govern and protect relations among market participants who are owed duties under the securities laws into a federal common law governing and protecting any and all trust relationships."[12]

2.   The "in connection with" requirement; herein of *Central Bank*

According to the Eighth Circuit's O'Hagan opinion, "the misappropriation theory does not require 'deception,' and, even assuming that it does, it renders nugatory the requirement that the 'deception' be 'in connection with the purchase or sale of any security,' " as required by the text of § 10(b).[13] The Eighth Circuit therefore held that the theory ran afoul of the Supreme Court's *Central Bank* decision.

In *Central Bank of Denver v. First Interstate Bank*,[14] the Supreme Court held that there was no implied private right of action against those who aid and abet violations of Rule 10b–5. *Central Bank* thus substantially limited the scope of secondary liability under the rule, at least insofar as private party causes of

---

[10] 58 F.3d at 946.

[11] On *Santa Fe* and its implications for the insider trading regime, see Chapter 6.A.1.

[12] Id. at 950.

[13] *O'Hagan*, 92 F.3d at 617.

[14] 511 U.S. 164 (1994).

action are concerned. For our purposes, however, the case is more significant for its methodology than its holding.

Until *Central Bank*, courts and commentators viewed Rule 10b–5 as an example of interstitial lawmaking in which courts used common law adjudicatory methods to flesh out the text's bare bones.[15] In *Central Bank*, however, the Supreme Court held the scope of conduct prohibited by § 10(b) (and thus the rule) is controlled by the text of the statute. Where the plain text does not resolve some aspect of the Rule 10b–5 cause of action, courts must "infer 'how the 1934 Congress would have addressed the issue had the 10b–5 action been included as an express provision of the 1934 Act.' "[16] The court elsewhere acknowledged this is an "awkward task,"[17] but Justice Scalia put it more colorfully by quipping that "[w]e are imagining here."[18] Central Bank constrained this imaginative process by requiring courts to "use the express causes of action in the securities acts as the primary model for the § 10(b) action."[19]

Invoking *Central Bank*, the Eighth Circuit's *O'Hagan* decision interpreted the statutory prohibition of fraud created by § 10(b) narrowly to exclude conduct constituting a "mere breach of a fiduciary duty."[20] Instead, the prohibition captures only conduct constituting a material misrepresentation or the nondisclosure of material information in violation of the duty to disclose. Because the misappropriation theory permits the imposition of § 10(b) liability based upon a breach of fiduciary duty without any such deception, the Eighth Circuit held that the theory was inconsistent with the plain statutory text of § 10(b) and, accordingly, invalid as per *Central Bank*.

The Eighth Circuit's principal rationale for rejecting the misappropriation theory, however, was based on the statutory limitation that the fraud be committed "in connection with" a

---

[15] See, e.g., A.C. Pritchard, Justice Lewis F. Powell, Jr., and the Counterrevolution in the Federal Securities Laws, 52 Duke L.J. 841, 865 (2003) (arguing that that Justice Powell "considered the judge-made remedy under Rule 10b–5 to be a species of federal common law, and thus appropriate for judges to consider policy in defining its limits"); Louis Loss, The Assault on Securities Act Section 12(2), 105 Harv. L. Rev. 908, 910–11 (1992) (arguing that courts are creating "federal common law in order to invent appropriate" elements of the Rule 10b–5 cause of action); see also Blue Chip Stamps v. Manor Drug Stores, 421 U.S. 723, 737 (1975) ("When we deal with private actions under Rule 10b–5, we deal with a judicial oak which has grown from little more than a legislative acorn.").

[16] *Central Bank*, 511 U.S. at 173 (quoting Musick, Peeler & Garrett v. Employers Ins. of Wausau, 508 U.S. 286, 294 (1993)).

[17] Lampf, Pleva, Lipkind, Prupis & Petigrow v. Gilbertson, 501 U.S. 350, 359 (1991).

[18] Id. at 366.

[19] *Central Bank*, 511 U.S. at 178.

[20] *O'Hagan*, 92 F.3d at 618.

securities transaction. Again relying upon the Supreme Court's *Central Bank* decision, the *O'Hagan court* gave this provision a narrow interpretation. Specifically, the court held that § 10(b) reaches "only a breach of a duty to parties to the securities transaction or, at the most, to other market participants such as investors."[21] Absent such a limitation, the court opined, § 10(b) would be transformed "into an expansive 'general fraud-on-the-source theory' which seemingly would apply to infinite number of trust relationships."[22] Such an expansive theory of liability, the court further opined, could not be justified by the text of statute.

In the typical misappropriation case, of course, the source of the information is not the affected purchaser or seller. Often the source is not even a contemporaneous purchaser or seller and frequently has no stake in any affected securities transaction. In *Carpenter*, for example, the Wall Street Journal was neither a purchaser nor seller of the affected securities, nor did it have any financial stake in any of the affected transactions. Similarly, in *Bryan*, the state of West Virginia was not a purchaser or seller, and had no direct stake in Bryan's securities transactions. In neither case did the defendant fail to disclose material information to a market participant to whom he owed a duty of disclosure. One thus must stretch the phrase "in connection with" pretty far in order to bring a misappropriator's alleged fraud within the statute's ambit, even assuming the misappropriator has deceived the source of the information. As the Fourth Circuit put it, the "misappropriation of information from an individual who is in no way connected to, or even interested in, securities is simply not the kind of conduct with which the securities laws, as presently written, are concerned."[23]

The Eighth and Fourth Circuits' interpretation of § 10(b) has much to commend it. The courts carefully considered the Supreme Court's relevant precedents, especially *Santa Fe* and *Central Bank*. Insofar as the misappropriation theory imposes liability solely on the basis of a breach of fiduciary duty to the source of the information, without any requirement that the alleged perpetrator have deceived the persons with whom he traded or other market participants, it ran afoul of those precedents. As the Eighth Circuit opined, the lower court decisions endorsing the misappropriation theory had generally failed to conduct a rigorous analysis of § 10(b)'s text or the pertinent Supreme Court decisions. On those few occasions when courts had done so, moreover, they had cast

---

[21] Id. In *Bryan*, the Fourth Circuit similarly opined § 10(b) is primarily concerned with deception of purchasers and sellers of securities, and at most extends to fraud committed against other persons closely linked to, and with a stake in, a securities transaction. *Bryan*, 58 F.3d at 946.

[22] *O'Hagan*, 92 F.3d at 619.

[23] *Bryan*, 58 F.3d at 950.

doubt on the misappropriation theory's validity. In his partial dissent to a leading Second Circuit opinion endorsing and fleshing out the misappropriation theory, for example, Judge Winter (a former corporate law professor at Yale) stated the misappropriation theory lacked "any obvious relationship" to the statutory text of § 10(b) because "theft rather than fraud or deceit" had become "the gravamen of the prohibition."[24]

Yet, there were problems with applying *Central Bank* to the insider trading prohibition. Although the Fourth Circuit was careful to opine that its opinion in *Bryan* left intact both the disclose or abstain theory of liability and tipping liability thereunder, arguably this was not the case. As we have seen, the duty at issue in tipping cases is not a duty to disclose, but rather, a duty to refrain from self-dealing in confidential information owed by the tipper to the source of the information.[25] As such, the prohibition on tipping under the disclose or abstain theory was subject to the same line of attack as the Fourth and Eighth Circuits invoked against the misappropriation theory.

Even the basic disclose or abstain theory of liability was called into question by those courts' decisions. Granted, insider trading in violation of the disclose or abstain rule involves an element of deception. By definition, the defendant has failed to disclose nonpublic information before trading. As we have seen, however, the insider trading prohibition generally collapses into a rule to abstain from trading rather than a rule requiring disclosure or abstention.[26] In other words, given that defendant had no right to disclose, it is the failure to abstain from trading, rather than any deception, which is the basis for imposing liability.

Put another way, the claim that insider trading involves deception is circular. As *Chiarella* made clear, and *Dirks* affirmed, not all failures to disclose are fraudulent. Rather, a nondisclosure is actionable only if the trader is subject to a duty to disclose. In turn, a duty to disclose exists only where the trader is subject to a fiduciary duty to refrain from self-dealing in confidential information. Absent such a fiduciary duty, insider trading simply is not fraudulent. Once again, this leaves the disclose or abstain rule subject to the same line of attack as was adopted by the Fourth and Eighth Circuits.

A further problem is that the texts in fact provide little guidance as to the scope of insider trading liability. Recall that

---

[24] U.S. v. Chestman, 947 F.2d 551, 578 (2d Cir. 1991) (Winter, J., concurring in part and dissenting in part), cert. denied, 503 U.S. 1004 (1992).

[25] See Chapter 5.B.

[26] See Chapter 4.B.

under *Central Bank*, where the text does not resolve some aspect of the Rule 10b–5 cause of action, courts must infer how the 1934 Congress would have addressed the issue if Rule 10b–5 had been included as an express provision of the 1934 Act. *Central Bank* somewhat constrained the imaginative process by requiring courts to use the express causes of action in the securities acts as the primary model for interpreting Rule 10b–5. As applied to insider trading, however, this approach is not especially helpful. The short-swing profits cause of action under Section 16(b) of the Exchange Act regulates insider trading only indirectly, does not seek to define insider trading, and does not involve questions of fiduciary duty. Section 20A of that Act provides an express private right of action for those who trade contemporaneously with an insider and Section 21A thereof provides a treble money civil fine for insider trading, but both were adopted more than 50 years after Section 10(b) and, moreover, neither provides a substantive definition of insider trading.

Non-textual evidence of congressional intent suggests that extension of *Central Bank* to the insider trading context in fact would be inconsistent with the will of Congress. Granted, there is a strong argument that Congress in 1934 did not intend to regulate insider trading in any way other than through the short-swing profit provisions of Section 16(b).[27] Since 1934, however, Congress has twice amended the Exchange Act for the specific purpose of enhancing the penalties associated with insider trading.[28] On both occasions, Congress strongly supported vigorous SEC enforcement of the federal insider trading prohibition.[29] Although ex post facto indications of legislative intent often are viewed skeptically, the recent amendments arguably constitute an authoritative congressional endorsement of the insider trading prohibition generally and the misappropriation theory in particular.

Under the so-called re-enactment doctrine, where Congress has revised a statute without reversing prior on-point judicial holdings, that failure has been taken as evidence of congressional approval of those holdings.[30] In adopting neither the 1984 Insider Trading Sanctions Act (ITSA)[31] nor the 1988 Insider Trading and Securities

---

[27] Stephen M. Bainbridge, Incorporating State Law Fiduciary Duties into the Federal Insider Trading Prohibition, 52 Wash. & Lee L. Rev. 1189, 1228–31 (1995).

[28] Insider Trading and Securities Fraud Enforcement Act of 1988, Pub. L. No. 100–704, 102 Stat. 4677 (1988); Insider Trading Sanctions Act of 1984, Pub. L. No. 98–376, 98 Stat. 1264 (1984).

[29] See, e.g., H.R. Rep. No. 910, 100th Cong., 2d Sess. 11–16 (1988).

[30] See, e.g., Merrill Lynch, Pierce, Fenner & Smith, Inc. v. Curran, 456 U.S. 353 (1982).

[31] Pub. L. No. 98–376, 98 Stat. 1264 (1984).

Fraud Enforcement Act (ITSFEA),[32] did Congress see fit to reverse the misappropriation theory. To the contrary, the legislative history of both acts is replete with statements of congressional approval of that theory.[33] Indeed, ITSFEA § 2 itself provides an express congressional finding that the SEC's rules "governing trading while in possession of material, nonpublic information are, as required by the Act, necessary and appropriate in the public interest and for the protection of investors."[34] The accompanying House Report further states that "these findings are intended as an expression of congressional support for these regulations."[35]

On the substantive level, ITSFEA overruled *Moss v. Morgan Stanley, Inc.,*[36] in which the Second Circuit had held that private parties did not have standing to sue under the misappropriation theory. ITSFEA expressly created a private party cause of action for insider trading cases. Because an implied private party cause of action already existed as to violations of the disclose or abstain rule, however, Congress's action amounts to an express legislative endorsement of the misappropriation theory.[37]

On the other hand, *Central Bank* significantly undercut the reenactment doctrine, by remarking that arguments based on the re-enactment doctrine "deserve little weight in the interpretive process."[38] The Court also held that because "Congress has not reenacted the language of § 10(b) since 1934" the Court need not "determine whether the other conditions for applying the reenactment doctrine are present."[39] Hence, even if Congress had intended that ITSA and ITSFEA expressly endorse the misappropriation theory, that action arguably would not be binding on the courts.

Extension of this aspect of *Central Bank* to the insider trading context, however, is just as problematic as extension of its main holding thereto. Rejecting the reenactment doctrine as authority for the misappropriation theory simply because § 10(b) has never been

---

[32] Pub. L. No. 100–704, 102 Stat. 4677 (1988).

[33] See, e.g., H.R. Rep. No. 910, supra note 29, at 10, 26; H.R. Rep. No. 355, 98th Cong., 1st Sess. 4–5 (1983).

[34] Pub. L. No. 100–704, 102 Stat. 4677 (1988). As suggested by the congressional use of the plural form, these findings and legislative history apparently were intended to validate SEC Rule 14e–3 as well as the misappropriation theory.

[35] H.R. Rep. No. 910, supra note 29, at 35.

[36] 719 F.2d 5 (2d Cir. 1983), cert. denied, 465 U.S. 1025 (1984).

[37] See H.R. Rep. No. 910, supra note 29, at 38–39 ("This codification of a right of action for all contemporaneous traders is intended, in part, to overturn court cases which have precluded recovery by plaintiffs who were victims of misappropriation. See, e.g., Moss v. Morgan Stanley, Inc., 719 F.2d 5 (2d Cir.1983).").

[38] *Central Bank,* 511 U.S. at 187.

[39] Id. at 185.

re-enacted ignores highly relevant congressional action elsewhere in the act and thus flouts the apparent congressional intent. If only the intent of the 1934 Congress is relevant, after all, the evidence suggests that § 10(b) was not concerned with insider trading and the prohibition as a whole should be overturned. This would negate the subsequently adopted statutory penalties for insider trading because there no longer would be any underlying violation to which they could be applied, which is an anomalous result, at best. Should penalties Congress adopted with the clear intent that they be applied to misappropriation of information be rendered nugatory by judicial rejection of the underlying cause of action?

In light of these considerations, reconciling the insider trading prohibition with *Central Bank* loomed as one of the major doctrinal problems facing the Supreme Court in *O'Hagan*.

C. The Supreme Court Holding

In *O'Hagan*, a majority of the Supreme Court upheld the misappropriation theory as a valid basis on which to impose insider trading liability. A fiduciary's undisclosed use of information belonging to his principal, without disclosure of such use to the principal, for personal gain constitutes fraud in connection with the purchase or sale of a security, the majority (per Justice Ginsburg) opined, and thus violates Rule 10b–5.[40]

The court acknowledged that misappropriators such as O'Hagan have no disclosure obligation running to the persons with whom they trade. Instead, it grounded liability under the misappropriation theory on deception of the source of the information. As the majority interpreted the theory, it addresses the use of "confidential information for securities trading purposes, in breach of a duty owed to the source of the information."[41] Under this theory, the majority explained, "a fiduciary's undisclosed, self-serving use of a principal's information to purchase or sell securities, in breach of a duty of loyalty and confidentiality, defrauds the principal of the exclusive use of that information."[42] So defined, the majority held, the misappropriation theory satisfies § 10(b)'s requirement that there be a "deceptive device or contrivance" used "in connection with" a securities transaction.[43]

---

[40] U.S. v. O'Hagan, 521 U.S. 642 (1997).

[41] Id. at 652.

[42] Id.

[43] Id. at 653. The Supreme Court thus rejected Chief Justice Burger's argument in *Chiarella* that the misappropriation theory created disclosure obligation running to those with whom the misappropriator trades. Id. at 655 n.6. Instead, it is the failure to disclose one's intentions to the source of the information that constitutes the requisite disclosure violation under the *O'Hagan* version of the misappropriation theory. Id. at 655.

1. Status of *Central Bank*

As we have just seen, the tension between *Central Bank* and the insider trading prohibition was a major doctrinal issue facing the court in *O'Hagan*. Surprisingly, however, the majority essentially punted on this issue. The majority essentially ignored both the statutory text and the cogent arguments advanced by both the Eighth and Fourth Circuits with respect to the implications of *Central Bank* for the misappropriation theory. To the limited extent the majority discussed *Central Bank*'s implications for the problem at hand, it focused solely on the Eighth Circuit's argument that *Central Bank* limited Rule 10b–5's regulatory purview to purchasers and sellers. The interpretive methodology expounded in *Central Bank* was essentially ignored.

The majority's failure to more carefully evaluate *Central Bank*'s implications for the phrase "in connection with," as used in § 10(b), is especially troubling. By virtue of the majority's holding that deception on the source of the information satisfies the "in connection with" requirement, fraudulent conduct having only tenuous connections to a securities transaction is brought within Rule 10b–5's scope. There has long been a risk that Rule 10b–5 will become a universal solvent, encompassing not only virtually the entire universe of securities fraud, but also much of state corporate law. The minimal contacts *O'Hagan* requires between the fraudulent act and a securities transaction substantially exacerbate that risk. In addition to the risk that much of state corporate law may be preempted by federal developments under Rule 10b–5, the uncertainty created as to Rule 10b–5's parameters fairly raises vagueness and related due process issues, despite the majority's rather glib dismissal of such concerns.

2. Status of *Santa Fe*

The majority opinion treated *Santa Fe* as a mere disclosure case, asserting: "in *Santa Fe Industries*, all pertinent facts were disclosed by the persons charged with violating § 10(b) and Rule 10b–5; therefore, there was no deception through nondisclosure to which liability under those provisions could attach."[44] The court thus wholly ignored the important federalism concerns upon which *Santa Fe* rested and which are implicated by the misappropriation theory (indeed, by the insider trading prohibition as a whole).

3. O'Hagan's liability

O'Hagan was not liable because he failed to disclose the material nonpublic information to the investors with whom he

---

[44] Id. at 655.

traded. Instead, he was liable because he failed to disclose his intention to trade to the source of the information on the basis of which he traded. As also required by the misappropriation theory, O'Hagan's duty to disclose arose out of a fiduciary duty to that source. As a partner, he had a fiduciary relationship with his law firm. As an attorney, he had a fiduciary duty to his firm's client. On the facts of *O'Hagan*, as the majority indicated, he thus needed to disclose his trading activity to both Dorsey & Whitney and Grand Met in order to escape Rule 10b–5 liability.[45]

D. Questions Left Open

In many respects, *O'Hagan* posed more new questions than it answered old ones. In this section, we discuss some of the more interesting and important issues it left open and the way lower courts have resolved them.

1.   Liability for brazen misappropriators?

The *O'Hagan* majority made clear that disclosure to the source of the information is all that is required under Rule 10b–5. Accordingly, it logically follows that if a misappropriator brazenly discloses his trading plans to the source, and then trades on that information, Rule 10b–5 is not violated, even if the source of the information refused permission to trade and objected vigorously.[46]

If this rule seems odd, so did the majority's justification for it. According to the majority, "investors likely would hesitate to venture their capital in a market where trading based on misappropriated nonpublic information is unchecked by law." The majority went on to opine that the investor on the other side of the transaction suffers from "a disadvantage that cannot be overcome with research or skill." As such, the majority claimed that the misappropriation theory advances "an animating purpose of the Exchange Act: to insure [sic] honest securities markets and thereby promote investor confidence."

The difficulties with this argument should be readily apparent. Investors who trade with a brazen misappropriator presumably will not feel any greater confidence in the integrity of the securities

---

[45] See id. at 655 n.6 ("Under the misappropriation theory urged in this case, the disclosure obligation runs to the source of the information, here, Dorsey & Whitney and Grand Met."). Notice the interesting question presented by the requirement that O'Hagan disclose his intentions to Dorsey & Whitney. Given that O'Hagan was a partner in Dorsey & Whitney, query whether his knowledge of his intentions would be imputed to the firm. As a practical matter, of course, O'Hagan should have informed the lawyer with the principal responsibility for the Grand Met transaction and/or the firm's managing partner.

[46] O'Hagan, 521 U.S. at 655 ("full disclosure forecloses liability under the misappropriation theory . . . if the fiduciary discloses to the source that he plans to trade on nonpublic information, there is no 'deceptive device' and thus no § 10(b) violation").

market if they later find out that the misappropriator had disclosed his intentions to the source of the information. Worse yet, both the phraseology and the substance of the majority's argument plausibly could be interpreted as resurrecting the long-discredited equal access test. If the goal of insider trading law in fact is to insulate investors from information asymmetries that cannot be overcome by research or skill, the equal access test is far better suited to doing so than the current test.

Merely requiring the prospective misappropriator to disclose his intentions before trading also provides only weak protection of the source of the information's property rights therein. To be sure, because of the disclosure requirement concerns about detecting improper trading are alleviated. As the majority pointed out, moreover, the source may have state law claims against the misappropriator. In particular, the agency law prohibition on the use of confidential information for personal gain will often provide a remedy to the source. In some jurisdictions, however, it is far from clear whether inside trading by a fiduciary violates state law. Even where state law proscribes such trading, the Supreme Court's approach means that in brazen misappropriator cases we lose the comparative advantage the SEC has in litigating insider trading cases and, moreover, also lose the comparative advantage provided by the well-developed and relatively liberal remedy under Rule 10b–5.

These issues were addressed in *SEC v. Rocklage*,[47] in which the SEC brought a misappropriation theory-based insider trading charge against the spouse of a CEO who had passed material nonpublic information about her husband's company to her brother and his friend who then traded. As the court summarized the issue:

> The defendants' view is that a pre-tip disclosure to the source of an intention to trade or tip completely eliminates any deception involved in the transaction. They rely on *O'Hagan*'s language that "if the fiduciary discloses to the source that he plans to trade on the nonpublic information, there is no 'deceptive device' and thus no § 10(b) violation." The defendants argue that *O'Hagan* put no qualifiers on what is meant by "disclos[ure] to the source" of a plan to trade on nonpublic information, and so the SEC is not free to qualify the concept.

> The SEC disagrees, arguing that the disclosure referenced in O'Hagan must mean disclosure that is "useful" to the fiduciary's principal. The SEC draws support from a footnote in O'Hagan which may be read as implying that disclosure

---

[47] 470 F.3d 1 (1st Cir. 2006).

enables a source to take remedial action. As the SEC sees it, disclosure to the source serves a useful purpose when "the source of material non-public information reasonably could be expected to, and reasonably could, prevent the unauthorized use of the information for securities trading."[48]

The First Circuit rejected both positions. Instead, the court opined that:

> Unlike this case, *O'Hagan* was not a case which involved the deceptive acquisition of information. Arguably, the language in *O'Hagan* can be read to create a "safe harbor" if there is disclosure to the fiduciary principal of an intention to trade on or tip legitimately acquired information. This is because under *O'Hagan*'s logic such a "safe harbor" applies, if at all, when the alleged deception is in the undisclosed trading or tipping of information. In those cases, disclosure of the intent to trade arguably will eliminate the sole source of deception. But a case of deceptive acquisition of information followed by deceptive tipping and trading is different. It makes little sense to assume that disclosure of an intention to tip using deceptively acquired information would necessarily negate the original deception.[49]

This reading of *O'Hagan* likely guts the brazen misappropriator loophole. If the "safe harbor" is limited to cases in which the alleged misappropriator "legitimately" acquires the information, the vast majority of misappropriation cases likely will be ineligible for the safe harbor.

Suppose for example that a CEO discloses material nonpublic information to the company's CLO. At the time the CLO receives the information, she plans to trade on the basis of it, but she does not disclose that intent to the CEO at that time. Sometime later, just as the CLO is about to trade, she discloses her plans to the CEO. Presumably, the First Circuit would tell us that the failure to disclose her intentions at the time she first received the information meant that she committed deception in acquiring the information and that her subsequent disclosure therefore does not preclude liability.

2.   Liability for authorized trading?

Suppose a takeover bidder authorized a speculator to trade in target company's stock on the basis of material nonpublic information about the prospective bidder's intentions. Warehousing of this sort is proscribed by Rule 14e–3, but only insofar as the

---

[48] Id. at 11.

[49] Id. at 12.

information relates to a perspective tender offer.[50] Whether such trading in a non-tender offer context violated Rule 10b–5 was unclear before *O'Hagan.*

The *O'Hagan* majority at least implicitly validated authorized trading. It approvingly quoted, for example, the statement of the government's counsel that "to satisfy the common law rule the trustee may not use the property that [has] been entrusted [to] him, there would have to be consent."[51] Is it plausible that Grand Met might have given O'Hagan such approval, if he had asked? Maybe. Warehousing of takeover stocks and tipping acquisition plans to friendly parties were once common—hence the need for Rule 14e–3—and doubtless still occurs, albeit probably not using the bidder's attorney.

The authorized trading dictum has significant, but as yet little-noticed, implications. Query, for example, whether it applies to all insider trading cases or just to misappropriation cases. Suppose that in a classic disclose or abstain case, such as *Texas Gulf Sulphur*, the issuer's board of directors adopted a policy of allowing insider trading by managers. If they did so, the corporation has consented to any such inside trading, which under Justice Ginsburg's analysis appears to vitiate any deception. The corporate policy itself presumably would have to be disclosed, just as broad disclosure respecting executive compensation is already required, but the implication is that authorized trading should not result in 10b–5 liability under either misappropriation or disclose or abstain.

On the other hand, the two theories can be distinguished in ways that undermine application of the authorized trading dictum to disclose or abstain cases. In a misappropriation case, such as *Carpenter*, liability is premised on fraud on the source of the information. In *Carpenter*, acting through appropriate decision-making processes, the Journal presumably could authorize inside trading by its agents. By contrast, however, *Chiarella* focused the classic disclose or abstain rule on fraud perpetrated on the specific investors with whom the insiders trade. Authorization of inside trading by the issuer's board of directors, or even a majority of the shareholders, does not constitute consent by the specific investors with whom the insider trades. Nothing in *O'Hagan* suggests an intent to undermine the *Chiarella* interpretation of the traditional disclose or abstain rule. Indeed, to the contrary, Justice Ginsburg expressly stated that the two theories are "complementary."[52] Because the disclose or abstain rule thus remains conceptually

---

[50] See Chapter 10 (discussing Rule 14e–3).

[51] *O'Hagan*, 521 U.S. at 654.

[52] *O'Hagan*, 521 U.S. at 652.

distinct from the misappropriation theory, the authorized trading dictum can be plausibly limited to the latter context.

3.   The fiduciary relationship requirement

Does a duty to disclose to the source of the information arise before trading in all fiduciary relationships? Consider ABA Model Rule of Professional Conduct 1.8(b), which states: "A lawyer shall not use information relating to representation of a client to the disadvantage of the client unless the client consents after consultation. . . ." Does a lawyer's use of confidential client information for insider trading purposes always operate to the client's disadvantage? If not, and assuming the Model Rule accurately states the lawyer's fiduciary obligation, O'Hagan did not violate § 10(b).

The *O'Hagan* majority, however, failed to inquire into the nature of O'Hagan's duties, if any, to Grand Met. Instead, the majority assumed that lawyers are fiduciaries, all fiduciaries are subject to a duty to refrain from self-dealing in confidential information, and, accordingly, that the misappropriation theory applies to lawyers and all other fiduciaries. The majority's approach, of course, begs the question—how do we know O'Hagan is a fiduciary? We will return to this problem in Chapter 8 below.

4.   Criminal or civil?

In rejecting the Eighth Circuit's argument that Rule 10b–5 is primarily concerned with deception of market participants, the *O'Hagan* majority noted that the discussion in *Central Bank* upon which the Eighth Circuit relied dealt only with private civil litigation under § 10(b). The court then went on to discuss its holding in *Blue Chip Stamps*[53] that only actual purchasers or sellers of securities have standing to bring private causes of action under Rule 10b–5. The court concluded: "Criminal prosecutions do not present the dangers the Court addressed in Blue Chip Stamps, so that decision is 'inapplicable' to indictments for violations of § 10(b) and Rule 10b–5."[54]

This passage opened the door for misappropriators to argue that *O'Hagan* should be limited to criminal prosecutions. As a practical matter, however, it was never likely that the misappropriation theory would be limited to criminal cases. Among other things, although the majority declined to address the significance of the 1988 statute and its legislative history for the validity of the misappropriation theory, interpreting *O'Hagan* as

---

[53] Blue Chip Stamps v. Manor Drug Stores, 421 U.S. 723 (1975).

[54] O'Hagan, 521 U.S. at 665.

validating the misappropriation theory only as to criminal actions would render the private party cause of action created by Exchange Act § 20A nugatory. Not surprisingly, subsequent lower court cases have routinely applied the misappropriation theory in both criminal and civil cases.

E. Tipping by Misappropriators

Although the SEC has occasionally urged courts to adopt a more liberal standard for tipping under the misappropriation theory than the *Dirks* regime, courts have generally opined that the *Dirks* test applies to cases brought under the misappropriation theory as well as to those brought under the classic disclose or abstain theory.[55] The vast bulk of these statements, however, were dicta. The leading precedent squarely addressing the issue is *SEC v. Yun*,[56] in which the Eleventh Circuit explicitly rejected an SEC argument that "the benefit requirement has no application in misappropriation cases."[57] In doing so, moreover, the Court established the important proposition that courts should attempt whenever possible to harmonize the law under both the disclose or abstain and misappropriation theories by applying precedents from one theory to the other.[58] Accordingly, the first place one should look for answers to open questions under one of the two theories is the case law under the other theory.

F. Is There Misappropriation Theory Liability for Trading in Debt Securities?

We saw in Chapter 6.C.5 that there is considerable doubt as to whether insider trading liability under the disclose or abstain theory arises when the insider trades in debt securities. As discussed therein, the principal argument against extending the insider trading prohibition to those cases is that the insider owes no

---

[55] Compare SEC v. Obus, 693 F.3d 276, 285–86 (2d Cir. 2012) (stating that the personal benefit requirement applies both to "an insider or a misappropriator"); U.S. v. Newman, 2013 WL 1943342 (S.D.N.Y. 2013) (rejecting defendant's argument that the personal benefit test did not apply to criminal cases under the misappropriation theory); SEC v. Gonzalez de Castilla, 184 F. Supp. 2d 365, 375 (S.D.N.Y. 2002) (stating that the personal benefit requirement applies to misappropriation cases); SEC v. Lambert, 38 F. Supp. 2d 1348, 1351–52 (S.D. Fla. 1999) (same) with SEC v. Rocklage, 470 F.3d 1, 7 n.4 (1st Cir. 2006) (noting that the court's prior precedents had "left open" the applicability of the personal benefit requirement in misappropriation cases). Professors Nagy and Painter observe that, "since *O'Hagan* was decided, no court has ever extended misappropriation theory liability to a putative tipper in the absence of evidence that he or she conveyed the material nonpublic information in exchange for a direct or indirect personal benefit." Donna M. Nagy & Richard W. Painter, Selective Disclosure by Federal Officials and the Case for an FGD (Fairer Government Disclosure) Regime, 2012 Wis. L. Rev. 1285, 1318.

[56] 327 F.3d 1263 (11th Cir. 2003).

[57] Id. at 1275.

[58] Id. at 1276.

fiduciary duties to debt holders, whose rights are solely contractual. This argument would not preclude applying the misappropriation theory to trading in debt securities, however, because liability under that theory is based not on the relationship between the trader and those with whom he trades but on the relationship between the trader and the source of the information. So long as that relationship gives rise to the requisite duty to disclose to the source before trading, the misappropriation theory's key prerequisite is satisfied.

In *Salovaara v. Jackson Nat. Life Ins. Co.*,[59] however, a federal district judge declined "to extend the Court's decision in *O'Hagan* to a civil case involving a transaction for high yield debt securities."[60] The judge justified his refusal to do so on grounds that the "[c]ase law clearly establishes that a corporation does not have a fiduciary relationship with its debt security holders, as with its shareholders."[61] For the reasons just discussed, however, this rationale is inapt in this context.

On the other hand, in this private party lawsuit, the plaintiffs were not the source of the information on which the defendant traded and the defendant owed them no fiduciary duties. According to the trial judge, this precluded application of the misappropriation theory. This basis for the judge's decision is sound, but obviously would not preclude the use of the misappropriation theory in other cases involving trading in debt securities.[62]

---

[59] 66 F. Supp.2d 593 (D. N.J. 1999), aff'd on other grounds, 246 F.3d 289 (3rd Cir. 2001).

[60] Id. at 601.

[61] Id.

[62] Cf. Donald C. Langevoort, Insider Trading: Regulation, Enforcement & Prevention § 3.12 at 3–27 (2012) ("The approach more consistent with *Chiarella* is that no abstain or disclose obligation arises in connection with trading in debt securities, leaving liability in such a case to rest on the misappropriation theory. . . .").

Chapter 8

THE FIDUCIARY DUTY REQUIREMENT AND NONTRADITIONAL RELATIONSHIPS

As we have seen, the predicate for insider trading liability under either the disclose or abstain rule or the misappropriation theory is the breach of a duty of disclosure arising out of a fiduciary relationship or similar relationship of trust and confidence between the insider and the person with whom he trades, in the former case, or the source of the information, in the latter case. Obviously, the initial task therefore is to determine whether a fiduciary relationship exists between the inside trader and the requisite counterpart. Whether that determination is made as a matter of state or federal law, unfortunately, is unclear. Likewise, which relationships qualify as fiduciary—as opposed to arms-length—remains unclear. *O'Hagan* informs us that the attorney-client relationship is a fiduciary one. Dictum in all three Supreme Court precedents tells us that corporate officers and directors are fiduciaries of their shareholders. Once we get outside the traditional categories of Rule 10b–5 defendants—insiders, constructive insiders, and their tippees—things get much more complicated. As the Second Circuit cogently observed in *U.S. v. Chestman*[1]:

> [F]iduciary duties are circumscribed with some clarity in the context of shareholder relations but lack definition in other contexts. Tethered to the field of shareholder relations, fiduciary obligations arise within a narrow, principled sphere. The existence of fiduciary duties in other common law settings, however, is anything but clear. Our Rule 10b–5 precedents ..., moreover, provide little guidance with respect to the question of fiduciary breach, because they involved egregious fiduciary breaches arising solely in the context of employer/employee associations.[2]

Although the case law attempting to determine which relationships are fiduciary in character was decided primarily under the misappropriation theory, the principles also should apply to any

---

[1] 947 F.2d 551 (2d Cir.1991), cert. denied 503 U.S. 1004 (1992).

[2] Id. at 567 (citations omitted). *Chestman* was a misappropriation theory case, as have been most of the nontraditional relationship cases. The problem it addressed and the principles announced therein, however, are applicable to insider trading cases generally. Accordingly, it seems appropriate to treat this issue here.

non-traditional fiduciary relationships arising under the disclose or abstain rule.[3]

A. *Chestman*

The best guidance to date on this issue in fact remains the *Chestman* decision. Ira Waldbaum was the president and controlling shareholder of Waldbaum, Inc., a publicly-traded supermarket chain. Ira decided to sell Waldbaum to A & P at $50 per share, a 100% premium over the prevailing market price. Ira informed his sister Shirley of the forthcoming transaction. Shirley told her daughter Susan Loeb, who in turn told her husband Keith Loeb. Each person in the chain told the next to keep the information confidential. Keith passed an edited version of the information to his stockbroker, one Robert Chestman, who then bought Waldbaum stock for his own account and the accounts of other clients. Chestman was accused of violating Rule 10b–5. According to the Government's theory of the case, Keith Loeb owed fiduciary duties to his wife Susan, which he violated by trading and tipping Chestman.

The Second Circuit held that in the absence of any evidence that Keith regularly participated in confidential business discussions, the familial relationship standing alone did not create a fiduciary relationship between Keith and Susan or any members of her family.[4] Likewise, unilaterally entrusting someone with confidential information does not by itself create a fiduciary relationship, even if the disclosure is accompanied by an admonition such as "don't tell," which Susan's statements to Keith included.[5] Since Keith had no fiduciary duty, his use of the information for personal gain did not violate Rule 10b–5.

In reaching that conclusion, the court laid out a general framework for dealing with nontraditional relationships. The court began by listing a number of "inherently fiduciary"[6] associations: "Counted among these hornbook fiduciary relations are those existing between attorney and client, executor and heir, guardian and ward, principal and agent, trustee and trust beneficiary, and

---

[3] See SEC v. Yun, 327 F.3d 1263, 1276 (11th Cir. 2003) (holding that courts should "attempt to synthesize, rather than polarize, insider trading law" and therefore should not "precedent involving the classical theory of liability whenever the SEC brings its actions under a misappropriation theory, and vice versa").

[4] See id. at 568 (holding that "marriage does not, without more, create a fiduciary relationship").

[5] See id. at 567 (holding that "a fiduciary duty cannot be imposed unilaterally by entrusting a person with confidential information"). Repeated disclosures of business secrets, however, could substitute for a factual finding of dependence and influence and, accordingly, sustain a finding that a fiduciary relationship existed in the case at bar. Id. at 569. On the facts of the case at bar, however, there was no evidence of such repeated disclosures as between Keith and Susan or her family.

[6] Id. at 568.

senior corporate official and shareholder."[7] If the relationship at bar falls within any such category, the inquiry is complete. In *O'Hagan*, for example, defendant O'Hagan, by virtue of his position as a partner in the law firm representing a potential acquirer, was deemed a fiduciary for purposes of Rule 10b–5. Of course, O'Hagan was a fiduciary of the acquirer, not the issuer or its shareholders. Although O'Hagan could not be prosecuted under the classic disclose or abstain theory, his fiduciary relationship with the source of the information on the basis of which he traded sufficed for liability under the misappropriation theory. In contrast, in *Chestman*, the court held that it was "clear that the relationships involved in this case—those between Keith and Susan Loeb and between Keith Loeb and the Waldbaum family—were not traditional fiduciary relationships."[8]

Once one moves beyond the class of "hornbook" fiduciary relationships, *Chestman* held that:

> A fiduciary relationship involves discretionary authority and dependency: One person depends on another—the fiduciary—to serve his interests. In relying on a fiduciary to act for his benefit, the beneficiary of the relation may entrust the fiduciary with custody over property of one sort or another. Because the fiduciary obtains access to this property to serve the ends of the fiduciary relationship, he becomes duty-bound not to appropriate the property for his own use.[9]

In the insider trading context, of course, the relevant property is confidential information belonging to the principal. Because the relationship between Keith and Susan did not involve either discretionary authority or dependency of this sort, their relationship was not fiduciary in character.

Accordingly, under *Chestman*, fiduciary "relationships are marked by the fact that the party in whom confidence is reposed has entered into a relationship in which he or she acts to serve the interests of the party entrusting him or her with such information."[10] Put another way, "*Chestman* requires the influence

---

[7] Id. (citations omitted).

[8] 947 F.2d at 568. The *Chestman* framework is yet another area in which the federalism concerns raised by *Santa Fe* ought to have figured more prominently than they did. As we have seen, the requisite fiduciary duty cannot be derived from Rule 10b–5 itself without making the rule incoherently circular and, moreover, violating *Santa Fe*. Unfortunately, the *Chestman* court simply ignored this problem. The court created a generic framework for deciding whether a fiduciary relationship is present, which purports to take its "cues as to what is required to create the requisite relationship from the securities fraud precedents and the common law." Id. The court thus mixed both federal and state law sources without much regard either for potential circularity or federalism.

[9] Id. at 569.

[10] U.S. v. Falcone, 257 F.3d 226, 234–35 (2d Cir.2001).

of a superior or dominating nature—not the 'influence' one peer might exert on another."[11] Relationships qualifying under that standard are "characterized by superiority, dominance, or control," they "are not relationships among equals."[12] The requisite dominance "arises out of some combination of 1) disparate knowledge and expertise, 2) a persuasive need to share confidential information, and 3) a legal duty to render competent aid."[13]

B. Rule 10b5–2

In 2000, the SEC addressed the *Chestman* problem insofar as cases arising under the misappropriation theory are concerned by adopting Rule 10b5–2, which provides "a nonexclusive list of three situations in which a person has a duty of trust or confidence for purposes of the 'misappropriation' theory. . . ."[14] First, such a duty exists whenever someone agrees to maintain information in confidence. Second, such a duty exists between two people who have a pattern or practice of sharing confidences such that the recipient of the information knows or reasonably should know that the speaker expects the recipient to maintain the information's confidentiality. Third, such a duty exists when someone receives or obtains material nonpublic information from a spouse, parent, child, or sibling. On the facts of *Chestman*, accordingly, Rule 10b5–2 would result in the imposition of liability because Keith received the information from his spouse who, in turn, had received it from her parent.

There is, however, some doubt as to the validity of the Rule. First, while it is true that the court in *Chestman* court observed that the requisite relationship could be satisfied either by a fiduciary relationship or a "similar relationship of trust and confidence," the court recognized that so expanding the class of relationships giving rise to liability could lead to results-oriented applications.[15] If a court wishes to impose liability, it need simply conclude that the relationship in question involves trust and confidence, even though the relationship bears no resemblance to those in which fiduciary-like duties are normally imposed. Accordingly, courts should be loath to use this phraseology as a mechanism for expanding the scope of liability. The *Chestman* court was sensitive to this possibility, holding that a relationship of trust and confidence must be "the functional equivalent of a fiduciary

---

[11] U.S. v. Kim, 184 F. Supp.2d 1006, 1011 (N.D.Cal.2002).

[12] Id.

[13] Id.

[14] Exchange Act Rel. No. 43,154 (Aug. 15, 2000).

[15] *Chestman*, 947 F.2d at 568.

relationship" before liability can be imposed.[16] *Chestman* also held that, at least as to criminal cases, it would not expand the class of relationships from which liability might arise to encompass those outside the traditional core of fiduciary obligation.[17] Rule 10b5–2, however, goes far beyond relationships that are the functional equivalent of fiduciary relationships by capturing, for example, purely contractual arrangements. Nevertheless, at least one court has upheld the Rule as a valid exercise of the SEC's rulemaking authority.[18]

C. Specific Relationships

1. Employees and other agents

Agency is a fiduciary relationship.[19] There is thus no dispute that employees and other agents have a fiduciary relationship with their employer out of which arises a duty to disclose sufficient to justify insider trading liability.[20] This is true even of low level employees.[21] The Second Circuit has held that journalists stand in a fiduciary relationship to the magazine or newspaper that employs them, rejecting a defendant journalist's argument that doing so interfered with the freedom of the press.[22]

---

[16] Id.

[17] Id. at 570.

[18] U.S. v. Corbin, 729 F. Supp.2d (S.D.N.Y.2011).

[19] Restatement (Third) of Agency § 1.01 (2012).

[20] See *Chestman*, 947 F.2d at 567 ("Our Rule 10b–5 precedents under the misappropriation theory . . . involved egregious fiduciary breaches arising solely in the context of employer/employee associations.").

[21] See SEC v. Falbo, 14 F. Supp.2d 508 (S.D.N.Y. 1998) (holding a secretary liable under misappropriation theory for using information learned from employer).

[22] U.S. v. Carpenter, 791 F.2d 1024, 1034 (2d Cir.1986) ("The First Amendment generally empowers a journalist with no 'special privilege' merely for the exercise of his craft . . . and the securities laws require of him, no less than of others, compliance therewith in the pursuit of his financial interests."), aff'd by an equally divided court, 484 U.S. 19 (1987). Interestingly, at least one court has held that a journalist has a duty to his readers his financial stake in the impact of his columns. Zweig v. The Hearst Corp., 521 F.2d 1129 (9th Cir.), cert. denied, 423 U.S. 1025, 96 S.Ct. 469, 46 L.Ed.2d 399 (1975). That opinion, however, has been sharply criticized. See, e.g., Note, A Financial Columnist's Duty to the Market Under Rule 10b–5: Civil Damages for Trading on a Misleading Investment Recommendation, 26 Wayne L. Rev. 1021, 1031 (1980) ("No precedent exists for the [Zweig] court's extension of a fiduciary duty of disclosure to an unlimited class, the reading-investing public, with whom defendant has not even a contractual or agency relationship.").

The *Zweig* decision pre-dated *Chiarella* and, according to many observers, is inconsistent with the Supreme Court's limitation of the duty to disclose or abstain to fiduciary relationships. See, e.g., Feldman v. Simkins Indus., 679 F.2d 1299, 1304 (9th Cir. 1982) (noting doubt at to the continuing validity of *Zweig* post-*Chiarella*); Note, Insider Trading and the Misappropriation Theory: Has the Second Circuit Gone Too Far, 61 St. John's L. Rev. 78, 101 n.90 (1986) ("The viability of the *Zweig* holding . . . has been seriously undercut by the Supreme Court's reinforcement of common law fiduciary relationship principles in *Chiarella*."). At least one court, however, believes *Zweig* is still good law, at least as applied to paid investment advisers. SEC v. Park, 99 F. Supp.2d 889, 899 (N.D.Ill. 2000) (stating that *Chiarella* "nowhere held that someone who encourages people to buy certain stocks and who

2.   Spouses and other family members

In *SEC v. Yun*,[23] the Eleventh Circuit disagreed with the *Chestman* result.[24] Without delving into the analysis of discretion and vulnerability contemplated by *Chestman*, the *Yun* court simply opined that spouses have reasonable and legitimate expectations of confidentiality.[25] In so holding, however, the *Yun* court relied heavily on Rule 10b5–2.[26] Although the trading at issue in *Yun* had taken place before the Rule went into effect, and thus was not directly subject to the Rule, the Eleventh Circuit found the SEC analysis of familial relationships codified in the Rule to be persuasive authority.

3.   Physicians

In *U.S. v. Willis*,[27] for example, the court determined that a psychiatrist violated the prohibition by trading on information learned from a patient. In determining that the requisite breach of fiduciary duty had occurred, the court relied in large measure on the Hippocratic Oath. In relevant part, the Oath states that "[w]hatsoever things I see or hear concerning the life of men, in my attendance on the sick or even apart therefrom, which ought not to be noised abroad, I will keep silence thereon, counting such things to be as sacred secrets."[28] As the *Willis* court noted, "[a]lmost every member of the public is aware of the promise of discretion contained in the Hippocratic oath, and every patient has a right to rely upon this warranty of silence."[29] The court concluded that the Oath therefore created a fiduciary relationship between physician and patient sufficient to justify holding the psychiatrist liable under the misappropriation theory.

---

also charges a fee to these people for this advice has no duty to disclose his interest in the stock").

[23] 327 F.3d 1263, 1272 (11th Cir. 2003) (holding that "the *Chestman* decision too narrowly defined the circumstances in which a duty of loyalty and confidentiality is created between husband and wife").

[24] In a footnote, the *Yun* court observed "that the *Chestman* majority emphasized that it was determining what constitutes a fiduciary relationship in the context of a criminal case." Id. at 1272 n.22. According to the *Yun* court, this suggested that even the *Chestman* majority "would expand the definition of a duty of loyalty and confidentiality in the civil context." Id. On the other hand, as the *Yun* court further observed, "many courts have employed *Chestman*'s narrow approach to determining the existence of a duty of loyalty and confidentiality to civil actions." Id. "Without commenting on the majority's analysis in *Chestman* as it pertains to the criminal context," the *Yun* court declined "to follow its analysis in the civil context." Id.

[25] Id. at 1273.

[26] See id. at 1273 n.23 ("Our conclusion is bolstered by statements the SEC has made since the trading in this case took place.").

[27] 737 F. Supp. 269 (S.D.N.Y.1990).

[28] Id. at 272.

[29] Id. (quoting Hammonds v. Aetna Casualty & Surety Co., 243 F. Supp. 793, 801 (N.D.Ohio 1965)).

4. The representative plaintiff in shareholder litigation

When a plaintiff's class action or derivative lawyer tells the representative shareholder material nonpublic information about the status of the litigation, on the basis of which the shareholder then trades in the issuer's stock, state courts have taken strong action. In *Steinhardt v. Howard-Anderson*,[30] several of the named representative plaintiffs in a state class action received confidential case status information from the plaintiff's class counsel. The plaintiffs then traded in the corporate defendant's' stock on the basis of that information. Upon discovering the improper trading, the court dismissed the plaintiffs from the case with prejudice, barred them from receiving any recovery from the litigation, required them to self-report their trades to the Securities and Exchange Commission, directed to disclose their improper trading in any future application to serve as lead plaintiff, and ordered to disgorge over half a million dollars in trading profits.

Query, however, whether the trading representative shareholders violated the federal insider trading prohibition. As always our analysis of this issue starts with the question of whether the relationship in question is fiduciary in character. In *Steinhardt*, the Chancery Court held that:

> When a stockholder of a Delaware corporation files suit as a representative plaintiff for a class of similarly situated stockholders, the plaintiff voluntarily assumes the role of fiduciary for the class. As a fiduciary, the representative plaintiff "owes to those whose cause he advocates a duty of the finest loyalty."[31]

Assuming that we can therefore count the relationship between the representative plaintiff and the class members as a textbook example of a fiduciary relationship, the misappropriation theory seemingly would apply to the representative plaintiff's trading.

Yet, there are at least two potential problems with applying the misappropriation theory in this context. First, does the relationship at issue here involve "discretionary authority and dependency," as required by *Chestman*?[32] In theory, the representative plaintiff has some discretionary authority over the litigation and the other shareholders depend on the representative shareholder to serve their interests. In practice, however, the real

---

[30] 2012 WL 29340 (Del. Ch. 2012).

[31] Id. at *8.

[32] U.S. v. Chestman, 947 F.2d 551, 568 (2d Cir.1991), cert. denied 503 U.S. 1004 (1992).

party in interest in shareholder litigation is the class counsel. It is
the class counsel who really runs the show and upon whom the
class members really depend; the representative shareholder is
simply the name on the lawsuit's title.[33] Accordingly, perhaps
trading by a representative plaintiff should be left to the tender
mercies of a court wielding its powers to control its docket.[34]

5.   Grand jurors

In 2006, the U.S. Attorney for the Southern District of New
York announced that his office had brought insider trading charges
against a grand juror. Defendant Jason Smith allegedly tipped
confidential information concerning the grand jury's investigation of
accounting fraud at Bristol-Myers Squibb Company to Eugene
Plotkin, an associate at Goldman Sachs & Co., and David Pajcin.
Their arrangement apparently was part of a broader effort by
Plotkin and Pajcin to trade on inside information obtained from
numerous sources. In any event, after receiving the tips from Smith
concerning the progress of the grand jury's investigation, Pajcin and
Plotkin, traded in Bristol-Meyers securities, betting that the stock

---

[33] See Jonathan R. Macey & Geoffrey P. Miller, The Plaintiffs' Attorney's Role
in Class Action and Derivative Litigation: Economic Analysis and Recommendations
for Reform, 58 U.Chi.L.Rev. 1, 3 (1991) (stating that plaintiffs' class and derivative
action attorneys "subject to only minimal monitoring by their ostensible 'clients' who
are either dispersed and disorganized (in the case of class litigation) or under the
control of hostile forces (in the case of derivative litigation)."); Geoffrey P. Miller,
Some Agency Problems in Settlement, 16 J.Legal Stud. 189, 190 (1987) (pointing out
that "the interests of plaintiff and attorney are never perfectly aligned"); Deborah L.
Rhode, Class Conflicts in Class Actions, 34 Stan.L.Rev. 1183, 1203 (1982) (asserting
that, "as a practical matter, once a class is certified, named plaintiffs generally are
neither highly motivated nor well situated to monitor the congruence between
counsel's conduct and class preferences"); Ralph K. Winter, Paying Lawyers,
Empowering Prosecutors, and Protecting Managers: Raising the Cost of Capital in
America, 42 Duke L.J. 945, 948 (1993) (stating that, in derivative actions, "plaintiffs
are generally figureheads").

[34] The Delaware Chancery Court's practitioner guidelines state that:

Litigation in the Court of Chancery often involves the production in
discovery of very sensitive, non-public information. When litigants and their
counsel and advisors obtain access to such information, it is their responsibility
to abide strictly by the terms of the confidentiality order in place. Particularly
troubling have been situations when litigants have had access to confidential,
non-public information about the value of a public corporation and have traded
in the securities of that corporation. If a litigant or a litigant's advisor engages
in such trading, they should expect to be subject to intensive scrutiny and, at
minimum, to face the requirement of reporting themselves to the Securities and
Exchange Commission and possibly even worse sanctions, including the
mandatory disgorgement of any trading profits and a potential bar to acting as
a class representative in future class or derivative actions in this Court. To
avoid these situations, counsel for litigants and their advisors who receive
access to confidential, non-public information should discuss these principles
with them and advise them that procedures need to be in place to avoid
violations of the order and trading in securities on the basis of confidential,
non-public information.

Delaware Court of Chancery, Guidelines to Help Lawyers Practicing in the Court of
Chancery 25 (undated), http://courts.delaware.gov/Chancery/docs/CompleteGuide
lines. pdf.

price would decline once the outcome of the grand jury's investigation became public.[35]

Does a grand juror stand in a fiduciary relationship to the source of the information (here, presumably, the government)? Although the case is not squarely on point, *U.S. v. Brenson*,[36] suggests an affirmative answer to that question. In it, the Eleventh Circuit held that a grand juror who provided ongoing information to an individual under grand jury investigation for drug smuggling and money laundering had violated a position of public trust and thus warranted an enhanced criminal penalty under the federal sentencing guidelines.[37]

In addition, the training process for grand jurors typically includes "an admonition as to the confidentiality of [the grand jury's] proceedings."[38] The SEC likely would take the position that that admonition constitutes an agreement of confidentiality for purposes of Rule 10b5–2(b).[39]

6.   Government officials

A 2004 study of the results of stock trading by United States Senators during the 1990s, however, found that senators on average beat the market by 12% a year.[40] In sharp contrast, U.S. households on average underperformed the market by 1.4% a year and even corporate insiders on average beat the market by only about 6% a year during that period.[41] A reasonable inference is that some Senators had access to—and were using—material nonpublic information about the companies in whose stock they trade:

> Looking at the timing of cumulative returns, the senators also appeared to know exactly when to buy or sell their holdings. Senators would buy stocks just before the shares suddenly would outperform the market by more than 25%. Conversely, senators would sell stocks that had been beating the market by about 25% for the past year just when the shares would fall back in line with the market's performance.

---

[35] Peter Lattman, Bizarre Insider-Trading Case Takes Another Bizarre Turn, The Wall Street Journal Law Blog (May 11, 2006), http:// blogs.wsj.com/law/2006/05/11/bizarre-insider-trading-case-takes-another-bizarre-turn/.

[36] 104 F.3d 1267 (11th Cir.), cert. denied, 522 U.S. 884 (1997).

[37] Id. at 1287–88.

[38] U.S. v. Diaz, 922 F.2d 998, 1003 (2d Cir. 1990).

[39] 17 C.F.R. § 240.10b5–2(b) (providing that "a 'duty of trust or confidence' exists in the following circumstances, among others: 1. Whenever a person agrees to maintain information in confidence").

[40] Alan J. Ziobrowski et al., Abnormal Returns from the Common Stock Investments of the U.S. Senate, 39 J. Fin. & Quant. Anal. 661 (2004).

[41] Jane J. Kim, U.S. Senators' Stock Picks Outperform the Pro's, Wall. St. J., Oct. 26, 2004.

The researchers say senators' uncanny ability to know when to buy or sell their shares seems to stem from having access to information that other investors wouldn't have. "I don't think you need much of an imagination to realize that they're in the know," says Alan Ziobrowski, a business professor at Georgia State University in Atlanta and one of the four authors of the study.[42]

Members of Congress can obtain material nonpublic information in many ways. They can learn inside information when, for example, a company confidentially discloses it during the course of a Congressional hearing or investigation. In most cases, however, members of Congress likely trade on the basis of market information, such as knowing that "tax legislation is apt to pass and which companies might benefit," being aware "that a particular company soon will be awarded a government contract or that a certain drug might get regulatory approval. . . ."[43]

Cases in which members of Congress or other government officials qualify as classical insiders or constructive insiders present no enforcement difficulties under current law. Nothing in the existing rules precludes their application in such cases. Such cases, however, presumably are quite rare. According to the House Ethics Manual, for example, members of Congress and their senior staff may not, *inter alia,* "serve for compensation as an officer or member of the board of an association, corporation, or other entity."[44] Opportunities to serve as a classical insider thus are unlikely to arise.

In contrast, it seems plausible that Congressmen or other government officials might sometimes receive tips from corporate insiders. Such a tip would be the functional equivalent of a bribe. Nothing in current law would prohibit prosecution of both tipper and tippee in such cases. Instead, it would be treated the same way as gifts of information.[45]

---

[42] Id. The extent of Congressional trading on material nonpublic information is uncertain. "Just over a third of the senators bought or sold individual stocks in any one year in the study, and the vast majority of stock transactions were less than $15,000." Id.

[43] Id.

[44] Committee on Standards of Official Conduct, Restrictions on Outside Employment Applicable To Members and Senior Staff (2010).

[45] Suppose the insider claimed that he gave the tip not for personal benefit, however, but so that the company would benefit. In effect, the tipper claims, he bribed the Congressman so the Congressman would do a favor for the company. The logic of *Dirks* suggests there could be no insider trading liability in such a case. Cf. 65 Fed. Reg. 51,716 n.7 (2000) (acknowledging how selective disclosures to analysts was viewed as protected from insider trader liability because tipper received no personal benefit but rather provided the tip so as to benefit corporation).

The more difficult question is whether members of Congress and other government officials can be held liable under the misappropriation theory. Because the vast majority of abuses of nonpublic information by government officials likely would be subject solely to the misappropriation theory, however, this long was a critical question.

Where a member of Congress, a Congressional staffer, or other government information obtains material nonpublic information in the course of their duties and then uses it to trade in the stock of the relevant issuer, their conduct could be colloquially described as a theft of the information, but any potential insider trading liability under the misappropriation theory would require proof of a fiduciary duty between the official and the source of the information. In this regard, an important distinction arises between members of Congress and other government officials. The Standards of Ethical Conduct For Employees of the Executive Branch provide that: "Public service is a public trust, requiring employees to place loyalty to the Constitution, the laws and ethical principles above private gain."[46] Accordingly, an employee of the Executive Branch should be deemed an agent of the government or, at least, to stand in a similar relationship of trust and confidence with the government.[47] The Standards further provide that: "An employee shall not engage in a financial transaction using nonpublic information, nor allow the improper use of nonpublic information to further his own private interest or that of another, whether through advice or recommendation, or by knowing unauthorized disclosure."[48]

Turning to Congress, both members of a Congressman's staff and Committee staffers are employees of their respective houses. They are subject to an ethical obligation never to "use any information received confidentially in the performance of governmental duties as a means for making private profit."[49] These employment relationships suffice for Congressional staffers to be deemed to have an agency or other relationship of trust and confidence with their employing agency. In *S.E.C. v. Cherif*,[50] for example, the court held that "a person violates Rule 10b–5 and

---

[46] 5 C.F.R. § 2635.101.

[47] Joseph Kalo, Deterring Misuse of Confidential Government Information: A Proposed Citizens' Action, 72 Mich. L. Rev. 1577, 1581 (1974) ("The application of fiduciary duties to activities of government employees is not novel.").

[48] 5 C.F.R. § 2634.703(a). Nonpublic information is defined for this purpose as "information that the employee gains by reason of Federal employment and that he knows or reasonably should know has not been made available to the general public." Id. at § 2634.703(b).

[49] House Ethics Manual 249 (2008).

[50] 933 F.2d 403 (7th Cir. 1991), cert. denied, 502 U.S. 1071 (1992).

Section 10(b) by misappropriating and trading upon material information entrusted to him by virtue of a fiduciary relationship such as employment."[51] Put into *O'Hagan*'s terminology, "a [staffer's] undisclosed, self serving use of [Congressional] information to purchase or sell securities, in breach of a duty of loyalty and confidentiality, defrauds the [Congress]."[52]

Of whom are members of Congress agents or fiduciaries, however? With whom do they have the requisite relationship of trust and confidence out of which the requisite duty to disclose before trading arises? The only logical candidate is the electorate. Although there is some precedent in other contexts for the proposition that "a public official . . . owe[s] a fiduciary duty to the public to make governmental decisions in the public's best interest,"[53] the predominant view, as stated by former SEC enforcement official Thomas Newkirk, is that "[i]f a congressman learns that his committee is about to do something that would affect a company, he can go trade on that because he is not obligated to keep that information confidential. . . . He is not breaching a duty of confidentiality to anybody."[54] Accordingly, most commentators concluded that insider trading by members of Congress was not illegal under the misappropriation theory.[55]

In response to considerable criticism of this loophole, Congress in 2012 passed the Stop Trading on Congressional Knowledge Act (STOCK Act).[56] The Act provides that "solely for purposes of the insider trading prohibitions arising under [the Securities Exchange] Act, including section 10(b) and Rule 10b–5 thereunder, each Member of Congress or employee of Congress owes a duty arising from a relationship of trust and confidence to the Congress, the United States Government, and the citizens of the United States

---

[51] Id. at 410. See also SEC v. Clark, 915 F.2d 439, 453 (9th Cir. 1990) ("[A]n employee's knowing misappropriation and use of his employer's material nonpublic information regarding its intention to acquire another firm constitutes a violation of § 10(b) and Rule 10b–5.").

[52] U.S. v. O'Hagan, 521 U.S. 642, 652 (1997). See generally Andrew George, Public (Self)-Service: Illegal Trading on Confidential Congressional Information, 2 Harv. L. & Poly' Rev. 161, 165–66 (2008) (concluding that staffers can be held liable either for trading on or tipping of material nonpublic information learned on the job).

[53] United States v. Woodard, 459 F.3d 1078, 1086 (11th Cir. 2006).

[54] Brody Mullins, Bill Seeks to Ban Insider Trading by Lawmakers and Their Aides, Wall St. J., Mar. 28, 2006, at A1.

[55] See, e.g., Stephen M. Bainbridge, Insider Trading Inside the Beltway, 36 J. Corp. L. 281 (2011)[hereinafter Bainbridge, Inside the Beltway] (describing the "predominant view"); Matthew Barbabella et al., Insider Trading in Congress: The Need for Regulation, 9 J. Bus. & Sec. L. 199 (2009); Bud W. Jerke, Comment, Cashing in on Capitol Hill: Insider Trading and the Use of Political Intelligence for Profit, 158 U. Pa. L. Rev. 1451 (2010). For a contrary view, see Sung Hui Kim, The Last Temptation of Congress: Legislator Insider Trading and the Fiduciary Norm Against Corruption, 98 Cornell L. Rev. 845 (2013); Donna M. Nagy, Insider Trading, Congressional Officials, and Duties of Entrustment, 91 B.U. L. Rev. 1105 (2011).

[56] Pub.L. 112–105, 126 Stat. 291 (2012).

with respect to material, nonpublic information derived from such person's position as a Member of Congress or employee of Congress or gained from the performance of such person's official responsibilities." The intent of doing so was to expose Congress members and employees to insider trading liability by creating the requisite duty of trust and confidence.

Chapter 9

SELECTIVE DISCLOSURE AND REGULATION FD

The SEC long has been concerned that selective disclosure to analysts undermines public confidence in the integrity of the stock markets:

> [M]any issuers are disclosing important nonpublic information, such as advance warnings of earnings results, to securities analysts or selected institutional investors or both, before making full disclosure of the same information to the general public. Where this has happened, those who were privy to the information beforehand were able to make a profit or avoid a loss at the expense of those kept in the dark.
>
> We believe that the practice of selective disclosure leads to a loss of investor confidence in the integrity of our capital markets. Investors who see a security's price change dramatically and only later are given access to the information responsible for that move rightly question whether they are on a level playing field with market insiders.[1]

Unfortunately for the SEC, the *Dirks* tipping regime was an inadequate constraint on the selective disclosure practice because, inter alia, it can be difficult to prove that the tipper received a personal benefit in connection with a disclosure.

A. Selective Disclosure under *Dirks*

Recall that *Dirks v. SEC* held that not at tips by corporate insiders are illegal. Instead, tipping is illegal, inter alia, only if the tipper receives a personal benefit in exchange for making the tip.[2] Where representatives of an issuer were authorized to disclose information to selected analysts or investors and did so for the issuer's benefit, rather than personal gain, this essential element is absent.[3] Because the tipper committed no breach, the tipper faced

---

[1] Selective Disclosure and Insider Trading, Exchange Act Rel. No. 43,154 (Aug. 15, 2000). On the relationship between investment analysis and insider trading, see Daniel R. Fischel, Insider Trading and Investment Analysts: An Economic Analysis of Dirks v. SEC, 13 Hofstra L. Rev. 127 (1984); Donald C. Langevoort, Investment Analysts and the Law of Insider Trading, 76 Va. L. Rev. 1023 (1990).

[2] 463 U.S. 646 (1983). See Chapter 6.B.

[3] Stephen J. Choi, A Framework for the Regulation of Securities Market Intermediaries, 1 Berkeley Bus. L.J. 45, 56–57 (2004) (explaining that the absence of a personal benefit to the tipper "corporate officers the ability to pass inside information freely to analysts"); Clay Richards, Selective Disclosure: "A Fencing Match Conducted on a Tightrope" and Regulation FD—The SEC's Latest Attempt to "Electrify the Tightrope," 70 Miss. L.J. 417, 425 (2000) (noting that Dirks was widely

no liability and the tippee was free to trade on the basis of the information or tip the information to someone else with impunity. Only where the SEC could show some sort of mixed motive on the tipper's part, as where the tipper was motivated by personal gain as well as pursuing corporate advantage. would liability be appropriate.[4]

B. Reg FD

In 2000, the SEC adopted Regulation FD (commonly known as Reg FD) to create a non-insider trading-based mechanism for restricting selective disclosure.[5] If someone acting on behalf of a public corporation discloses material nonpublic information to securities market professionals or "holders of the issuer's securities who may well trade on the basis of the information," the issuer must also disclose that information to the public.[6]

The rule does not define what constitutes "material information," instead incorporating the standard securities law definition of materiality.[7] In adopting Reg FD, however, the SEC specifically pointed to certain areas especially likely to be deemed material: (1) earnings announcements; (2) merger and acquisition negotiations; (3) new products or discoveries; (4) a change in control or top management; (5) a change in the issuer's outside auditors; (6) major events affecting the issuer's securities, such as a default on debt securities or a stock split; and (7) the company entering bankruptcy or a receivership.[8]

Where the issuer intentionally discloses such information in a covered communication, it must simultaneously disclose the

---

believed to have insulated corporate officers and analysts from liability because the "personal benefit" test was not satisfied in selective disclosure cases); Scott Russell, Note, Regulation Fair Disclosure: The Death of the Efficient Capital Market Hypothesis and the Birth of Herd Behavior, 82 B.U. L. Rev. 527, 531 (2002) (explaining that "corporations have engaged in selective disclosure under the apparent protection of . . . *Dirks v. SEC*").

[4] SEC v. Phillip J. Stevens, SEC Litig. Rel. No. 12,813, 1991 WL 296537 at *1 (Mar. 19, 1991) (stating that the tip was illegal because it "was seen by [defendant] Stevens as having direct, tangible benefit to his status as a corporate manager").

[5] 17 C.F.R. § 243.100–.103. See Donald C. Langevoort, Insider Trading: Regulation, Enforcement, and Prevention § 12.12 at 12–37 (2012) (explaining that Reg FD "is not an insider trading rule, but rather a contingent affirmative disclosure obligation designed to force companies either to publicize information or keep it completely confidential"); see generally Marc I. Steinberg, Insider Trading, Selective Disclosure, and Prompt Disclosure: A Comparative Analysis, 22 U. Penn. J. Int'l Econ. L. 635 (2001).

[6] 17 C.F.R. § 243.100(b)(1). Specifically, Reg FD applies to issuers that have a class of securities registered with the SEC pursuant to § 12 of the Exchange Act or is subjected to the SEC periodic disclosure regime under § 15(d) of the Act. 17 C.F.R. § 240.101(b). Mutual funds, foreign governments, and foreign private issuers are explicitly excluded from coverage by Reg FD. Id.

[7] See Chapter 6.C.1 (discussing the definition of materiality under the securities laws).

[8] Rel. No. 43,154, supra note 1.

information in a manner designed to convey it to the general public.[9] Hence, for example, if the issuer holds a briefing for selected analysts, it must simultaneously announce the same information by filing a Form 8–K with the SEC or "through another method (or combination of methods) of disclosure that is reasonably designed to provide broad, non-exclusionary distribution of the information to the public."[10]

> As a general matter, acceptable methods of public disclosure for purposes of Regulation FD will include press releases distributed through a widely circulated news or wire service, or announcements made through press conferences or conference calls that interested members of the public may attend or listen to either in person, by telephonic transmission, or by other electronic transmission (including use of the Internet). The public must be given adequate notice of the conference or call and the means for accessing it.[11]

The SEC suggested that issuers consider following a three-step model "for making a planned disclosure of material information, such as a scheduled earnings release":[12]

- First, issue a press release, distributed through regular channels, containing the information;

- Second, provide adequate notice, by a press release and/or website posting, of a scheduled conference call to discuss the announced results, giving investors both the time and date of the conference call, and instructions on how to access the call; and

- Third, hold the conference call in an open manner, permitting investors to listen in either by telephonic means or through Internet webcasting.[13]

Where the disclosure was not intentional, as where a corporate officer let something slip in casual conversation with an analyst, the issuer must make public disclosure "promptly" after a senior officer learns of the disclosure.[14] " 'Promptly' means as soon as reasonably practicable (but in no event after the later of 24 hours or the commencement of the next day's trading on the New York Stock

---

[9] Id. at § 243.100(a)(1). According to Reg FD, "[a] selective disclosure of material nonpublic information is 'intentional' when the person making the disclosure either knows, or is reckless in not knowing, that the information he or she is communicating is both material and nonpublic." Id. at § 243.101(a).

[10] Id. at § 243.101(e).

[11] Selective Disclosure and Insider Trading, supra note 1.

[12] Id.

[13] Id. (footnotes omitted).

[14] Id. at § 243.100(a)(2).

Exchange) after a senior official of the issuer (or, in the case of a closed-end investment company, a senior official of the issuer's investment adviser) learns that there has been a non-intentional disclosure by the issuer or person acting on behalf of the issuer of information that the senior official knows, or is reckless in not knowing, is both material and nonpublic."[15] In turn, senior official "means any director, executive officer . . . , investor relations or public relations officer, or other person with similar functions."[16]

The communications that trigger a Reg FD disclosure obligation are those made to a person outside the issuer who falls into one (or more) of four categories. First, a broker or dealer, or a person associated with a broker or dealer. Second, an investment adviser, an institutional investment manager, or someone associated with either such person. Third, an investment company, a hedge fund, or a person affiliated with either such fund. Finally, "a holder of the issuer's securities, but only under circumstances in which it is reasonably foreseeable that the person will purchase or sell the issuer's securities on the basis of the information."[17]

The purpose of limiting Reg FD to such communications is to permit the issuer to make ordinary business conversations with stakeholders such as clients, consultants, journalists, regulators, and the like who are unlikely to use the disclosed information for trading purposes. Towards that end, the Regulation explicitly exempts three commercially important categories of business communications. First, disclosures to "a person who owes a duty of trust or confidence to the issuer (such as an attorney, investment banker, or accountant)" are exempt.[18] Second, communications to any person who expressly agrees to keep the disclosed information confidential are exempt. Finally, the Regulation exempts a broad range of communications commonly made in connection with a registered offering of securities.

Where an issuer fails to comply with its Reg FD disclosure obligations, the SEC typically seeks limited relief in the form of a cease and desist order.[19] The Regulation specifically provides that a failure to comply is not of itself a violation of Rule 10b–5.[20] It

---

[15] Id. at § 243.101(d).

[16] Id. at § 243.101(f). "Executive officer" is defined in Rule 3b–7 under the Exchange Act of 1934 as the issuer's "president, any vice president of the registrant in charge of a principal business unit, division or function (such as sales, administration or finance), any other officer who performs a policy making function or any other person who performs similar policy making functions for the registrant." 17 C.F.R. 240.3b–7.

[17] 17 C.F.R. § 243.100(b)(1).

[18] Id. at § 243.100(b)(2)(i).

[19] Langevoort, supra note 5, at § 12.19.

[20] 17 C.F.R. § 243.102.

likewise provides that a failure to comply does not adversely affect the issuer's ability to use S–2 or S–8 short form registration statements.[21]

C. Reg FD and Social Media

It took the SEC almost a decade to decide that corporations could use the internet to disclose information. Not until 2008 did the SEC conclude that posting information to the company's website was even potentially a sufficient way of complying with Reg FD.[22] Whether such disclosure suffices is determined on a case-by-case basis, considering factors such as "(1) whether the company website was 'a recognized channel of distribution;' (2) whether the website posting made the information available to the general marketplace; and (3) whether there was a reasonable waiting period for investors and the market to react to the posted information."[23]

When it came to social media, however, the SEC moved a bit faster. As the WSJ reported on April 2, 2013:

> In a ruling that portends changes to how companies communicate with investors, the Securities and Exchange Commission said Tuesday that postings on sites such as Facebook and Twitter are just as good as news releases and company websites as long as the companies have told investors which outlets they intend to use.

> The move was sparked by an investigation into a July Facebook posting from Netflix Inc. Chief Executive Reed Hastings, who boasted on the social-media site that the streaming-video company had exceeded one billion hours in a month for the first time, sending the firm's shares higher. The SEC opened the investigation in December to determine if the post had violated rules that bar companies from selectively disclosing information. . . .

> In its Tuesday ruling, the agency said social-media sites would also suffice—in some circumstances. It blessed sites as long as companies make clear to investors they plan to use them. It also suggested a corporate executive's personal Facebook page wasn't as likely as a company's social-media page to be a channel through which companies would be allowed to make important announcements. . . .

---

[21] Id. at § 243.103.

[22] See Jill Fisch, Regulation FD: An Alternative Approach to Addressing Information Asymmetry, in Research Handbook on Insider Trading 112, 127 (Stephen M. Bainbridge ed. 2012).

[23] Id.

Joseph Grundfest, a former member of the commission who now teaches at Stanford Law School, said the SEC is bowing to reality in blessing social media. Twitter, where users can post comments of 140 characters or less, says more than 200 million people world-wide use the service at least twice a month. Facebook says it has more than one billion users. "As a practical matter, Reed Hastings' personal Web page probably informed more people more quickly of the information than" a formal SEC filing, said Mr. Grundfest, who published a paper in January urging the SEC not to pursue an enforcement action against Mr. Hastings. "You don't have 200,000 people a day checking Netflix filings on" the SEC's electronic-document site.[24]

The SEC announcement explained that:

The SEC's report of investigation confirms that Regulation FD applies to social media and other emerging means of communication used by public companies the same way it applies to company websites. The SEC issued guidance in 2008 clarifying that websites can serve as an effective means for disseminating information to investors if they've been made aware that's where to look for it. Today's report clarifies that company communications made through social media channels could constitute selective disclosures and, therefore, require careful Regulation FD analysis. . . .

Regulation FD requires companies to distribute material information in a manner reasonably designed to get that information out to the general public broadly and non-exclusively. It is intended to ensure that all investors have the ability to gain access to material information at the same time.[25]

Corporate law professor Usha Rodrigues observed that:

This move seems easy and right. . . . There seems to be no stopping social media.

Next question: how broadly will companies authorize social media disclosure? Dealbook's Michael J. de la Merced observes that "the new move may reduce spontaneity because companies may limit their communications to official corporate

---

[24] Jessica Holzer & Greg Bensinger, SEC Embraces Social Media, Wall St. J., April 2, 2013, at A1.

[25] Press Release, SEC Says Social Media OK for Company Announcements if Investors are Alerted (Apr. 2, 2013), http://www.sec.gov/news/press/2013/2013–51.htm.

accounts and file the information with the agency at the same time."[26]

Corporate commentator Broc Romanek opined that:

> Even though the SEC's press release touts the new report as a greenlight for companies—the press release's title is "SEC Says Social Media OK for Company Announcements if Investors are Alerted"—I'm dubious that companies and their advisors will see it that way. For starters, the new guidance comes from an Enforcement report (here's an explanation of what a Section 21(a) report is)—perhaps not the best vehicle to encourage new practices. [Not surprisingly, many mass media reporters were fooled by the SEC's title and report that the SEC has "new" disclosure rules.]
>
> And it doesn't get into the nitty gritty like IM's new guidance does. Given the slow adoption rate of social media by IR, finance and governance professionals—compared to the rest of the world—I'm not convinced this will be enough to get folks moving. . . .[27]

---

[26] Usha Rodrigues, From the "Inevitable File," The Conglomerate (Apr. 3, 2013), http://www.theconglomerate.org/2013/04/from-the-inevitable-file.html.

[27] Broc Romanek, Social Media: SEC Issues Reg FD Guidance (In Form of Enforcement Report), The CorporateCounsel.net (Apr. 3, 2013), http://www.the corporatecounsel.net/Blog/2013/04/tech.html.

Chapter 10

RULE 14e–3

The SEC adopted Rule 14e–3 in response to the wave of insider trading activity associated with the increase in merger and acquisition activity during the 1980s. In that era, insider trading and corporate takeovers seemed to go hand in hand.[1] Indeed, in light of the enormous profits that can be made by persons with advance knowledge of impending corporate takeover bids, it would have been more surprising if there had been no such correlation.

The view that insider trading was common in the takeover game was confirmed by the results of a study of 172 successful tender offers between 1981 and 1985 by the SEC's Chief Economist, which found abnormal price increases as early as seventeen days before the announcement of a takeover bid.[2] By the close of trading the day before the announcement, the price of a target's stock, on average, increased by an amount equal to almost forty percent of the eventual control premium paid by the offeror. The SEC study asserted that some of the pre-announcement run-up could be explained by factors other than insider trading, including media speculation, rumors and pre-announcement acquisitions by the bidder. However, the study admitted that the authors were "unable to explain a great deal of the pre-bid trading," and that "it is possible, and logical to many, that illegal insider behavior could affect simultaneously runup [sic] and these other factors.[3] Indeed, the most logical conclusion to be drawn from the study's raw data was that trading on the basis of nonpublic takeover information is common."

This view was shared by a number of members of Congress and SEC officials, perhaps most notably by former SEC Chairman John S. Shad. In 1983, he stated that "[t]he large number of mergers and tender offers has been an important factor in the increased incidence of insider trading."[4] In the wake of the SEC Chief

---

[1] See generally Robert D. Rosenbaum & Stephen M. Bainbridge, The Corporate Takeover Game and Recent Legislative Attempts to Define Insider Trading, 26 American Crim. L. Rev. 229 (1988).

[2] SEC Office of the Chief Economist, Stock Trading Before the Announcement of Tender Offers: Insider Trading or Market Anticipation? 3 (Feb. 24, 1984). The study also found that average trading volume measurably increases about 10 days prior to public announcement of a takeover bid. Id.

[3] Id. at 33–34.

[4] Insider Trading Sanctions and SEC Enforcement Legislation: Hearing on H.R. 559 Before the Subcomm. on Telecommunications, Consumer Protection, and Finance of the House Comm. on Energy and Commerce, 98th Cong., 1st Sess. 14, 19 (1983) (statement of John S. Shad, SEC Chairman).

Economist's study, Chairman Shad again observed that "[t]he large increase [in insider trading cases in the 1980s was] due principally to the increase in corporate takeovers," as well as better SEC enforcement efforts.[5] Similarly, in releasing a Congressional Research Service study of the issue on July 15, 1987, Congressman Edward J. Markey (D-Mass.), Chairman of the Telecommunications and Finance Subcommittee of the House Energy and Commerce Committee, stated that "[c]orporate takeovers seem to have become a principal catalyst for insider trading."[6]

A. Takeover Trading Falling through the Gaps in the *Chiarella/Dirks Regime*

Much insider trading in connection with corporate takeovers was (and still is) attributable to the misappropriation of information from investment bankers, law firms, printers and similar sources, in breach of employment-related fiduciary duties. Such cases could be readily dealt with under the misappropriation theory. But not all insider trading relating to takeovers involved the requisite breach of duty.[7]

There was considerable evidence, for example, that some bidders (or their agents) have tipped takeover speculators about the bidder's plans so that arbitragers could begin accumulating blocks of target stock before the bid is announced publicly. By tipping the arbitrager prior to announcing his bid, the bidder enables the arbitrager to buy large blocks at the lower pre-announcement price, thereby locking in a likely profit for the latter and putting a substantial amount of stock in friendly hands. Such an arrangement materially advances the bidder's objective of obtaining control. Pre-announcement tips may also be intended to put the target company in play, by stimulating artificially high interest and trading activity in the target's stock and by initiating takeover rumors and speculation relating to the target. Stimulating such interest on the part of speculators and potential other bidders was often part of a scheme by the bidder/tipper to extract greenmail from the putative target by coercing the company to repurchase the bidder's shares at a premium in order to end takeover speculation.[8]

---

[5] Securities Regulation Issues: Hearings Before the Subcomm. on Telecommunications and Finance of the House Comm. on Energy and Commerce, 100th Cong., 1st Sess. 44 (1987) (statement of John S. Shad, SEC Chairman).

[6] Daily Rep. for Executives, DER 136, at A2, July 17, 1987.

[7] See generally Rosenbaum & Bainbridge, supra note 1, at 236.

[8] Greenmail is defined as causing a "target company to buy the shares already obtained by the hostile would-be acquirer at a substantial premium over the latter's cost, with the understanding that he, she, or it will stop the takeover attempt." Robert C. Clark, Corporate Law 574 (1986).

In general, these forms of collusion do not violate the insider trading laws under the duty-based analysis, since neither the bidder nor its allies owe any fiduciary duty to the target company's stockholders. Outsiders to the corporation generally can be charged only with such a duty where they receive information from the target and there is both an affirmative expectation on the part of the target that the information will be used solely for its benefit and the recipient assents in some way to that obligation.[9] None of these requirements are likely to be satisfied with respect to the typical bidder or takeover speculator. Similarly, it is unlikely that shareholders of an issuer can be said to have placed their trust and confidence in an undisclosed acquirer or other takeover player who buys target shares on the open market. Likewise, these types of collusion presumably do not violate the misappropriation theory, because the bidder or arbitrager's trades do not violate any duty owed to the source of the information.[10]

A closely related practice is known as "parking" (a.k.a. warehousing) in which one entity or person holds stock in a prospective target corporation on behalf of the potential bidder. The goal of investors who park stock with one another frequently is to avoid compliance with these disclosure requirements by making it appear that no member of the group has acquired more than five percent of a company's stock or to avoid other legal requirements.[11] If a securities firm was restricted from trading in a company's stock because it had inside information about the company, it might park stock with an investor in order secretly to acquire stock in the potential takeover target and then attempt to set in motion a tender offer in which the firm would have a role; or, the firm might use the stock reserves to obtain favors from a client. In either case, by keeping both parties' stockholdings below the five percent threshold the conspirators not only avoid the disclosure requirements of the Williams Act, but also make it more difficult to detect their accumulation of large blocks of target stock. The result, of course, is that the parties are able to accumulate stock relatively

---

[9] See Dirks v. SEC, 463 U.S. 646 (1983) (creating the so-called "constructive insider" rule, pursuant to which, where corporate information is revealed legitimately to underwriters, accountants, lawyers, or consultants working for corporation, such outsiders may become fiduciaries of the corporation); see also § Chapter 6.A.3 (discussing constructive insiders).

[10] See Chapter 7.D.2 (discussing status of authorized trading under the misappropriation theory).

[11] Pursuant to Exchange Act § 13(d) and the SEC rules thereunder anyone who beneficially owns 5 percent or more of a class of equity securities must file a Schedule 13D with the SEC disclosing their holdings and, inter alia, any contracts or arrangements with respect to those shares. As such, undisclosed parking violates the Exchange Act. The modest penalties applicable to parking cases, however, failed to deter the practice. See Rosenbaum & Bainbridge, supra note 1, at 238–40.

inexpensively before the market is alerted to a potential takeover play, with the consequent usual run up in the price of the stock.

B. Adoption of Rule 14e–3

In 1980, the SEC announced its intention to specifically address insider trading in connection with tender offers:

> In view of the potential harm to investors and the securities markets which results from trading on material, nonpublic information, the Commission will continue diligently to discharge its enforcement responsibilities in this area with particular emphasis on corporate insiders and securities professionals involved in tender offers. The Commission and the self-regulatory organizations will continue to monitor insider trading and to investigate allegations of unlawful trading on material, nonpublic information.

> The abuses which result from trading in securities by persons in possession of material, nonpublic information are particularly troublesome in the context of tender offers. Such trading was a matter of concern to Congress when it enacted the Williams Act and is of ongoing concern to the Commission in administering the Exchange Act. . . . [The] testimony in the Senate and House Hearings on the legislation which became the Williams Act highlighted the market disruption and abusive practices associated with leaks by a bidder relating to a tender offer. . . .

> In view of the continued trading and potential for trading by persons while in possession of material, nonpublic information relating to tender offers and the detrimental impact which such trading has on tender offer practice, shareholder protection and the securities markets, the Commission has determined that Rule 14e–3 is necessary and appropriate in the public interest and for the protection of investors. As adopted, Rule 14e–3 pertains to both the person who receives the information, the tippee, and the person who transmits the information, the tipper.[12]

The rule thus prohibits insiders of the bidder and target from divulging confidential information about a tender offer to persons that are likely to violate the rule by trading on the basis of that information.[13] It also prohibits any person that possesses material information relating to a tender offer by another person from trading in target company securities if the bidder has commenced or

---

[12] Tender Offers, Exchange Act Release No. 17,120 (Sept. 4, 1980), 1980 SEC LEXIS 775 at *16–17.

[13] 17 C.F.R. § 240.14e–3(d)(1).

has taken substantial steps towards commencement of the bid, subject to specific narrow exceptions, which are identified below.[14]

C. The Disclose or Abstain Provision

Rule 14e–3(a) provides that:

If any person has taken a substantial step or steps to commence, or has commenced, a tender offer (the "offering person"), it shall constitute a fraudulent, deceptive or manipulative act or practice within the meaning of section 14(e) of the Act for any other person who is in possession of material information relating to such tender offer which information he knows or has reason to know is nonpublic and which he knows or has reason to know has been acquired directly or indirectly from:

1. the offering person,

2. the issuer of the securities sought or to be sought by such tender offer, or

3. any officer, director, partner or employee or any other person acting on behalf of the offering person or such issuer, to purchase or sell or cause to be purchased or sold any of such securities or any securities convertible into or exchangeable for any such securities or any option or right to obtain or to dispose of any of the foregoing securities, unless within a reasonable time prior to any purchase or sale such information and its source are publicly disclosed by press release or otherwise.[15]

1. Exemptions

Because the rule on its face applies only to "any other person"—i.e., someone other than the bidder—the rule does not prohibit the bidder from acquiring target shares. Rule 14e–3(c)(1) likewise exempts purchases of target securities by a broker or other agent on behalf of the bidder.[16] "This exception addresses the concern by some commentators that a broker or other agent making purchases on behalf of an offering person would violate the proposed rule if the offering person disclosed material, nonpublic information to such broker or agent."[17] In addition, Rule 14e–3(c)(2) exempts sales by any person of target shares to the bidder.[18] The SEC explained that:

---

[14] 17 C.F.R. § 240.14e–3(a).

[15] 17 C.F.R. § 240.14e–3(a).

[16] 17 C.F.R. § 240.14e–3(c)(1).

[17] Release No. 17120, supra note 12, 1980 SEC LEXIS 775 at *37.

[18] 17 C.F.R. § 240.14e–3(c)(2).

This exception permits a person who has received material, nonpublic information from a particular offering person relating to a tender offer to sell securities to that offering person prior to the date of commencement of the tender offer as well as to tender securities to that offering person pursuant to the tender offer and to have those securities accepted for payment by the offering person pursuant to the tender offer. Since the potential for misuse of the information is negligible in these instances, liability is not imposed on the seller in this type of transaction.

The exception in Rule 14e–3(c)(2) is designed to permit the following transactions without a violation of Rule 14e–3(a). In the situation where the offering person acquires the securities of an insider prior to the commencement of a tender offer and the insider is informed of the offering person's nonpublic intention to make a tender offer, then paragraph (a) would prohibit the sale to the offering person by the insider without disclosure. However, the exception in Rule 14e–3(c)(2) would permit the sale by the insider to the offering person. This exception would also permit any person to tender securities to the offering person in the tender offer, where such person knows material, nonpublic information relating to the tender offer, such as an increase in consideration or an extension of the tender offer, without complying with the disclosure requirements of paragraph (a).[19]

The SEC further explained that "the scope of the exceptions from liability provided by [Rule 14e(3)(c)] is limited."[20]

Rule 14e–3(c) provides an exception for only those persons named in Rule 14e–3(c) and an exception from liability for violations of only Rule 14e–3(a). Rule 14e–3(c) does not have any effect on the duties imposed on an offering person under other provisions of the federal securities laws such as Rule 10b–13 [17 C.F.R. § 240.10b–13]. Rule 10b–13 prohibits an offering person from directly or indirectly purchasing or arranging to purchase certain securities otherwise than pursuant to a tender offer from the time the tender offer is publicly announced or otherwise made known by the offering person until the expiration of the offer. Therefore, if Rule 10b–13 is applicable, the offering person would be unable to purchase the securities notwithstanding that Rules 14e–3(c)(1) or 14e–3(c)(2) will render the provisions of Rule 14e–3(a) inapplicable. In such instances, the transaction would not

---

[19] Release No. 17120, supra note 12, 1980 SEC LEXIS 775 at *37–38.
[20] Id. at *35.

occur because the offering person would be unable to purchase or arrange for the purchase of the securities.[21]

Rule 14e–3(b) exempts certain transactions by corporations and other legal persons—but not natural persons—who can satisfy two requirements:

> (1) The individual(s) making the investment decision on behalf of such person to purchase or sell any security described in paragraph (a) of this section or to cause any such security to be purchased or sold by or on behalf of others did not know the material, nonpublic information; and

> (2) Such person had implemented one or a combination of policies and procedures, reasonable under the circumstances, taking into consideration the nature of the person's business, to ensure that individual(s) making investment decision(s) would not violate paragraph (a) of this section, which policies and procedures may include, but are not limited to, (i) those which restrict any purchase, sale and causing any purchase and sale of any such security or (ii) those which prevent such individual(s) from knowing such information.[22]

The SEC explained that:

> The abuse at which Rule 14e–3(a) is directed is the actual misuse of material, nonpublic information in connection with a sale or purchase. The Commission recognizes that the rule is capable of being applied to a person that is not a natural person even though the individuals making the investment decision on behalf of such person did not know the material, nonpublic information. This could occur, for example, where one department of a multi-service financial institution received material, nonpublic information relating to a tender offer while a separate and independent department of the same organization made the decision to purchase (or sell) securities

---

[21] Id. at *35–36. Rule 10b–13 prohibits a bidder from making open market or private purchases of target stock during the pendency of a tender offer. Under the rule, a bidder may purchase target stock prior to commencing the tender offer. See, e.g., Heine v. Signal Companies, Inc., [1976–77 Transfer Binder] Fed.Sec.L.Rep. (CCH) ¶ 95,898, 1977 WL 930 (S.D.N.Y.1977) (delaying announcement of a self tender offer in order to purchase a block of its shares in a privately negotiated transaction did not violate the rule; inter alia, because Signal had obtained a no action letter from the SEC staff in connection with the proposed series of transactions). Likewise, entering into option agreements to purchase target shares prior to the commencement of a tender offer should not violate the rule, provided the option period does not extend into the tender offer period, since the rule does not prohibit such arrangements until the tender offer period begins to run.

[22] 17 C.F.R. § 240.14e–3(b).

of the subject company without any knowledge of such information. In the instance where the prohibition would be applicable to a person other than a natural person, and the individuals making the investment decision did not know the material, nonpublic information, there would be no actual misuse of the information, yet it could be said that the institution was in possession of the information and did purchase or sell in apparent violation of Rule 14e–3(a).[23]

In order to qualify for the 14e–3(b) exemption, the financial institution (or other legal person) must carry the burden of proof under both elements of the rule. First, the institution must prove that the person who decided to trade in the target securities did not know the information at the time the investment decision was made. Second, the institution must prove that it had established policies and procedures, which are reasonable under the circumstances, to prevent its employees from using inside information when making trading decisions on behalf of the institution. "These policies and procedures may include but are not limited to (i) those which restrict any purchase, sale and causing any purchase or sale of any security and (ii) those which prevent the individual decision maker(s) from knowing such information."[24]

2. Commencing or taking substantial steps towards commencing a tender offer

Rule 14e–3(a) applies only when the bidder has commenced a tender offer or taken substantial steps towards the commencement of a tender offer. The rule thus implicates three distinct definitional questions. First, what constitutes a tender offer? Second, what constitutes commencement of a tender offer? Third, what constitutes substantial steps towards commencing a tender offer?

Tender Offer. The Exchange Act nowhere defines the term "tender offer." No one doubts that the term encompasses a public offer to purchase at a specified price and terms during a specified period of time all or part of a class or classes of equity securities of a publicly held corporation. As for transactions that do not fall squarely within that definition, courts have used a variety of standards to determine whether they constitute a tender offer. In *Wellman v. Dickinson,*[25] for example, the court set out a widely used eight-factor standard:

---

[23] Release No. 17120, supra note 12, 1980 SEC LEXIS 775 at *25–26.

[24] Id. at *29. For more on such practices and procedures, see Chapter 11.E.4.

[25] 475 F. Supp. 783 (S.D.N.Y. 1979), aff'd on other grounds, 682 F.2d 355 (2d Cir.1982).

(1) [A]ctive and widespread solicitation of public shareholders; (2) for a substantial percentage of the issuer's stock; (3) at a premium over the prevailing market price; (4) offer terms fixed, rather than negotiable; (5) offer contingent on the tender of a fixed minimum or limited to a maximum number of shares to be purchased; (6) offer open for only a limited time period; (7) offeree subjected to pressure to sell; and (8) public announcement of a purchasing program preceding or accompanying a rapid accumulation of a large amount of the target's securities.[26]

Not all factors need be present for a transaction to be deemed a tender offer. Indeed, one may not even need a majority to be present, as the court emphasized that identifying the determinative factors is to be done on a case-by-case basis. Having said that, however, the factors that usually seem most important are publicity and pressure to sell. These are the factors that make a purchase program most look like a tender offer.

The ambiguity inherent in the *Wellman* test has not precluded its widespread use. Although the SEC has not formally adopted the *Wellman* test, the SEC enforcement staff developed the test for use in litigation and the SEC staff has often urged its adoption by the courts on a case-by-case basis.[27] In *Hanson Trust PLC v. SCM Corp.*,[28] however, the Second Circuit called the validity of the *Wellman* test into question, arguing that a "mandatory 'litmus test' appears to be both unwise and unnecessary."[29] In lieu of the *Wellman* factors, the Second Circuit invoked the guidelines used to determine whether an offering of securities is eligible for the private placement exemption under Securities Act § 4(1). As such, the main issue is whether the offerees are sophisticated investors who do not need the Williams Act's protections.

Commencement. SEC Rule 14d–2 governs the commencement of a tender offer.[30] It identifies two basic events that may constitute the commencement of a tender offer; whichever event takes place first in a particular offer will be the commencement date for that offer. Under Rule 14d–2(a), publishing or transmitting offering materials to the shareholders commences the offer. Under Rule 14d–2(b), subject to limited exceptions, any public announcement of

---

[26] Id. at 823.

[27] David J. Segre, Open-Market and Privately Negotiated Purchase Programs and the Market for Corporate Control, 42 Bus. Law. 715, 727 (1987).

[28] 774 F.2d 47 (2d Cir. 1985).

[29] Id. at 57.

[30] 17 C.F.R. § 240.14d–2.

takeover plans commences the offer.[31] Accordingly, if the bidder discloses such information as its identity, the target's identity, the amount of securities it will offer to buy, and the price it is willing to pay, the bidder has just commenced the tender offer.

Substantial Steps. According to the SEC, substantial steps include such things as the bidder's board of directors voting on a resolution relating to the tender offer, the bidder having formulated a plan or proposal to make a tender offer, or the bidder having undertaken activities that substantially facilitate the tender offer, such as arranging financing or authorizing the preparation of tender offer documentation.[32] Court decisions identify a number of combinations that collectively constitute the requisite substantial steps. In *SEC v. Mayhew*,[33] for example, the bidders were deemed to have taken steps where they "had retained a consulting firm, signed confidentiality agreements, and held meetings between top officials."[34] In *SEC v. Ginsburg*,[35] the substantial steps requirement was deemed to be satisfied where "there was a meeting between executives, which was followed by due diligence procedures, [and] a confidentiality agreement," even though those actions did "not fall into the specifically enumerated examples of activities described as 'substantial steps' in the SEC release."[36] As the court explained, the SEC's adopting "release makes it clear that the examples listed are only that; they are not a complete list of 'substantial steps.' "[37] In *SEC v. Maio*,[38] the court likewise concluded that a meeting between officers of the target and acquiring companies, which was held after the target had solicited an offer from the acquiring company and was "much more serious than any previous discussion between the parties," and which was followed the next day by the bidder beginning its due diligence process, collectively constituted substantial steps.[39]

On its face, the rule merely requires that the bidder have taken substantial steps towards commencing a tender offer. The rule thus seemingly permits imposition of liability even if a tender offer never actually takes place. In *O'Connor & Associates v. Dean Witter*

---

[31] The Rule provides that pre-offer communications are exempted if they (1) do not identify the means by which target shareholders may tender their stock and (2) all written communications are filed with the SEC and issuer. 17 C.F.R. § 240.14d–2(b).

[32] Release No. 17120, supra note 12, 1980 SEC LEXIS 775 at *20.

[33] 121 F.3d 44 (2d Cir. 1997).

[34] Id. at 53.

[35] 362 F.3d 1292 (11th Cir. 2004).

[36] Id. at 1303–04.

[37] Id. at 1303.

[38] 51 F.3d 623 (7th Cir.1995).

[39] Id. at 636.

Reynolds, Inc.,[40] a federal district court held that liability could be imposed even though the tender offer never became effective.[41]

3. The prohibition

Under Rule 14e–3(a), the trader must know or have reason to know that the information is nonpublic. The definition of nonpublic in this context presumably is the same as under Rule 10b–5.[42] Interestingly, however, the Rule states that the trader can avoid liability if "within a reasonable time prior to any purchase or sale [the nonpublic] information and its source are publicly disclosed by press release or otherwise."[43] The SEC thus seemingly contemplates that the trader can opt to disclose the information before trading. Where the trader is an agent or other fiduciary of the source of the information, however, an unauthorized disclosure of such information would violate his state law fiduciary duties.[44]

The trader also must know or have reason to know the information was acquired from the bidder, the target company, or agents of either.[45] Acquired includes "information received as well as information obtained by conversion, misappropriation and other means. . . ."[46] As guidance for applying this prohibition, the SEC offered the following examples:

(1) If an offering person tells another person that the offering person will make a tender offer which information is nonpublic, the other person has acquired material, nonpublic information directly from the offering person and has a duty under Rule 14e–3(a).

(2) If an offering person delegates the authority to determine whether such offering person should take a substantial step or steps to commence or should commence a tender offer to an officer, employee, director or partner and such person decides to implement the tender offer, such person will be deemed to have acquired information relating to the tender offer from the offering person and therefore will have a duty under Rule 14e–3(a) to disclose or abstain from trading.

---

[40] 529 F. Supp. 1179 (S.D.N.Y. 1981).

[41] Id. at 1192.

[42] Donald C. Langevoort, Insider Trading: Regulation, Enforcement & Prevention § 7.5 at 7–7 (2012).

[43] 17 C.F.R. § 240.14e–3(a)(3).

[44] See Stephen M. Bainbridge, Insider Trading Regulation: The Path Dependent Choice between Property Rights and Securities Fraud, 52 SMU L. Rev. 1589, 1642 (1999) (explaining that "persons subject to the disclose or abstain theory are also often subject to a state law-based fiduciary duty of confidentiality, which precludes them from disclosing the information").

[45] 17 C.F.R. § 240.14e–3(a)(1)–(3).

[46] Release No. 17120, supra note 12, 1980 SEC LEXIS 775 at *20 n.37.

(3) If the offering person sends a nonpublic letter to a subject company notifying the subject company of a proposed tender offer at a specified price and upon specified terms and the management of the subject company learns the contents of the letter, the management of the subject company has acquired material, nonpublic information directly from the offering person. An individual member of such management will violate Rule 14e–3(a) if he purchases or sells or causes the purchase or sale of the securities to be sought in the tender offer.

(4) If, under the facts in the preceding example, the management of the subject company also tells other persons not affiliated with management of the letter, then those other persons have acquired material, nonpublic information indirectly from the offering person and are under a duty to disclose or abstain from trading under Rule 14e–3(a).

(5) If a person receives material information from the subject company relating to its response to another person's tender offer for the subject company's securities, such person will be under a duty to disclose or abstain from trading provided that such person knows or has reason to know the information is nonpublic.

(6) If a person steals, converts or otherwise misappropriates material, non-public information relating to a tender offer from an offering person, such person will have acquired the information directly from the offering person and has a duty under Rule 14e–3(a).

(7) If an offering person tells another person of his intention to make a tender offer, and such other person subsequently tells a third person that a tender offer will be made and this third person knows or has reason to know that this non-public information came indirectly from the offering person, then this third person has a duty under Rule 14e–3(a).[47]

Note that the absence of any fiduciary duty requirement in Rule 14e–3 means that liability can be imposed under that Rule in situations in which neither the disclose or abstain nor the misappropriation theory would permit liability to be imposed under Rule 10b–5. In the first three examples, one could plausibly infer that the bidder intended to authorize the recipient to trade on the basis of the disclosed information. As discussed in Chapter 7 above, however, authorized trading should not violate the

---

[47] Id. at *22–24.

misappropriation theory.[48] Likewise, as discussed below, one who trades on the basis of stolen information has not violated the misappropriation theory.[49]

As we have seen, in addition to being nonpublic and being acquired from one or more of the requisite sources, the information also must be material and relate to a tender offer. The SEC takes the position that a knowledge requirement applies only to the first two requirements.[50] Accordingly, one can be held liable even if one is unaware that the information is material or even that it relates to a tender offer. In *SEC v. Ginsburg*,[51] for example, the court held that "Rule 14e–3, by its terms, does not require that the offender know or have reason to know that the information relates to a tender offer, so long as the information in fact does relate to a tender offer and the offender knows or has reason to know the information is nonpublic and was acquired by a person with the required status."[52] A defendant who believed the bidder planned to effect the acquisition via merger, for example, thus could still be held liable so long as the information actually related to a tender offer and the other requirements of the rule are met. Likewise, in *U.S. v. O'Hagan*,[53] the court held that while "Rule 14e–3(a) requires that 'any person' must have taken 'a substantial step or steps' towards the tender offer," it "does not require the defendant to have knowledge of these acts."[54] A defendant thus can be held liable even if he does not know or have reason to know that the bidder has commenced or taken substantial steps towards commencing a tender offer.

D. The Tipping Prohibition

Rule 14e(3)(d)(1) provides that:

> As a means reasonably designed to prevent fraudulent, deceptive or manipulative acts or practices within the meaning of section 14(e) of the Act, it shall be unlawful for any person described in paragraph (d)(2) of this section to communicate material, nonpublic information relating to a tender offer to any other person under circumstances in which it is reasonably foreseeable that such communication is likely to result in a

---

[48] See Chapter 7.D.2.

[49] See Chapter 12.D.3.

[50] See Release No. 17120, supra note 12, 1980 SEC LEXIS 775 at *21 ("For the first two requisites, i.e., materiality and relation to a tender offer, there is no 'knows or has reason to know' standard.").

[51] 362 F.3d 1292 (11th Cir. 2004).

[52] Id. at 1304.

[53] 139 F.3d 641 (8th Cir. 1998), on remand from, 521 U.S. 642 (1997).

[54] Id. at 650.

violation of this section except that this paragraph shall not apply to a communication made in good faith,

(i) To the officers, directors, partners or employees of the offering person, to its advisors or to other persons, involved in the planning, financing, preparation or execution of such tender offer;

(ii) To the issuer whose securities are sought or to be sought by such tender offer, to its officers, directors, partners, employees or advisors or to other persons, involved in the planning, financing, preparation or execution of the activities of the issuer with respect to such tender offer; or

(iii) To any person pursuant to a requirement of any statute or rule or regulation promulgated thereunder.[55]

Rule 14e–3(d) is intended as a broad prohibition of tipping information relating to a tender offer, whether the source of the tip is affiliated with either the bidder or the target:

> The proscription consists of two elements. First, such person must possess material, nonpublic information relating to a tender offer. Such person may create the information, e.g., the offering person or the subject company, or he may have acquired the information from the offering person or the subject company or from a person who is in a chain from the offering person or the subject company. Second, such person tips the information to another. The tipping occurs where it is reasonably foreseeable that the communication is likely to result in a violation of Rule 14e–3. The standard of reasonably foreseeable is premised on what a reasonable man would view as reasonably foreseeable.[56]

The rule exempts a number of disclosures unlikely to result in the abuses to which the rule is aimed and that are necessary and appropriate in virtually all transactions. Rule 14e–3(d)(1)(i), for example, allows the bidder to disclose information internally to its officer, directors and agents. Likewise, that provision permits the bidder to disclose confidential information relating to the planned tender offer to its legal and financial advisers. Subsection (ii) allows the bidder to disclose confidential information to the target and its affiliates, which is common in the course of negotiations relating to a prospective acquisition. Subsection (iii) recognizes that the bidder often will need to disclose information to a variety of federal and state regulators, such as antitrust authorities.

---

[55] 17 C.F.R. § 240.14e–3(d)(1).

[56] Release No. 17120, supra note 12, 1980 SEC LEXIS 775 at *41–42.

What the rule thus prohibits is tipping of information to persons who are likely to buy target shares for their own account. In particular, the rule was intended to strike at the practice known as warehousing. Anecdotal evidence suggests that before Rule 14e–3 was on the books bidders frequently tipped their intentions to friendly parties. Warehousing increased the odds a hostile takeover bid would succeed by increasing the number of shares likely to support the bidder's proposal.[57]

1.   The tippers and tippees to whom the rule applies

Rule 14e–3(d)(2) provides that only the following classes of persons are subject to the rule:

(i) The offering person or its officers, directors, partners, employees or advisors;

(ii) The issuer of the securities sought or to be sought by such tender offer or its officers, directors, partners, employees or advisors;

(iii) Anyone acting on behalf of the persons in paragraph (d)(2)(i) of this section or the issuer or persons in paragraph (d)(2)(ii) of this section; and

(iv) Any person in possession of material information relating to a tender offer which information he knows or has reason to know is nonpublic and which he knows or has reason to know has been acquired directly or indirectly from any of the above.[58]

As the SEC explained, the rule thus applies to two basic categories of persons:

The first category consists of those persons who occupy a certain status such as the offering person, the subject company, or an officer, director, partner or employee or any other person acting on behalf of the offering person or the issuer. The second category consists of tippees of the persons in the status category. As a result, Rule 14e–3(d)(2) would reach intermediate level tippees, regardless of whether they trade on the basis of the information. For example, a person who receives such information from the offering person such as a broker or dealer not involved in the tender offer will violate Rule 14e–3 if he communicates such information to another

---

[57] In U.S. v. O'Hagan, 521 U.S. 642 (1997), however, the Supreme Court declined to determine "the legitimacy of Rule 14e–3(a) as applied to 'warehousing,' which the Government describes as 'the practice by which bidders leak advance information of a tender offer to allies and encourage them to purchase the target company's stock before the bid is announced.' " Id. at 673 n.17.

[58] 17 C.F.R. § 240.14e–3(d)(1).

person under circumstances where it is reasonably foreseeable that such other person will trade on the basis of the information or such other person will tip someone else.[59]

E. The Validity of Rule 14e–3

Unlike both the disclose or abstain rule and the misappropriation theory under Rule 10b–5, Rule 14e–3 liability is not premised on breach of a fiduciary duty.[60] As a result, there is no need for a showing that the trading party or tipper was subject to any duty of confidentiality, and no need to show that a tipper personally benefited from the tip. In addition, in adopting the rule, the SEC specifically invoked the equal access standard:

> The Commission has previously expressed and continues to have serious concerns about trading by persons in possession of material, nonpublic information relating to a tender offer. This practice results in unfair disparities in market information and market disruption. Security holders who purchase from or sell to such persons are effectively denied the benefits of disclosure and the substantive protections of the Williams Act. If furnished with the information, these security holders would be able to make an informed investment decision, which could involve deferring the purchase or sale of the securities until the material information had been disseminated or until the tender offer had been commenced or terminated.[61]

In light of the well-established fiduciary duty requirement under Rule 10b–5 and the Supreme Court's explicit rejection of the equal access standard, Rule 14e–3 arguably ran afoul of *Schreiber v. Burlington Northern, Inc.*,[62] in which the Supreme Court held that § 14(e) was modeled on § 10(b) and, like that section, requires a showing of misrepresentation or nondisclosure. If the two sections are to be interpreted in pari materia, as *Schreiber* indicated, and § 10(b) requires a showing of a breach of a duty in order for liability to arise, the SEC appeared to have exceeded its statutory authority by adopting a rule that makes illegal a variety of trading practices that do not involve any breach of duty.

---

[59] Release No. 17120, supra note 12, 1980 SEC LEXIS 775 at *42–43.

[60] United States v. Chestman, 947 F.2d 551, 557 (1991) (en banc) (holding that Rule 14e–3 "creates a duty in those traders who fall within its ambit to abstain or disclose, without regard to whether the trader owes a pre-existing fiduciary duty to respect the confidentiality of the information"), cert. denied, 503 U.S. 1004 (1992).

[61] Release No. 17120, supra note 12, 1980 SEC LEXIS 775 at *17.

[62] 472 U.S. 1 (1985).

In *U.S. v. O'Hagan*,[63] however, the Supreme Court nevertheless upheld Rule 14e–3 as a valid exercise of the SEC's rulemaking authority despite the absence of a fiduciary duty element. The Supreme Court emphasized that the SEC's rule making authority under § 14(e) is broad. Under § 10(b), the SEC's authority is limited to rules proscribing manipulative and deceptive devices. Under § 14(e), however, the SEC's authority extends to regulating non-deceptive devices in ways "reasonably designed" to prevent fraud and manipulation.[64] In turn, Rule 14e–3 was deemed to be a "means reasonably designed to prevent" fraudulent trading on material, nonpublic information in the tender offer context.[65] Noting that a "prophylactic measure," because its mission is to prevent, typically encompasses more than the core activity prohibited, the Court held that, "under § 14(e), the Commission may prohibit acts not themselves fraudulent under the common law or § 10(b), if the prohibition is 'reasonably designed to prevent . . . acts and practices [that] are fraudulent.' "[66] Although the Supreme Court's holding was limited to the validity of the trading prohibition under Rule 14e–3(a), the logic of the court's opinion is widely assumed to extend to the tipping prohibition under Rule 14e–3(d).[67]

F. The Rule's Limited Scope

Although Rule 14e–3 is broader than Rule 10b–5 in one since, because the former lacks the latter's fiduciary relationship requirement, Rule 14e–3 otherwise is quite limited in scope. One prong of the rule (the prohibition on trading while in possession of material nonpublic information) does not apply until the offeror has taken substantial steps towards making the offer. More important, both prongs of the rule are limited to information relating to a tender offer. As a result, most types of inside information remain subject to the duty-based analysis of *Chiarella* and its progeny.

G. Is there an Implied Private Party Cause of Action under the Rule?

Although most lawsuits under Rule 14e–3 have been brought by the SEC, most courts to address the issue have concluded that an implied private right of action exists under the rule and is

---

[63] 521 U.S. 642 (1997).

[64] Id. at 672.

[65] Id. at 672.

[66] Id. at 672–73.

[67] See Langevoort, supra note 43, § 7:10 at 7–18 ("Assuming that the abstain or disclose portion of the rule is valid, i.e., that trading while in possession of tender offer related information can be fraudulent within the meaning of the section, it does follow that seeking to control leaks and selective dissemination to persons reasonably likely to trade unlawfully is a means reasonably designed to prevent unlawful trading.").

available to investors trading in the target's securities at the same time as the persons who violated the rule.[68] In addition, persons who trade contemporaneously with someone who violates Rule 14e–3 by trading on the basis of information relating to a tender offer may avail themselves of the express statutory cause of action under Exchange Act § 20A.[69]

---

[68] William K.S. Wang & Marc I. Steinberg, Insider Trading § 9.4 at 737 (3rd ed. 2010).

[69] Id. See also Chapter 11.G (discussing the private right of action under 20A).

Chapter 11

REMEDIES AND PENALTIES

An inside trader faces three potential opponents. The Justice Department may pursue criminal charges. The SEC may pursue a variety of civil penalties. Private party litigants may bring damage actions under both federal and state law. Taken together, the penalties and other liabilities to which an inside trader is potentially subject in such litigation are extensive and severe.

A. Civil and Criminal Liability

The SEC has no authority to prosecute criminal actions against inside traders, but it is authorized by Exchange Act § 21(d)(1) to ask the Justice Department to initiate a criminal prosecution.[1] In addition, the Justice Department may bring such a prosecution on its own initiative. Under § 32(a) of the Act, a willful violation of Rule 10b–5 or 14e–3 is a felony that can be punished by a $5 million fine ($25 million in the case of corporations) and up to 20 years in jail.[2] Since the mid-1980s insider trading scandals, criminal prosecutions have become fairly common in this area.

The SEC long has had the authority to pursue various civil penalties in insider trading cases. Under Exchange Act § 21(d), the SEC may seek a permanent or temporary injunction whenever "it shall appear to the Commission that any person is engaged or is about to engage in any acts or practices constituting a violation" of the Act or any rules promulgated thereunder.[3] Courts have made it quite easy for the SEC to obtain injunctions under § 21(d). The SEC must make a "proper showing," but that merely requires the SEC to demonstrate that a violation of the securities laws occurred and there is a reasonable likelihood of future violations.[4] At least in the

---

[1] 15 U.S.C. § 78(d)(1) ("The Commission may transmit such evidence as may be available concerning . . . a violation of any provision of this chapter or the rules or regulations thereunder to the Attorney General, who may, in his discretion, institute the necessary criminal proceedings under this chapter.").

[2] 15 U.S.C. § 78ff(a). "The 'willfulness' requirement of § 32(a) of the Exchange Act does not require the Government to prove specific intent to violate the act. . . . The Government must, however, prove an intent to commit the act which constitutes a violation of that section of the statute under which the defendant is charged." U.S. v. Koenig, 388 F. Supp. 670, 711 (S.D.N.Y. 1974).

[3] 15 U.S.C. § 78(d)(1).

[4] See SEC v. Commonwealth Chem. Sec., Inc., 574 F.2d 90, 99–100 (2d Cir.1978) ("Our recent decisions have emphasized, perhaps more than older ones, the need for the SEC to go beyond the mere facts of past violations and demonstrate a realistic likelihood of recurrence."); SEC v. Lund, 570 F. Supp. 1397, 1404 (C.D.Cal.1983) (court denied an injunction on the grounds that the defendant's action was "an isolated occurrence" and that his "profession [was] not likely to lead him into future violations"). In addition to the likelihood of future violations, courts weighing an SEC request to enjoin the defendant have also considered such factors

Second Circuit, the SEC is not required to meet traditional requirements for equitable relief, such as irreparable harm, which is significant because so much insider trading litigation takes place in the federal courts in New York, which are within the Second Circuit.[5]

Once the court's equity jurisdiction "has been properly invoked by the showing of a securities law violation, the court possesses the necessary power to fashion an appropriate remedy."[6] Thus, in addition to or in place of injunctive relief, the SEC may seek disgorgement of profits, correction of misleading statements, disclosure of material information, or other special remedies.[7] In the insider trading context, disgorgement of profits to the government is the most commonly used enforcement tool.

> The primary purpose of disgorgement orders is to deter violations of the securities laws by depriving violators of their ill-gotten gains. "The effective enforcement of the federal securities laws requires that the SEC be able to make violations unprofitable. The deterrent effect of an SEC enforcement action would be greatly undermined if securities law violators were not required to disgorge illicit profits."[8]

Consistent with the principle that disgorgement is intended to deter insider trading, courts have held that tippers can be forced to disgorge an amount equivalent to their tippee's profits.[9]

The SEC can ask the court to direct any money disgorged by inside traders into a so-called "Fair Fund," the proceeds of which can be distributed to victims of the inside trader's illegal conduct as

---

as "the degree of scienter involved, the sincerity of defendant's assurances against future violations, the isolated or recurrent nature of the infraction, [and the] defendant's recognition of the wrongful nature of his conduct. . . ." SEC v. Universal Major Industries, 546 F.2d 1044, 1048 (2d Cir. 1976).

[5] See SEC v. Management Dynamics, Inc., 515 F.2d 801 (2d Cir.1975); SEC v. Manor Nursing Centers, Inc., 458 F.2d 1082 (2d Cir.1972). See also SEC v. Chapman, 826 F. Supp.2d 847, 857 (D.Md.2011) ("The SEC need not prove irreparable injury or inadequacy of other remedies. . . . Instead, the Court must issue an injunction if the SEC 'demonstrates a reasonable and substantial likelihood that the defendant, if not enjoined, will violate securities laws in the future.'"). But see SEC v. Fife, 311 F.3d 1, 9 (1st Cir. 2002) ("Unlike the Second Circuit, we have not removed irreparable harm from the preliminary injunction inquiry in SEC preliminary injunction actions.")

[6] SEC v. Manor Nursing Centers, 458 F.2d 1082, 1103 (2d Cir.1972).

[7] See 15 U.S.C. § 78(d)(5) ("In any action or proceeding brought or instituted by the Commission under any provision of the securities laws, the Commission may seek, and any Federal court may grant, any equitable relief that may be appropriate or necessary for the benefit of investors.").

[8] SEC v. Fischbach Corp., 133 F.3d 170, 175 (2d Cir.1997) (citations omitted).

[9] See SEC v. Clark, 915 F.2d 439, 454 (9th Cir.1990) ("It is well settled that a tipper can be required to disgorge his tippees' profits. . . . Such a rule is a necessary deterrent to evasion of Rule 10b–5 liability by either: (1) enriching a friend or relative; or (2) tipping others with the expectation of reciprocity.").

partial restitution of their losses.[10] "The primary purpose of disgorgement orders is to deter violations of the securities laws by depriving violators of their ill-gotten gains," however.[11] Reimbursement of victim losses is a "distinctly secondary goal."[12] The focus on punishment and deterrence explains why the amount to be disgorged is measured by the defendant's profits, rather than the victims' losses.[13]

Although "a general practice of awarding disgorged funds to the victims of the illegal conduct appears to have emerged,"[14] the SEC has discretion as to whether or not to direct the proceeds of a disgorgement proceeding into a fund for victims.[15] Likewise, the court always has the "discretion to refuse to order that a disgorgement fund be paid out as restitution."[16] Where there is a large number of victims each with small claims, for example, the costs of administering such a fund can justify a refusal to create a fund.[17] Where no fund is created, the proceeds of the disgorgement proceeding are paid into the U.S. Treasury.[18]

In addition to the civil sanctions to which all inside traders are subject, the SEC may punish insider trading by regulated market professionals through administrative proceedings. Under § 15(b)(4) of the 1934 Act, for example, the SEC may censure, limit the activities of, suspend, or revoke the registration of a broker or dealer who willfully violates the insider trading prohibition.[19] Similar sanctions may be imposed on those associated with the broker or dealer in such activities. The SEC may issue a report of its investigation of the incident even if it decides not to pursue judicial or administrative proceedings, which may lead to private litigation.[20]

---

[10] See SEC v. Cioffi, 868 F. Supp.2d 65, 70 (E.D.N.Y.2012) ("Disgorgement can be used as a restitutionary remedy by the creation of a 'Fair Fund' from which victims can be paid."); see, e.g., SEC v. Fischbach Corp., 133 F.3d 170, 176 (2d Cir.1997) (noting that "disgorged funds may often go to compensate securities fraud victims for their losses").

[11] *Fischbach Corp.,* 133 F.3d at 175.

[12] Id.

[13] Official Comm. of Unsecured Creditors of WorldCom, Inc. v. SEC, 467 F.3d 73, 82 (2d Cir.2006).

[14] SEC. v. Bhagat, 2008 WL 4890890 at *1 (N.D.Cal.2008).

[15] See *Official Comm. of Unsecured Creditors,* 467 F.3d at 83.

[16] *Fischbach Corp.,* 133 F.3d at 176.

[17] *Bhagat,* 2008 WL 4890890 at *1.

[18] Id. at *2.

[19] 15 U.S.C. § 78o(b)(4).

[20] 15 U.S.C. § 78u(a).

B. Statutory Sanctions

During the 1980s, Congress significantly expanded the civil sanctions available to the SEC for use against inside traders. The Insider Trading Sanctions Act of 1984 (ITSA) created a civil monetary penalty of up to three times the profit gained or loss avoided by a person who violates rules 10b–5 or 14e–3 "by purchasing or selling a security while in the possession of material non-public information."[21] An action to impose such a penalty may be brought in addition to or in lieu of any other actions that the SEC or Justice Department is entitled to bring. Because the SEC thus may seek both disgorgement and treble damages, an inside trader faces potential civil liability of up to four times the profit gained.

In the Insider Trading and Securities Fraud Act of 1988 (ITSFEA), Congress made a number of further changes designed to augment the enforcement resources and penalties available to the SEC.[22] Among other things, it authorized the SEC to pay a bounty to informers of up to 10 percent of any penalty collected by the SEC. The treble money fine was extended to controlling persons, so as to provide brokerage houses, for example, with greater incentives to monitor the activities of their employees.

1.　ITSA

As we have seen, a merger or acquisition provides an opportunity for individuals with advance knowledge of the transaction to reap enormous profits. Because target share prices almost always rise toward the bid price once an offer is made public, corporate insiders and associated parties such as lawyers, investment bankers, accountants, financial printers, and their employees can use their informational advantage to buy target shares at the pre-bid price with little risk of financial loss.

The 1980s were a period of intense corporate takeover activity. Partly as a result, that decade also saw a significant increase in SEC enforcement activity directed at insider trading in connection with corporate takeovers. Between 1979 and 1981 alone, for example, the SEC charged thirty-three individuals with insider trading violations.[23] The emphasis on insider trading increased further with the 1981 appointment of John Shad as Chairman of the SEC. Chairman Shad promised to make insider trading a top priority of his administration and "to come down with hobnail boots

---

[21] Pub. L. No. 98–376, 98 Stat. 1264 (1984).

[22] Pub. L. No. 100–704, 102 Stat. 4677 (1988).

[23] The Economist, June 30, 1984, at 67.

to give some startling examples to inhibit" insider trading.[24] As a result, between 1982 and 1984, forty-nine individuals were charged with insider trading offenses, which at that time represented almost one-third of all the insider trading cases in the SEC's history.[25]

In assessing the results of this enforcement program, the SEC concluded that an increase in the penalties for insider trading was necessary.[26] On September 1, 1982, the commissioners unanimously approved a request to Congress for legislation increasing the penalties for insider trading. On September 27th, the SEC forwarded a draft bill to Congress that would impose a civil treble damage penalty and increase the criminal fine for securities violations.[27]

The House opened subcommittee hearings on the bill, H.R. 559, on April 13, 1983.[28] During the hearings, a consensus emerged for the need for some legislation in this area. The principal point of contention proved not to be the desirability of an enhanced penalty but whether the statute should define insider trading. On July 27, 1983, the subcommittee approved the bill, which was amended to include provisions insulating from liability brokers who unknowingly executed orders for clients trading on inside information, establishing a definition of profit and loss, and creating a statute of limitations applicable to the penalty.[29] It contained no substantive provisions, with the omission of a definition of insider trading having been a conscious decision by Congress.[30] The bill was reported out of committee on August 3 and

---

[24] Id.

[25] Id.

[26] Former Commissioner Thomas observed that "[i]nsider trading has been proliferating at an alarming rate, and we need a new weapon in our arsenal to stem this tide." Securities Sale Rule Extended, S.E.C., 2 to 1, Backs Shelf Registration, N.Y. Times, Sept. 2, 1982, at D1, col. 6 (quoting SEC Commissioner Barbara Thomas).

[27] H.R. Rep. No. 355, 98th Cong., 1st Sess. 19–21 (1983), reprinted in 1984 U.S. Code Cong. & Ad. News 2274.

[28] Insider Trading Sanctions Act and SEC Enforcement Legislation: Hearing on H.R. 559 Before the Subcomm. on Telecommunications, Consumer Protection, and Finance of the House Comm. on Energy and Commerce, 98th Cong., 1st Sess. (1983).

[29] See H.R. 559, 98th Cong., 1st Sess. § 2 (1983).

[30] The House committee asserted that the common law was sufficiently developed to warn traders of what was wrongful and that the problem of drafting a workable definition was so complex that "any effort to define insider trading would result in, at best, a slightly less generalized rule than 10b–5 and, at worst, a rule that leaves gaping holes 'large enough to drive a truck through.'" H.R. Rep. No. 355, supra note 27, at 14. The committee also feared that any definition would have to be either so broad as to be unworkable or so narrow as to reduce the SEC's and the courts' flexibility to address new forms of trading. Moreover, it was concerned that any definition, even if limited to the treble damage penalty, would ultimately control all situations. Id. at 13.

The Senate chose not to include a definition because of its acceptance of the SEC's testimony that it was satisfied with existing law and because of its concern

was passed without objection by the House on September 9.[31] The Senate made several changes to the House bill, expanding the SEC's administrative proceedings power to include takeover and proxy violations, making liability for the use of inside information on options or other derivative securities coextensive with liability for such use with regard to the underlying security, and giving the SEC power to exclude violators of commodity market rules from the securities market.[32] The House adopted all three amendments. The bill was passed on July 25, 1984, and signed into law by President Reagan on August 10, 1984.[33]

As ultimately passed, ITSA increased both the civil and the criminal penalties for insider trading. The Act gave the SEC authority to seek a civil monetary penalty of up to "three times the profit gained or loss avoided" by a person who violates the prohibition "by purchasing or selling a security while in the possession of material, nonpublic information."[34] This action may be brought in addition to or in lieu of any other actions that the SEC or Justice Department is entitled to bring. The SEC's other civil, as well as its administrative and criminal remedies, remain available.

Because the SEC may seek both disgorgement and treble damages, the inside trader now faces a potential civil liability of up to four times the profit gained.[35] The SEC is not required, however, to seek the maximum penalty in every case. Moreover, the Act gives the presiding court "discretion to determine the amount of the penalty, within the maximum amount, in light of the facts and

---

that a statutory definition would produce a substantial amount of interpretive litigation and limit the SEC's flexibility. The legislative history in the Senate indicates that an additional concern was "the complexity of the undertaking, and the necessity for prompt action on the bill." 130 Cong. Rec. S8913 (daily ed. June 29, 1984) (remarks of Sen. D'Amato).

[31] N.Y. Times, Sept. 20, 1983, at D13, col. 1.

[32] S. 910, 98th Cong., 1st Sess. (1983).

[33] The Insider Trading Sanctions Act: Some Unfinished Business Ahead, Nat'l L.J., Oct. 15, 1984, at 18, col. 1. See generally Stephen M. Bainbridge, Note, A Critique of the Insider Trading Sanctions Act of 1984, 71 Va. L. Rev. 455 (1985) (discussing Act's provisions).

[34] 15 U.S.C. § 78u–1.

[35] In appropriate insider trading cases, the SEC thus may seek a court order enjoining the individual from again violating the prohibition, disgorgement of "ill-gotten" gains, and the imposition of the ITSA civil penalty, or any combination thereof. H.R. Rep. No. 355, supra note 27, at 8. Section 308(a) of the Sarbanes-Oxley Act provides, in pertinent part, that:

> If in any judicial or administrative action brought by the Commission under the securities laws ... the Commission obtains an order requiring disgorgement against any person for a violation of such laws or the rules or regulations thereunder, or such person agrees in settlement of any such action to such disgorgement, and the Commission also obtains pursuant to such laws a civil penalty against such person, the amount of such civil penalty shall, on the motion or at the direction of the Commission, be added to and become part of the disgorgement fund for the benefit of the victims of such violation.

15 U.S.C. § 7246(a).

circumstances" of the case. In doing so, the court may consider factors such as the violator's level of culpability and the amount of proof demonstrated by the SEC in establishing its case.[36]

The creation of ITSA's treble profit penalty exacerbated a longstanding disagreement over how to measure the profit gained or loss avoided by the violator. To illustrate the problem assume that the insider illegally bought stock at four dollars per share and that throughout the month following the announcement of the information on which his purchase was based, the stock sold at five dollars per share.[37] If he sells during that month, there is general agreement that he may be required to disgorge one dollar of profit per share. If the share price later declines to three dollars, he can still be required to disgorge one dollar per share under a line of cases holding insiders liable for any profits they could have realized.[38] If the share price rises to ten dollars but then falls to three dollars, at which point the insider sells, the SEC will only request disgorgement of one dollar of profit per share, despite the "could have realized" line of cases. Where the insider sells at ten dollars, however, the SEC will demand that he disgorge six dollars per share.[39]

The SEC argued in *SEC v. MacDonald* that the appropriate standard was the difference between the purchase and sale prices, no matter how far distant in time or how much subsequent events may have affected the price.[40] In the SEC's view, it was necessary to include profits realized after public dissemination of the inside information to maximize deterrence. The First Circuit rejected the SEC's position, holding that the correct definition of profit gained was the difference between the purchase price and the market price a "reasonable time" after the information was generally disseminated.[41] The court saw "no legal or equitable difference" between the inside trader's decision to retain the stock "with the hope of further profit and a decision to sell it and invest in something else. In both cases the subsequent profits are purely a new matter."[42] A reasonable time was defined as ending on "the date by which the news had been fully digested and acted upon by

---

[36] Id. at 8–9.

[37] This example is taken from SEC v. MacDonald, 699 F.2d 47, 52–53 (1st Cir. 1983).

[38] See, e.g., SEC v. Shapiro, 494 F.2d 1301, 1309 (2d Cir. 1974).

[39] SEC v. MacDonald, 699 F.2d 47, 52–53 (1st Cir. 1983). There the court noted, "in passing, that inconsistencies do not bother the Commission." Id. at 53.

[40] 699 F.2d 47, 52–54 (1st Cir. 1983).

[41] Id. at 55.

[42] Id. at 54.

investors," as indicated by the volume and the price at which the shares were traded following disclosure.[43]

The SEC's proposed approach to measuring profit is even less persuasive when applied to the ITSA. The treble profits penalty should erase any subsequent profits made by the defendant. Moreover, because most inside traders sell shortly after disclosure, the *MacDonald* issue rarely arises in practice. Recognizing this, the SEC recommended that the *MacDonald* standard be adopted in the ITSA, and the House committee agreed. The Act therefore defined "profit gained" or "loss avoided" to be "the difference between the purchase or sale price of the security and the value of the security as measured by the trading price of the security a reasonable period after public dissemination of the nonpublic information."[44]

In addition to creating the new treble profit penalty, ITSA increased the maximum criminal fine from $10,000 to $100,000. The Act also provided that the use of material nonpublic information in connection with the "purchase or sale of a put, call, straddle, option, or privilege" in a way that would violate the insider trading ruled if used with respect to the underlying security is also a violation of the rules and will result in "comparable liability."[45] This provision was intended to "make clear that it is not possible to insulate oneself from the prohibition of insider trading by restricting activity to securities that are derivative of the securities to which the material nonpublic information relates."[46]

2.   ITSFEA

In the wake of several very high profile insider trading prosecutions in the mid-1980s, Congress in 1988 passed ITSFEA.[47] The Act extended ITSA liability to controlling persons, required securities industry firms to take affirmative steps to ensure insider trading compliance programs, increased the maximum criminal penalties under Exchange Act § 32(a), allowing the SEC to pay bounties to insider trading informants, and created an express private right of action for persons who trade contemporaneously

---

[43] Id. at 55. Cf. SEC v. Texas Gulf Sulphur Co., 312 F. Supp. 77 (S.D.N.Y. 1970) (insiders required only to disgorge those profits accrued prior to the time the inside information was disclosed), modified on other grounds, 446 F.2d 1301 (2d Cir.), cert. denied, 404 U.S. 105 (1971).

[44] 15 U.S.C. 78u–1(e).

[45] 15 U.S.C. § 78t(d).

[46] 130 Cong. Rec. H7758 (daily ed. July 25, 1984) (written explanation submitted by Rep. Dingell analyzing the ITSA as amended by the Senate).

[47] See H.R. Rep. No. 100–910, at 14 (1988) (stating that ITSFEA "represents the response of this Committee to a series of revelations over the last two years concerning serious episodes of abusive and illegal practices on Wall Street").

with an inside trader.[48] We'll examine these provisions in detail in the sections that follow.

C. Controlling Person Liability

Exchange Act § 20(a) provides that any "person who, directly or indirectly, controls any person liable under any provision of this chapter or of any rule or regulation thereunder shall also be liable jointly and severally with and to the same extent as such controlled person to any person to whom such controlled person is liable . . . , unless the controlling person acted in good faith and did not directly or indirectly induce the act or acts constituting the violation or cause of action."[49] Both liability of the controlled person to private persons and the SEC can trigger controlling person liability.

The Act does not define what constitutes control for this purpose. Some courts define a controlling person as someone who has "the power to control the general affairs of the entity primarily liable at the time the entity violated the securities laws . . . [and] had the requisite power to directly or indirectly control or influence the specific corporate policy which resulted in the primary liability."[50] Some courts require a showing that the allegedly controlling person actually exercised the power to control the primarily liable defendant, while others merely require the abstract ability to control.[51] Because the purpose of controlling person liability is to encourage employers and the like to supervise their employees so as to prevent violations by the latter, there is no need to show that the controlling person was involved in the wrongful conduct.[52]

---

[48] See generally Barbara Bader Aldave, The Insider Trading and Securities Fraud Enforcement Act of 1988: An Analysis and Appraisal, 52 Alb. L. Rev. 893 (1988); Howard M. Friedman, The Insider Trading and Securities Fraud Enforcement Act of 1988, 68 N.C. L. Rev. 465 (1990); Stuart J. Kaswell, An Insider's View of the Insider Trading and Securities Fraud Enforcement Act of 1988, 45 Bus. Law. 145 (1989); William K. S. Wang, ITSFEA's Effect on Either an Implied Cause of Action for Damages by Contemporaneous Traders or an Action for Damages or Rescission by the Party in Privity with the Inside Trader, 16 J. Corp. L. 445 (1991).

[49] 15 U.S.C. § 78t(a).

[50] Brown v. Enstar Group, Inc., 84 F.3d 393, 396 (11th Cir. 1996), cert. denied, 519 U.S. 1112 (1997).

[51] See id. at 396 n.6 ("The Eighth Circuit's test requires a plaintiff to prove that a defendant actually exercised power over the entity primarily liable. . . . [W]e do not need to decide here whether 'power to control the general affairs of the entity primarily liable' means simply abstract power to control, or actual exercise of the power to control.").

[52] See, e.g., Martin v. Shearson Lehman Hutton, Inc., 986 F.2d 242 (8th Cir. 1993) (holding that "that liability did not depend on the controlling person's having exercised control over the particular transaction that gave rise to the violation . . . Shearson had the ability to discipline O'Leary's conduct, and it was this conduct that gave rise to the loss."), cert. denied, 510 U.S. 861 (1993); see also In re Initial Public Offering Sec. Litig., 241 F. Supp. 2d 281, 392–97 (S.D.N.Y. 2003) (holding that "culpable participation" is not required for the controlling person to be liable under § 20(a)).

Good faith on the part of the controlling person is an affirmative defense under § 20(a).[53] In order to establish the good faith defense, the controlling person first must show that it did not induce the primary actor's violations. The controlling person then must show that it maintained and enforced a reasonable and proper system of supervision and internal control over the pertinent personnel.[54]

1.　ITSA exemption

In 1984, the securities industry opposed subjecting individuals who did not actually trade securities or tip inside information to ITSA's treble damage sanction. The SEC subsequently agreed, arguing that the deterrent objective underlying the Act did not require the imposition of the sanction on secondary actors. In response to these concerns, the bill was amended to provide the following exemption:

> No person shall be subject to a sanction [under the Act] solely because that person aided and abetted a transaction covered by [the Act] in a manner other than by communicating material nonpublic information. Section 20(a) of this title [which makes controlling persons liable for violations committed by their agents] shall not apply to an action brought under [the Act]. No person shall be liable under [the Act] solely by reason of employing a person who is liable under [it].

This exemption limited a financial firm's liability in several important ways. First, a brokerage firm would not be liable if an employee learned inside information legitimately released to the firm and then used it to trade for his own account. Second, the firm would be insulated from liability where an employee traded for a customer's account without the firm's knowledge or approval. Third, the firm was not liable where it executed trades for an insider without trading on the information for its own account or tipping it to other customers. Fourth, the firm was not liable if an adviser working for an investment company traded on the firm's account without the company's knowledge or approval.

2.　ITSFEA amendments

ITSFEA further revised controlling person liability in insider trading cases. On the one hand, it extended the ITSA treble money penalty to controlling persons.[55] On the other hand, before an ITSA penalty could be imposed on a controlling person, ITSFEA required

---

[53] Frank v. Dana Corp., 646 F.3d 954 (6th Cir. 2011).

[54] SEC v. First Jersey Securities, Inc., 101 F.3d 1450, 1473 (2d Cir.1996).

[55] 15 U.S.C. § 78u–1(a)(3).

the SEC to show that the controlling person "knew or recklessly disregarded the fact that such controlled person was likely to engage in the act or acts constituting the violation and failed to take appropriate steps to prevent such act or acts before they occurred" or, in the case of a broker or dealer, that the controlling person knowingly or recklessly failed to establish, maintain, or enforce "insider trading prevention compliance programs that such failure substantially contributed to or permitted the occurrence of the act or acts constituting the violation."[56]

D. Liability by Attribution

In 2013, the US Attorney for the Southern District of New York indicted SAC Capital Advisors, a major hedge fund advisor, and several affiliated entities. The companies were charged with criminal responsibility for insider trading offenses committed by numerous employees, which occurred over a period of over 10 years and involved the securities of more than 20 publicly-traded companies. According to the indictment, the employees' misconduct was made possible by institutional practices—followed at all of the defendant entities—encouraging widespread gathering and use of material, non-public information by employees in making trading decisions for the funds. According to the charges, the employees' allegedly illegal activity resulted in hundreds of millions of dollars in profits and avoided losses.

Curiously, the government did not rely on controlling person liability to hold the employers liable for their employee's misdeeds. Instead, they relied on the basic agency law principle of attribution:

> Persons who possess or receive material nonpublic information in the course of their employment might well decide to trade on the basis of that information for their employer's proprietary trading account. That could happen when the employer is the issuer itself, as in the case where management engages in a stock repurchase program at the same time that they are aware of undisclosed positive information about the company's prospects. Or, more frequently, it could be a case where an employee of an investment firm, a broker-dealer, for example, receives a tip from some company insider and buys or sells stock in the insider's company for his firm's account on the basis of the tip.

> In either case, liability under the federal securities laws would be fairly straightforward. Legally, the firm itself is the purchaser or seller of the securities; hence, this would be an issue of primary (not secondary) liability. When the issuer

---

[56] Id. at § 78u–1(b)(1).

itself is the purchaser, it is deemed to "know" all information known by its officers, directors and senior management—indeed, probably all agents and employees—unless such persons are acting outside the scope of their employment or contrary to its interests. As a result, the basic test for liability under Rule 10b–5 is readily satisfied in the typical case: the company is trading while in possession of material nonpublic information. . . .

The same result would follow in the case where the employer is trading in securities other than its own, assuming that the employee trading on its behalf is deemed a temporary insider or a tippee under the *Dirks* rationale or misappropriated the information in question. Again, the knowledge of the employee is attributed to the employer, since the information came to him or was used in the course of employment for the employer's benefit. The fiduciary duty imposed on the employee as a result of his tippee status would be attributed also. Thus, primary liability would exist, as in the SEC's action against the First Boston Corp. In that settled proceeding, First Boston learned confidential information about an increase in a client's loss reserves through its Corporate Finance department. That information made its way to the head trader in the firm's Equity Trading department (a managing director), who caused the firm to sell the client's stock. First Boston consented to disgorgement of profits of $132,138, a penalty of $264,276 and an undertaking to review and improve if necessary its procedures for handling confidential information.[57]

E. Compliance Programs

"A significant purpose of the Exchange Act was to eliminate the idea that use of inside information for personal advantage was a normal emolument of corporate office."[58] As a matter of good corporate practice, all publicly held corporations should adopt policies designed to prevent illegal trading by insiders—especially Section 16 officers. Such policies protect the insiders by providing guidance as to when trading is least likely to result in liability. Given the severe penalties for inside trading, and the inevitable temptation to profit from access to inside information, such policies are necessary to, in a sense, protect insiders from themselves. Even more important, however, such policies also protect the issuer itself

---

[57] Donald C. Langevoort, Insider Trading: Regulation, Enforcement & Prevention § 12.2 (2012).

[58] Dirks v. SEC, 463 U.S. 646, 653 n.10 (1983).

from potential controlling person liability. Not surprisingly, perhaps, most public corporations have adopted such policies.[59]

As we have seen, the good faith defense available under § 20(a) "provides an incentive [for issuers] to implement procedures to preserve confidential information and to deter insider trading."[60] The incentive to adopt such compliance programs was enhanced following the 1988 adoption of ITSFEA, because adoption and effective implementation of a reasonable compliance program makes it significantly more difficult for the SEC to show that the issuer acted recklessly and/or failed to take appropriate steps with respect to potential illegal trading by its insiders. Accordingly, good corporate practice mandates creation and rigorous enforcement of effective corporate compliance programs intended to prevent insider trading by officers and other employees of the issuer.[61]

Another consideration is that evidence of insider transactions is highly relevant to private securities litigation. Public corporations, especially in technology sectors, have become highly vulnerable to such litigation. A technology corporation that fails to meet its quarterly earnings projection will experience a drop in its stock price when that news is announced, and often will be sued shortly thereafter for fraud under Rule 10b–5.

In 1995, Congress adopted the Private Securities Litigation Reform Act (PSLRA) to curtail what Congress believed was a widespread problem of merit-less strike suits.[62] Of particular relevance to insider trading compliance programs, one of the PSLRA's provisions established a new (and arguably higher) pleading standard with respect to the scienter element of Rule 10b–5, requiring that a complaint detail facts giving rise to a "strong inference" of scienter.[63]

Post-PSLRA, plaintiffs' securities lawyers began routinely seeking to satisfy the scienter pleading standard by alleging that insiders sold shares in suspicious amounts and/or at suspicious

---

[59] See, e.g., Marc I. Steinberg & John Fletcher, Compliance Programs for Insider Trading, 47 SMU L. Rev. 1783, 1828 (1994); see also Alan J. Berkeley, Form of Summary Memorandum and Sample Corporate Policy on Insider Trading, ALI–ABA Course of Study on Securities Law for Nonsecurities Lawyers, SF43 ALI–ABA 457, 464 (2001) (stating that "companies are increasingly adopting and implementing insider trading compliance programs").

[60] Steinberg & Fletcher, supra note 59, at 1786.

[61] Id. at 1790 (stating that, "given the astronomical liability exposure and the emergence of organizational compliance programs directed against insider trading as an industry norm, the absence of a reasonably effective compliance program in this context makes little sense").

[62] Pub. L. 104–67, 109 Stat. 737 (1995).

[63] 15 U.S.C. § 78u–4(b)(2).

times.[64] Insider sales supposedly provide inferential evidence that senior management knew that earnings forecasts would not be met and sold to avoid the price drop that follows from announcements of lower than expected earnings. Evidence that transactions took place during a trading window established by a corporate insider trading compliance program will help rebut claims that the insider transactions establish the existence of scienter.[65]

1.   Basics of a reasonable compliance program

Insider trading compliance programs commonly have two components. First, corporate policies commonly limit trading by insiders to specified time periods. Second, at least as to directors and Section 16 officers, corporate insider trading compliance programs commonly require preapproval of proposed transactions by a specified compliance officer. As a matter of good corporate practice, an issuer's insider trading compliance program commonly will apply to any and all transactions in any of the issuer's securities, including not just common stock, but also preferred stock, convertible debentures, options, warrants, and any derivatives.

2.   Timing

As a matter of good corporate practice, an insider trading compliance program should create prophylactic rules governing the timing of insider transactions. Recall that under *Texas Gulf Sulphur*, an insider who possesses material nonpublic information may not trade until such information has been widely disseminated.[66] While the *Texas Gulf Sulphur* standard works well for the sort of dramatic, one-time event news at issue there, it works less well for the more mundane sorts of nonpublic information to which insiders routinely have access. An issuer always has undisclosed information about numerous different aspects of its business. By the time all of that information has been disseminated publicly, moreover, new undisclosed information doubtless will have been developed. In response to this concern, firms should develop policies limiting the periods within which insiders may trade.

---

[64] In addition, insider selling activity can be used as evidence that the nonpublic information in question was material. See Basic Inc. v. Levinson, 485 U.S. 224, 240 n.18 (1988) (stating that "trading and profit making by insiders can serve as *an* indication of materiality"; emphasis in original).

[65] Finally, the board of directors may have a state law fiduciary duty to ensure that the corporation has adopted an insider trading compliance program. See, e.g., In re Caremark Int'l Inc. Deriv. Litig., 698 A.2d 959 (Del. Ch. 1996) (suggesting in dicta that directors of a health care corporation had a duty to adopt programs ensuring corporate compliance with relevant state and federal regulations).

[66] See Chapter 6.C.2.

Prophylactic trading restrictions of this sort typically are tied to the company's periodic disclosure process. Per SEC regulations, public corporations must send an annual report to the shareholders and also file with the SEC a Form 10–Q after each of the first three quarters of their fiscal year and a Form 10–K after year's end. Because of the substantial and wide-ranging disclosures required in these reports, which are publicly available, there is a relatively low probability that an insider who trades during the time immediately following their dissemination will be deemed to have traded on material nonpublic information. As *Texas Gulf Sulphur* suggests, however, the insider may not trade the moment the report goes in the mail. Instead, the insider must wait until the market has had time to digest the report.

Corporate insider trading compliance policies typically create a "trading window" during which insiders are affirmatively permitted to trade. The window commonly opens a day or two after filing of the periodic report and closes a specified number of days later (commonly 10 to 30).[67] The premise underlying the delay between the release of operating results and the opening of the trading window a day or two later is that it takes time for information to be absorbed by the marketplace. As we have seen, providing the market with such an opportunity is effectively mandated by *Texas Gulf Sulphur*.

A corporate compliance program establishing a trading window, of course, may not trump the federal securities laws. Because corporations generally do not have an affirmative duty to disclose information simply because it is material, there will be many instances where insiders have access to material information that is not yet ripe for disclosure. An insider who possesses material information that has not been disclosed must refrain from trading at all times—whether or not a trading window is open. As a matter of good corporate practice, public corporations should prohibit trading during an otherwise open trading window whenever insiders have access to undisclosed material nonpublic information even though the company has timely released its financial operating results in a periodic disclosure statement. This is referred to as "closing the window" or as a "blackout period." The window can be closed either through a general announcement that trading should not occur or by declining to preclear specific proposed transactions.

A trading window is appropriately closed during the period prior to the announcement of a proposed merger or acquisition or

---

[67] See Alan L. Dye, Securities Law Compliance Programs, ALI–ABA Course of Study on Postgraduate Course in Federal Securities Law, SF05 ALI–ABA 1043, 1964 (2000).

the announcement of a significant joint venture or other strategic partnering relationship. Because the insider trading prohibition requires the insider to either disclose the information or abstain from trading, and because the insider has no right to disclose confidential corporate information, the insider is effectively obliged to comply with a company-imposed closure and refrain from trading during the period the issuer chooses to keep the information confidential.

A trading window approach contemplates a limited period in which insiders are permitted to trade, while prohibiting them from trading outside that period. In contrast, some corporations adopt so-called "blackout periods" during which insiders are prohibited from trading. A corporation might, for example, adopt a policy prohibiting insiders from trading during the period immediately prior to dissemination of a quarterly or annual report.[68] Outside the blackout period, insiders are presumptively free to trade, although transactions by officers and directors should be precleared on a case-by-case basis as described below.

An effective blackout policy obviously must preclude insiders from trading stock they hold directly. In order to ensure compliance, however, it should also apply to stock held indirectly, such as stock held in a 401(k) plan or other employee benefit program.

Abuse of just such a blackout policy was one of the most unsavory features of the infamous Enron scandal. As Enron was going down the tubes, rank-and-file Enron employees were prevented from selling Enron stock held in their 401(k) plans during a lengthy blackout period imposed while the plan changed administrators. At the same time, however, top Enron executives were selling large amounts of stock they owned directly.

Section 306 of the Sarbanes-Oxley Act was adopted in direct response to this part of the Enron saga. Under it, directors and executive officers of a corporation are forbidden from trading any of their company's equity securities during any blackout period in which 50% or more of the issuer's employees are banned from trading stocks held in pension and benefit accounts. In addition, subject to some minor exceptions, employees must be given 30 days notice before a blackout period commences.

If an executive officer or director violates the trading ban, the company can sue to recover any profit the executive earns from the trade. If the company fails to do so, § 306 expressly authorizes

---

[68] See, e.g., Steinberg & Fletcher, supra note 59, at 1832 (suggesting issuers adopt a blackout period prohibiting trading by officers and directors "three weeks before and forty-eight hours after public announcement (and dissemination) of the company's earnings").

shareholders of the company to sue derivatively on the company's behalf to force the executive to disgorge profits.[69]

3.　Preclearance

Many commentators argue that, as a matter of good corporate practice, the issuer should require preclearance of trading by corporate directors and § 16 officers even during an otherwise open trading window.[70] Non-officer employees are typically exempted from the preclearance requirement. In my opinion, the greater access of corporate directors and § 16 officers to material nonpublic information mandates the adoption of such policies as a matter of good corporate practice.

Corporate compliance programs directed at insider trading by directors and officers in fact customarily include a requirement for preclearance of their transactions by a specified corporate official. Typically, the compliance officer will be a very senior corporate officer, such as the general counsel, corporate secretary, or chief financial officer.[71] A director or officer wishing to trade in the company's securities should notify the compliance officer one or more business days before the proposed transaction is to be effected. In a trading window-based program, the compliance officer may disapprove the proposed transaction even though the trading window is open.

Clearly, the compliance officer should not approve a transaction when the insider seeking approval is known to possess material nonpublic information. As a matter of sound corporate practice, moreover, it would be appropriate for the compliance officer to disapprove a proposed transaction where there is material nonpublic information presently unknown to the insider requesting approval but to which that insider might have access. Indeed, because insider trading compliance programs have such a substantial prophylactic component, it would be appropriate for the compliance officer to disapprove a transaction even where the insider in question does not have authorized access to the material nonpublic information in question. Disapproval of a proposed transaction under such circumstances is appropriate because (1) it prevents subsequent litigation of the question "what did the insider know and when did he/she know it?" and (2) insiders without authorized access to nonpublic information nevertheless often come into possession of such information inadvertently or surreptitiously.

---

[69] 15 U.S.C. 7244.

[70] See, e.g., Dye, supra note 67, at 1065; Steinberg & Fletcher, supra note 58, at 1832.

[71] A different senior officer typically is appointed to review and approve trades by the compliance officer in the corporation's stock.

4.   Insulation walls

Sound compliance programs should include insulation walls so that only persons with need for material nonpublic information have access to such information. Such walls were formerly known in colloquial legal speech as "Chinese walls." As a California appellate judge aptly noted, however:

> "Chinese Wall" is [a] piece of legal flotsam that should be emphatically abandoned. The term has an ethnic focus that many would consider a subtle form of linguistic discrimination. Certainly, the continued use of the term would be insensitive to the ethnic identity of the many persons of Chinese descent. . . .

> Aside from this discriminatory flavor, the term "Chinese Wall" is being used to describe a barrier of silence and secrecy. . . . [But] "Chinese Wall" is not even an architecturally accurate metaphor for the barrier to communication created to preserve confidentiality. Such a barrier functions as a hermetic seal to prevent two-way communication between two groups. The Great Wall of China, on the other hand, was only a one-way barrier. It was built to keep outsiders out—not to keep insiders in.[72]

In law firms, terms such as "ethical wall" or "ethical screen" are emerging as alternatives.[73] In the present context, however, the term "insulation wall" seems superior.[74] First, it does not connote the professional responsibility aspects associated with the ethical wall terminology. Second, it provides a more exact "architecturally accurate metaphor" than does ethical wall.

Key features of such a wall would include organizational and physical separation of persons with access to information especially likely to be abused from persons who do not need such access. Prohibitions against and penalties for discussing confidential matters with unauthorized personnel or in locations where such discussions could be overheard are also an important part of the insulation wall. Likewise, procedures for preventing unapproved personnel from accessing confidential information and files, delinking approved personnel compensation from trading profits,

---

[72] Peat, Marwick, Mitchell & Co. v. Superior Court, 245 Cal. Rptr. (App. 1988) (Low, P.J., concurring).

[73] See, e.g., Ronald R. St. John, When an Ethical Screen Can Be Used to Avoid Vicarious Disqualification of a Law Firm Remains Unsettled, L.A. Lawyer, Feb. 2005, at 29 ("This technique has been referred to in the past as a Chinese wall and is now commonly called an ethical screen.").

[74] Cf. Bernard Shapiro & Neil D. Wyland, Ethical Quandaries of Professionals in Bankruptcy Cases, C836 ALI–ABA 15 (1993) (noting "the recently politically correct expression 'insulation wall' ").

and regular training of personnel on their legal and commercial responsibilities.[75]

F. Private Party Litigation under Rule 10b–5

Nothing in either § 10(b) or Rule 10b–5 explicitly authorizes a private party cause of action against violators. Lower federal courts recognized an implied right of action under Rule 10b–5 as early as 1946,[76] however, and the Supreme Court followed suit in 1971.[77] Today, of course, judicial implication of private rights of action is highly controversial and the current Supreme Court seems less inclined to create or preserve such rights of action than any of its recent predecessors. The private right of action under Rule 10b–5 nevertheless remains quite firmly established. As the late Supreme Court Justice Thurgood Marshall once observed, the "existence of this implied remedy is simply beyond peradventure."[78]

Although the Supreme Court has never addressed the application of the implied private right of action under § 10(b) to inside traders, the principle is widely accepted among the federal circuit courts of appeal. The Second Circuit long has held that "[t]he knowing use by corporate insiders of non-public information for their own benefit or that of 'tippees' by trading in corporate securities amounts to a violation of Rule 10b–5 which may give rise to a suit for damages by uninformed outsiders who trade during a period of tippee trading."[79] Note that liability is not limited to those who actually traded with the insider or tippee. Instead, because "identifying the party in actual privity with the insider is virtually impossible in trades occurring on an anonymous public market, the contemporaneous standard was developed as a more feasible avenue by which to sue insiders."[80] Under that standard, everyone

---

[75] See Henriksen v. Great Am. Sav. & Loan, 14 Cal. Rptr. 2d 184 (App. 1992) (discussing key elements of an insulation wall in a law firm). On the origin and development of insulation walls, see Stanislav Dolgopolov, Insider Trading, Chinese Walls, and Brokerage Commissions: The Origins of Modern Regulation of Information Flows in Securities Markets, 4 J.L. Econ. & Pol'y 311 (2008). To be sure, insulation walls often are imperfect. See H. Nejat Seyhun, Insider Trading and the Effectiveness of Chinese Walls in Securities Firms, 4 J.L. Econ. & Pol'y 369 (2008) (reporting on a study of investment banks with representatives on client boards of directors and concluding that the insulation walls at these banks were "porous"). But this is an argument for improving the wall, rather than doing away with it.

[76] Kardon v. Nat'l Gypsum Co., 69 F. Supp. 512 (E.D.Pa.1946).

[77] Superintendent of Insurance v. Bankers Life & Cas. Co., 404 U.S. 6, 13 n. 9 (1971).

[78] Herman & MacLean v. Huddleston, 459 U.S. 375, 380 (1983).

[79] Elkind v. Liggett & Myers, Inc., 635 F.2d 156, 165 (2d Cir. 1980).

[80] Buban v. O'Brien, 1994 WL 324093, at *3 (N.D. Cal. June 22, 1994). See also In re MicroStrategy, Inc., 115 F. Supp.2d 620, 662 (E.D. Va. 2000) ("Put differently, the contemporaneity requirement serves as a substitute for the traditional requirement that only those clearly ascertainable individuals who stand to be exploited by the insider trading—for example, by personally trading with the insider or, in the context of the federal law, by trading on the same market with the

who traded in the same time period as the insider or tippee—but only that period—is a proper member of the plaintiff class. As the Second Circuit later explained in *Wilson v. Comtech Telecommunications Corp.*:[81]

> To extend the period of liability well beyond the time of the insider's trading simply because disclosure was never made could make the insider liable to all the world. Any duty of disclosure is owed only to those investors trading contemporaneously with the insider; non-contemporaneous traders do not require the protection of the "disclose or abstain" rule because they do not suffer the disadvantage of trading with someone who has superior access to information.[82]

The obvious question thereby presented is how closely in time must the investors' trades coincide with those of the insider in order for them to be proper class members? In *Wilson*, the plaintiff had "purchased his Comtech stock approximately one month after [the insiders'] sales," and the court held that he therefore had not traded "contemporaneously with the insiders" therefore had no standing to sue.[83]

Subsequent courts have defined contemporaneous trading as taking place within a very narrow window around the insider's trades, explaining that a restrictive reading of the term serves the "privity-substitute function" of the provision while simultaneously "guard[ing] against 'mak[ing] the insider liable to the world.'"[84] Accordingly, a Texas federal district court concluded that "two or three days, certainly less than a week, constitute a reasonable period to measure the contemporaneity of a defendant's and a plaintiff's trades. . . ."[85] Indeed, a number of cases have been even

---

insider—can be said to have individual interests that are directly implicated by the insider trading for which they may seek direct redress.").

[81] 648 F.2d 88 (2d Cir. 1981).

[82] Id. at 94–94 (citations omitted). The *Wilson* court's rationale has been criticized on grounds that "there is little difference in causation between someone who traded within one minute of the insider's trade and someone who traded one month later. Each will suffer the same loss, and if the insider has caused harm to one, it is contradictory that he would not be deemed to have caused harm to the other." Stephanie F. Barkholz, Comment, Insider Trading, the Contemporaneous Trader, and the Corporate Acquirer: Entitlement to Profits Disgorged By the SEC, 40 Emory L.J. 537, 550 (1991). See also Donald C. Langevoort, Insider Trading and the Fiduciary Principle: A Post-*Chiarella* Restatement, 70 Calif. L. Rev. 1, 37 n.149 (1982) ("Once the privity requirement is abandoned, there is simply no principled basis for distinguishing between a person trading the day after (or 15 minutes after) the insider and one trading a week later, in terms of injury suffered. Both are equally disadvantaged by the lack of information, and if a finding of deception is justified for the former, it is no less so for the latter.").

[83] Id. at 95.

[84] In re MicroStrategy, 115 F. Supp.2d at 663.

[85] In re Enron Corp. Sec., Deriv. & ERISA Litig., 258 F. Supp.2d 576, 600 (S.D. Tex. 2003). Although the *Enron* decision was interpreting the meaning of the comparable contemporaneous trading requirement of Exchange Act § 20A, 15 U.S.C.

more restrictive, limiting the class to investors who trade on the same day as the insider or tippee.[86]

Wilson involved conduct violating the disclose or abstain rule. In *Moss v. Morgan Stanley Inc.*,[87] the Second Circuit declined to extend private party liability to cases in which the insider's conduct violated solely the misappropriation theory:

> Nothing in our [prior misappropriation cases] suggests that an employee's duty to "abstain or disclose" with respect to his employer should be stretched to encompass an employee's "duty of disclosure" to the general public. . . . Thus, the district court was correct in concluding that "plaintiff cannot hope to piggyback upon the duty owed by defendants to Morgan Stanley and Warner. There is no 'duty in the air' to which any plaintiff can attach his claim."[88]

G. Private Party Litigation under Exchange Act § 20A

In 1988, Congress adopted Exchange Act § 20A to provide an express private right of action for investors who trade contemporaneously with an insider or tippee.[89] Although Congress was motivated primarily by a desire to reverse *Moss* and thereby extend the private right of action to misappropriation cases,[90] § 20A applies to all insider trading cases involving a violation of the Exchange Act or the rules thereunder.[91] Section 20A(a) thus provides that:

> Any person who violates any provision of this chapter or the rules or regulations thereunder by purchasing or selling a security while in possession of material, nonpublic information shall be liable in an action in any court of competent

---

§ 78t–1, the legislative history of that provision indicates that Congress intended to adopt the prior judicial definition of that term in cases arising under § 10(b). See also In re Engineering Animation Sec. Litig., 110 F. Supp.2d 1183 (S.D. Iowa 2000)(three-day window); In re Oxford Health Plans, Inc., Sec. Litig., 187 F.R.D. 133, 138 (S.D.N.Y.1999)(five-day window); In re Cypress Semiconductor Litig., 836 F. Supp. 711 (N.D. Cal. 1993)(same).

[86] Copland v. Grumet, 88 F. Supp.2d 326, 338 (D. N.J. 1999); In re AST Research Sec. Litig., 887 F. Supp. 231, 234 (C.D. Cal. 1995).

[87] 719 F.2d 5 (2d Cir. 1983), cert. denied, 465 U.S. 1025 (1984).

[88] Id. at 13.

[89] 15 U.S.C. § 78t–1.

[90] H. Comm. on Energy and Commerce, Insider Trading and Securities Fraud Enforcement Act of 1988, H.R. Rep. No. 100–910, at 26–27 (2d Sess. 1988) (explaining that Congress intended to "overturn court cases which have precluded recovery for plaintiffs where the defendant's violation is premised upon the misappropriation theory").

[91] See 15 U.S.C. § 78t–1(a) (providing a private right of action for "[a]ny person who violates any provision of [the Exchange Act] or the rules or regulations thereunder by purchasing or selling a security while in possession of material, nonpublic information").

jurisdiction to any person who, contemporaneously with the purchase or sale of securities that is the subject of such violation, has purchased (where such violation is based on a sale of securities) or sold (where such violation is based on a purchase of securities) securities of the same class.[92]

---

[92] 15 U.S.C. § 78t–1(a).

Chapter 12

LIABILITY WITHOUT A FIDUCIARY RELATIONSHIP

As we have seen, in order to link insider trading to the goals of the federal securities laws, the Second Circuit claimed in *Texas Gulf Sulphur* that Congress intended those laws to ensure that "all investors trading on impersonal exchanges have relatively equal access to material information"[1] and "be subject to identical market risks."[2] This rationale presented a number of doctrinal and policy problems, but at least was linked to a core problem of securities regulation; namely, controlling flows of information to the capital markets.

In his *Chiarella*[3] and *Dirks*[4] opinions, Supreme Court Justice Lewis Powell led the Court in rejecting the equal access rationale in favor of a new focus on disclosure obligations arising out of fiduciary relationships. In doing so, Powell solved some of the problems created by the equal access rationale, but created a new set of doctrinal and policy issues. In particular, Powell's rationale largely severed the link between the insider trading prohibition and the core concerns of securities law.

Powell's fiduciary duty rationale met substantial resistance from the USA Securities and Exchange Commission (SEC) and the lower courts. Through both regulatory actions and judicial opinions, the SEC and the courts gradually chipped away at the fiduciary duty rationale.[5] In recent years, the trend has accelerated, with several developments having substantially eviscerated the fiduciary duty requirement.

A. Why Did Justice Powell Reject Equal Access?

One problem with equal access was that the *Texas Gulf Sulphur* court could point to no legislative history or statutory text supporting the equal access principle. As Michael Dooley later argued, moreover, "insider trading in no way resembles deceit. No representation is made, nor is there any reliance, change of

---

[1] SEC v. Texas Gulf Sulphur Co., 401 F.2d 833, 847 (2d Cir.), cert. denied, 394 U.S. 976 (1968).

[2] Id. at 852.

[3] Chiarella v. US, 445 U.S. 222 (1980).

[4] Dirks v. SEC, 463 U.S. 646 (1983).

[5] In an important article, Professor Donna Nagy first brought attention to this trend. Donna M. Nagy, Insider Trading and the Gradual Demise of Fiduciary Principles, 94 Iowa L. Rev. 1315 (2009).

position, or causal connection between the defendant's act and the plaintiff's losses."[6] Well-established state precedents thus had treated the problem as one implicating not concepts of deceit or manipulation, but rather the fiduciary duties of corporate officers and directors.[7] As such, equal access was not an inherent feature of the securities laws scheme as contemplated by Congress but rather simply the product of judicial fiat.

Equal access also implied a prohibition that swept far too broadly. In *Chiarella*, for example, Justice Powell noted that a broad equal access rule might "prohibit a tender offeror's purchases of target corporation stock before public announcement of the offer," a step Congress clearly had declined to take when it adopted the Williams Act to regulate tender offers.[8] In the subsequent *Dirks* opinion, Justice Powell further explained that such a broad policy basis for regulating insider trading implied a ban that "could have an inhibiting influence on the role of market analysts, which the SEC itself recognizes is necessary to the preservation of a healthy market."[9]

> It is commonplace for analysts to "ferret out and analyze information," and this often is done by meeting with and questioning corporate officers and others who are insiders. And information that the analysts obtain normally may be the basis for judgments as to the market worth of a corporation's securities. The analyst's judgment in this respect is made available in market letters or otherwise to clients of the firm. It is the nature of this type of information, and indeed of the markets themselves, that such information cannot be made simultaneously available to all of the corporation's stockholders or the public generally.[10]

It was in order to avoid chilling such legitimate activity that Powell sought out a policy rationale that would sweep far less broadly. He found it in the principle that the duty to disclose or abstain "arises from a specific relationship between two parties."[11] Accordingly, "there can be no duty to disclose where the person who has traded on inside information 'was not [the corporation's] agent,

---

[6] Michael P. Dooley, Enforcement of Insider Trading Restrictions, 66 Va. L. Rev. 1, 59 (1980).

[7] Stephen M. Bainbridge, Incorporating State Law Fiduciary Duties into the Federal Insider Trading Prohibition, 52 Wash. & Lee L. Rev. 1189, 1218–27 (1995).

[8] Chiarella v. US, 445 U.S. 222, 233 (1980).

[9] Dirks v. SEC, 463 U.S. 646, 658 (1983).

[10] Id. at 658–59 (citations and footnotes omitted).

[11] *Chiarella*, 445 U.S. at 233.

. . . was not a fiduciary, [or] was not a person in whom the sellers [of the securities] had placed their trust and confidence.' "[12]

B. Why Did Justice Powell Base Liability on a Fiduciary Relationship?

Just as there had been nothing inevitable about *Texas Gulf Sulphur's* imposition of the equal access standard, there equally was nothing inevitable about the Supreme Court's rejection of that standard. The equal access standard was consistent with a trend towards affirmative disclosure obligations and away from *caveat emptor* that was sweeping across a broad swath of the common law.[13] In rejecting this trend, Justice Powell arguably shifted the focus of insider trading liability from deceit to agency, a point that becomes especially significant later in our analysis.[14] Nothing in the text of the statute or the rule explicitly mandated that shift; nor did the relevant precedents require it.

To the contrary, Justice Powell's use of precedent in *Chiarella* and *Dirks* was highly suspect. In *Dirks*, for example, he opined:

> In the seminal case of *In re Cady, Roberts & Co.*, the SEC recognized that the common law in some jurisdictions imposes on "corporate 'insiders,' particularly officers, directors, or controlling shareholders" an "affirmative duty of disclosure . . . when dealing in securities." The SEC found that . . . breach of this common law duty also establish[ed] the elements of a Rule 10b–5 violation. . . .[15]

Although he acknowledged that the common law duty upon which *Cady, Roberts* purportedly rested existed only in "some jurisdictions,"[16] he failed to acknowledge that that duty was essentially limited to face-to-face transactions between the issuer's officers or directors and the issuer's current shareholders. With no analysis or citation of authority, moreover, Powell extrapolated from this limited state common law duty the all-encompassing federal rule that all "insiders [are] forbidden by their fiduciary relationship from personally using undisclosed corporate information to their advantage."[17]

---

[12] *Dirks*, 463 U.S. at 654 (quoting *Chiarella*, 445 U.S. at 232).

[13] Donald C. Langevoort, Words From on High About Rule 10b–5: Chiarella's History, Central Bank's Future, 20 Del. J. Corp. L. 865, 870–71 (1995).

[14] A. C. Pritchard, United States v. O'Hagan: Agency Law and Justice Powell's Legacy for the Law of Insider Trading, 78 Bos. Univ. L. Rev. 13 (1998).

[15] *Dirks*, 463 U.S. at 653.

[16] Id.

[17] Id. at 659.

Powell also failed to reconcile his fiduciary duty-based framework with a central principle of Rule 10b–5 jurisprudence; namely, that there is no such thing as a "federal fiduciary principle."[18] In *Santa Fe*, the Supreme Court had held that Rule 10b–5 did not reach claims "in which the essence of the complaint is that shareholders were treated unfairly by a fiduciary."[19] This is, of course, the very essence of the complaint made in insider trading cases. The Court also expressed reluctance "to federalize the substantial portion of the law of corporations that deals with transactions in securities, particularly where established state policies of corporate regulation would be overridden,"[20] which is precisely what the federal insider trading prohibition did.

Powell's reframing of insider trading law thus was no less problematic than the equal access principle it replaced. Like equal access, the fiduciary duty approach lacked any basis in the text or legislative history of the statute and rule. Instead, like equal access, basing insider trading liability on a fiduciary duty to disclose was essentially a matter of judicial fiat. It was the deference his colleagues paid Powell on securities law matters that turned it into law, rather than its intrinsic merits.[21] Unlike equal access, however, Powell's approach lacked any obvious link to the purposes of the securities laws and, moreover, created a clear conflict with the federalism-based limits on those laws.

C. The SEC Strikes Back

The SEC has powerful institutional reasons for favoring a broad insider trading prohibition. A vigorous enforcement program directed at a highly visible and unpopular law violation such as insider trading is an effective means of attracting political support for larger budgets. The SEC's prominent role in attacking insider trading also placed it in the vanguard of the movement to federalize corporate law and ensured that the Commission would have a leading role in any system of federal corporations law.[22]

It is thus not surprising that the SEC responded to the substantial narrowing of the insider trading prohibition effected by *Chiarella* and *Dirks* by developing new theories of liability that would recapture as much of the lost ground as possible. The process began with development of the so-called misappropriation theory. It

---

[18] Santa Fe Indus. v. Green, 430 U.S. 462, 479 (1977).

[19] Id. at 477.

[20] Id. at 479.

[21] See generally Stephen M. Bainbridge & G. Mitu Gulati, How Do Judges Maximize? (The Same Way Everybody Else Does—Boundedly): Rules of Thumb in Securities Fraud Opinions, 51 Emory L.J. 83 (2002).

[22] See generally § Chapter 13.A.3.

bans the use of "confidential information for securities trading purposes, in breach of a duty owed to the source of the information,"[23] even if the inside trader owed no duties to the persons with whom he traded or the issuer of the securities in which he traded. Someone thus can be held liable under this theory only where they have deceived the source of the information by failing to disclose to the source their intent to trade on the basis of the information learned from the source.[24]

The misappropriation theory perhaps complied with the letter of the *Chiarella/Dirks* fiduciary relationship-based framework, but it clearly evaded the spirit of Powell's intent. The misappropriation theory first reached the Supreme Court in *US v. Carpenter*.[25] After the court initially voted to deny certiorari, Justice Powell prepared a draft dissent arguing that the misappropriation theory was inconsistent with *Chiarella* and *Dirks*. In Powell's view, Rule 10b–5 had incorporated the common law principle that silence is fraudulent solely where one party to the transaction owes a fiduciary duty of disclosure to the other.[26] Breach of a duty owed to someone else, such as the source of the information, thus did not violate Rule 10b–5.

Powell's draft dissent was never published. The Supreme Court decided to grant certiorari in the Carpenter case. While the case was pending, however, Powell retired from the Court. The Court thereafter affirmed the defendant's misappropriation theory-based convictions by a 4–4 vote without opinion. Because *Carpenter* thus set no precedent, the way was left open for the misappropriation theory to continue chipping away at the *Chiarella/Dirks* framework.

When the Supreme Court finally ruled on the misappropriation theory in *O'Hagan*, Justice Ginsburg's opinion validating the theory confirmed that a far more sweeping prohibition had displaced Powell's approach to insider trading. In particular, Ginsburg expressly rejected "the notion that *Chiarella* required that the fraud be between parties to the securities transaction."[27] The misappropriation theory thereby significantly expanded the categories of persons covered by the insider trading prohibition. While the resulting prohibition perhaps was not quite as sweeping as equal access had been, the prospect of liability had been

---

[23] U.S. v. O'Hagan, 521 U.S. 642, 652 (1997).

[24] Id. at 2208.

[25] 484 U.S. 19 (1987).

[26] A.C. Pritchard, Justice Lewis F. Powell, Jr. and the Counter-Revolution in the Federal Securities Laws, 52 Duke L.J. 841, 944 (2003).

[27] A. C. Pritchard, United States v. O'Hagan: Agency Law and Justice Powell's Legacy for the Law of Insider Trading, 78 Bos. Univ. L. Rev. 13, 42 (1998).

resurrected with respect to most of the significant categories of potential defendants freed from that prospect by *Chiarella*.

As noted above, Powell's claim that liability required a duty of disclosure arising out a relationship between the parties to the transaction was not obviously required by the securities laws; it was mere judicial fiat. The same was true of Justice Ginsburg's claim that liability could be premised on a duty of disclosure owed to the source of the information.[28]

As was the case with both equal access and Powell's approach, moreover, Ginsburg's version of the misappropriation theory was difficult to square with the basic premises of securities regulation. Securities laws seek to protect investors and preserve investor confidence in the integrity of the securities markets.[29] As formulated by Justice Ginsburg, however, the misappropriation theory seems largely detached from those goals. Instead, it is mainly concerned with preventing an agent from abusing access to nonpublic information.

D. From Fiduciary Duty Back to Equal Access

In a rare moment of candor, a former SEC Commissioner admitted that the Commission's development of the misappropriation theory served "merely a pretext for enforcing equal opportunity in information."[30] Yet, so long as the ban on insider trading remained tethered to fiduciary relationships, it could not recapture all of the ground lost in *Chiarella*. It is thus not surprising that the SEC has repeatedly advanced new theories of liability that push the boundaries of fiduciary relationships to the breaking point and beyond and, especially in recent years, outright abandon the fiduciary duty-based framework.

1.   Stretching fiduciary duty to the breaking point

In *Chiarella*, Justice Powell had premised liability on "a fiduciary or other similar relation of trust and confidence between" the parties to the transaction.[31] This formulation posed two avenues for expanding the scope of the insider trading liability. First, as Professor Nagy observed, the *Chiarella*, *Dirks*, and *O'Hagan* trilogy

---

[28] See Nagy, supra note 5, at 1335 ("Unfortunately, the Court in *O'Hagan* never came to terms with why its misappropriation theory 'was limited to those who breached a recognized duty' and why 'feigning fidelity' to the information's source was essential.")

[29] See, e.g., Central Bank of Denver, N.A. v. First Interstate Bank of Denver, N.A., 511 U.S. 164, 173 (1994) ("the broad congressional purposes behind the [securities laws are] to protect investors from false and misleading practices that might injure them").

[30] Charles C. Cox & Kevin S. Fogarty, Bases of Insider Trading Law, 49 Ohio St. L.J. 353, 366 (1988).

[31] *Chiarella*, 445 U.S. at 228.

demonstrated that the Supreme Court was "willing to stretch fiduciary principles to no small degree, when doing so facilitates a desirable policy outcome."[32] In turn, this "emboldened lower courts to approach new issues with similar results-oriented reasoning" stretching the concept of a fiduciary relation to the breaking point.[33]

Second, the reference to a "similar relation of trust and confidence" suggested another avenue for policy-driven outcomes. If a court wished to impose liability, it simply needed to conclude that the relationship in question involves trust and confidence, even though the relationship bears no resemblance to those in which fiduciary-like duties are normally imposed. In *U.S. v. Chestman*,[34] the Second Circuit tried to prevent such outcomes by holding that a relationship of trust and confidence must be "the functional equivalent of a fiduciary relationship" before liability can be imposed.[35] In the case at bar, the relationship in question was a marital one between spouses. The court held that that relationship lacked the "discretionary authority and dependency" inherent in fiduciary relationships.[36] In addition, the Court emphasized that "entrusting confidential information to another does not, without more, create the necessary relationship and its correlative duty to maintain the confidence."[37]

In 2000, however, the SEC eviscerated *Chestman* by adopting Rule 10b5–2. It provides "a nonexclusive list of three situations in which a person has a duty of trust or confidence for purposes of the 'misappropriation' theory."[38] First, such a duty exists whenever someone agrees to maintain information in confidence. Second, such a duty exists between two people who have a pattern or practice of sharing confidences such that the recipient of the information knows or reasonably should know that the speaker expects the recipient to maintain the information's confidentiality. Third, such a duty exists when someone receives or obtains material nonpublic information from a spouse, parent, child, or sibling.

In adopting the rule, the SEC made a subtle move by turning the Supreme Court's conjunctive phrase "trust and confidence" into the disjunctive form "trust or confidence." As Professor Nagy explains:

---

[32] Nagy, supra note 5, at 1339–40.

[33] Id.

[34] 947 F.2d 551 (2d Cir.1991) (citations omitted), cert. denied, 503 U.S. 1004 (1992).

[35] Id. at 568.

[36] Id. at 569.

[37] Id. at 568.

[38] Exchange Act Rel. No. 43,154 (Aug. 15, 2000).

This change from the conjunctive to the disjunctive extends the scope of the misappropriation theory considerably. To be sure, the terms "trust" and "confidence" are often used synonymously to describe reliance on the character or ability of someone to act in a right and proper way. But as used in Rule 10b5–2, the term "confidence" may align more with an obligation of "confidentiality" than with obligations predicated on trust and loyalty.[39]

The potential significance of this move is illustrated by *SEC v. Cuban*.[40] Defendant Mark Cuban was a large shareholder in a firm called Mamma.com Inc. Cuban was informed by Mama.com's CEO that the company planned a private investment in public equity (PIPE) offering that would result in significant dilution of outstanding shares and concomitant drop in stock price. Cuban sold his shares before the PIPE offering was made public and thereby avoided a substantial loss. The SEC then brought suit, arguing that Cuban breached a "duty created by his agreement to keep confidential the information that Mamma.com's CEO provided him about the impending PIPE offering."[41] The district court partially rejected the SEC's position. Despite Rule 10b5–2, the court held that the relevant Supreme Court precedents contemplated liability based on breach of a contractual obligation but only if the contract imposed a duty of confidentiality and a duty of non-use. On appeal, the Fifth Circuit vacated the district court opinion and remanded for trial without reaching the issue of Rule 10b5–2's validity.

Even assuming the district court's restriction on 10b5–2 is eventually upheld, Rule 10b5–2 will still violate the *Chiarella/Dirks* framework. As the *Chestman* opinion correctly explained, those cases clearly require something more than a mere contract. They require a fiduciary relationship. If Rule 10b5–2 is valid, however, that requirement has been stretched to its breaking point.[42]

2.   Insider trading liability without a fiduciary relationship: Rule 14e–3

The SEC adopted Rule 14e–3 in response to the wave of insider trading activity associated with the increase in merger and acquisition activity during the 1980s. The rule prohibits insiders of the bidder and target from divulging confidential information about

---

[39] Nagy, supra note 5, at 1360.

[40] 634 F. Supp.2d 713 (N.D. Tex. 2009), vacated and remanded, 620 F.3d 551 (5th Cir. 2010). Along with several other insider trading scholars, the author signed amicus briefs in both the district and circuit court proceedings in support of defendant Cuban's interpretation of Rule 10b5–2.

[41] Id. at 721.

[42] For an argument that Rule 10b5–1 similarly eviscerates the fiduciary relationship requirement, see Nagy, supra note 5, at 1353–57.

a tender offer to persons that are likely to violate the rule by trading on the basis of that information. Rule 14e–3 also, with certain narrow and well-defined exceptions, prohibits any person that possesses material information relating to a tender offer by another person from trading in target company securities if the bidder has commenced or has taken substantial steps towards commencement of the bid.

Unlike both the disclose or abstain rule and the misappropriation theory under Rule 10b–5, Rule 14e–3 liability is not premised on breach of a fiduciary duty. There is no need for a showing that the trading party or tipper was subject to any duty of confidentiality, and no need to show that a tipper personally benefited from the tip. In light of the well-established fiduciary duty requirement under Rule 10b–5, however, the rule should have run afoul of *Schreiber v. Burlington Northern, Inc.*[43] In that case, the Supreme Court held that § 14(e) was modeled on § 10(b) and, like that section, requires a showing of misrepresentation or nondisclosure. As such, the two sections are to be interpreted *in pari materia.* Because § 10(b) requires a showing of a breach of a disclosure duty arising out of a fiduciary relationship, Rule 14e–3 appeared to exceed the SEC's statutory authority.

In *O'Hagan*, however, the Supreme Court upheld Rule 14e–3 as a valid exercise of the SEC's rulemaking authority despite the absence of a fiduciary duty element.[44] It thus set the stage for subsequent developments abandoning the fiduciary duty element.

3. Insider trading liability without a fiduciary relationship: Hackers and other non-fiduciary thieves

SEC v. Dorozhko[45] dealt with a question left open by *O'Hagan*; namely, the liability of persons who steal inside information but have no fiduciary duty to either the source of the information or the issuer of the securities in which the thief trades. In *Dorozhko*, the SEC alleged that a computer hacker broke into a health information company's computer system and stole confidential information about an undisclosed earnings decline. The hacker then made a substantial profit by selling the company's stock short. The Second Circuit tried to finesse the fiduciary duty requirement by arguing "that the SEC's claim against defendant—a corporate outsider who owed no fiduciary duties to the source of the information—is not based on either of the two generally accepted

---

[43] 472 U.S. 1 (1985).

[44] 521 U.S. at 667–77.

[45] 574 F.3d 42 (2d Cir. 2009).

theories of insider trading."[46] The problem is that the only hole into which this case fits is the one designed for an insider trading peg.

An affirmative misappropriation can be actionable under Section 10(b) and Rule 10b–5 if it is committed in connection with the purchase or sale of a security. In order to find that the hacker committed an affirmative misrepresentation, a court first must find a lie. Calling computer hacking a lie is a rather considerable stretch. At most, the hacker "lies" to a computer network, not a person. Hacking is theft; it is not fraud.

Even if hacking is fraudulent in the sense of an affirmative misrepresentation, the requisite misrepresentation must be made in connection with a purchase or sale of a security in order to be insider trading. In *SEC v. Zandford*,[47] the Supreme Court emphasized that "the statute must not be construed so broadly as to convert every common-law fraud that happens to involve securities into a violation of § 10(b)."[48] Accordingly, the district court in *Dorozhko* correctly "found it 'noteworthy' that in the over seventy years since the enactment of the Exchange Act of 1934, 'no federal court has ever held that those who steal material nonpublic information and then trade on it violate § 10(b),' even though 'traditional theft (e.g. breaking into an investment bank and stealing documents) is hardly a new phenomenon, and involves similar elements for purposes of our analysis here.' "[49]

"Traditional theft" has not given rise to insider trading liability because, the district court correctly noted, "the Supreme Court has in a number of opinions carefully established that the essential component of a § 10(b) violation is a breach of a fiduciary duty to disclose or abstain that coincides with a securities transaction."[50] *Dorozhko* thus is properly understood to be an end run by the SEC—aided and abetted by the Second Circuit—around that carefully established requirement. As such, it establishes an important precedent for the SEC and courts to collaborate on future inventive means of end-running the Supreme Court's clear insider trading jurisprudence.

4. Insider trading liability without a fiduciary relationship: SOX § 807

Section 807 of the Sarbanes-Oxley Act added a new § 1348 to the U.S. Criminal Code, which provides that:

---

[46] Id. at 45.

[47] 535 U.S. 813 (2002).

[48] Id. at 820.

[49] SEC v. Dorozhko, 606 F. Supp. 2d 321, 339 (S.D.N.Y. 2008).

[50] Id. at 323.

Whoever knowingly executes, or attempts to execute, a scheme or artifice—

(1) to defraud any person in connection with any security of an issuer with a class of securities registered under section 12 of the Exchange Act of 1934 or that is required to file reports under section 15(d) of the Exchange Act of 1934; or

(2) to obtain, by means of false or fraudulent pretenses, representations, or promises, any money or property in connection with the purchase or sale of any security of an issuer with a class of securities registered under section 12 of the Exchange Act of 1934 or that is required to file reports under section 15(d) of the Exchange Act of 1934

shall be fined under this title, or imprisoned not more than 25 years, or both.[51]

Neither the text nor its sparse legislative history shed much light on what Congress intended it to do. About all one can say for sure is that Congress intended to significantly increase the penalties in securities fraud cases and to make it easier for prosecutors to prove such cases by eliminating the so-called "technical elements" of existing provisions such as § 10(b) and Rule 10b–5.[52] Is Powell's fiduciary duty requirement such a technical element?

In *US v. Mahaffy*,[53] defendant stockbrokers tipped nonpublic information to defendant day traders in return for cash. The case could and should have been prosecuted under the misappropriation theory. In *Mahaffy*, however, the prosecutors charged the defendants with violation § 1348. In upholding the charge as a proper one, the district court did not require the prosecution to prove that the tippers had breached a duty of confidence arising out of a fiduciary relationship owed either to the source of the relationship or to the persons with whom the tippees traded. Indeed, of the Supreme Court trilogy, the district court mentioned only *O'Hagan* and only in passing.[54]

"The *Mahaffy* decision [thus] reflects the first step of a potential sea change in the elements required of the government to prove a criminal insider trading violation."[55] It casts aside, albeit *sub silentio*, the need for the prosecution to show a breach of a duty to disclose arising out of a fiduciary relationship or similar

---

[51] Sarbanes-Oxley Act of 2002 § 807, Pub. L. No. 107–204, 116 Stat. 745 (2002) (to be codified at 18 USC § 1348) (citation omitted).

[52] Kenneth M. Breen & Keith W. Miller, Securities Fraud, 32 Champion 49 (2009).

[53] 2006 WL 2224518 (E.D.N.Y. 2006).

[54] Id. at *12.

[55] Breen & Miller, supra note 52.

relationship of trust and confidence. Instead, by analogizing "§ 1348 to an honest services fraud case," *Mahaffy* "requires only a material misrepresentation, not a violation of confidence."[56] Because the SEC lacks power to bring criminal charges, the Commission will be unable to avail itself of § 1348 apparent gutting of the fiduciary duty requirement. Because it can be used by the Justice Department in criminal cases, however, § 1348 still must be counted as having knocked one more brick out of the wall.

---

[56] Id.

Chapter 13

WHY DO WE CARE? THE ECONOMICS OF INSIDER TRADING

The federal insider trading prohibition has not been cheap. The SEC and other law enforcement agencies have expended vast resources to detect and prosecute inside traders. The lives of those caught have been devastated. Courts have devoted considerable judicial resources to working out and applying the prohibition in all its intricate detail. Has it been worth it?

The policy case against insider trading traditionally sounded in the language of equity. In *Cady, Roberts*, for example, the SEC justified the prohibition as necessary to "the inherent unfairness" of insider trading.[1] But why is insider trading unfair? In *Texas Gulf Sulphur*, the Second Circuit opined that all investors were entitled to "relatively equal access to material information."[2] But whence comes this entitlement? The difficulty, of course, is that fairness and equality are high-sounding but essentially content-less words. We need some standard of reference by which to measure the fairness or lack thereof of insider trading.

In the search for an appropriate reference standard, the seminal event was the 1966 publication of Henry Manne's book *Insider Trading and the Stock Market*.[3] It is only a slight exaggeration to suggest that Manne stunned the corporate law world by daring to propose the deregulation of insider trading. The response by most law professors, lawyers, and regulators was "immediate and vitriolic" rejection.[4]

In one sense, Manne's project failed. Insider trading is still prohibited. Indeed, as we have seen, the sanctions for violating the prohibition have become more draconian—not less—since Manne's book was first published.[5] In another sense, however, Manne's daring was at least partially vindicated. He changed the terms of the debate. Today, the insider trading debate takes place almost

---

[1] In re Cady, Roberts & Co., 40 SEC 907, 912 (1961).

[2] SEC v. Texas Gulf Sulphur Co., 401 F.2d 833, 848 (2d. Cir. 1968), 394 U.S. 976 (1969).

[3] Henry G. Manne, Insider Trading and the Stock Market (1966). For an appreciation of Manne's contributions to the insider trading debate, see Stephen M. Bainbridge, Introduction, in 2 The Collected Works of Henry G. Manne: Insider Trading (2009).

[4] See Alexandra Padilla, How Do We Think About Insider Trading? An Economist's Perspective on the Insider Trading Debate and Its Impact, 4 Wash. & Lee J.L. Econ. & Pol. 239, 243 (2008).

[5] See supra Chapter 11 (discussing remedies and penalties for insider trading).

exclusively in the language of economics.[6] Even those who still insist on treating insider trading as an issue of fairness necessarily spend much of their time responding to those who see it in economic terms.

In essence, the argument of Manne and those subsequent scholars who also embraced the idea of deregulating insider trading is that insider trading promotes market efficiency and creates efficient incentives for innovative corporate managers.[7] Those scholars who favor regulating insider trading typically respond either by relying on fairness arguments or by asserting that insider trading has substantial economic costs.[8] In this chapter, we first take up the economic argument for deregulation. We then evaluate the noneconomic arguments for regulating insider trading. Finally, we evaluate the economic arguments for the pro-regulation position. In each case, we will ask two questions: Does the argument make sense? Can it explain the prohibition as it exists?

A pedagogical caveat—indeed, a warning—is in order: No effort will be made herein to hide the ball. Although this chapter canvases the major arguments for and against all three positions, my own view is that the insider trading prohibition can be justified, but only by an economic argument that treats insider trading as theft of confidential information in which someone other than the inside trader has a property right superior to that of the inside trader. This chapter concludes with an assessment of the implications of that policy position for the proper scope and content of the insider trading prohibition.

A. The Case for Deregulation

Manne identified two principal ways in which insider trading benefits society and/or the firm in whose stock the insider traded. First, he argued that insider trading causes the market price of the affected security to move toward the price that the security would

---

[6] See Jie Hu & Thomas Noe, The Insider Trading Debate, Federal Reserve Bank of Atlanta Economic Review 34, 34 (1997) (arguing that "insider trading remains, at least among economists and legal scholars, one of the most controversial economic transactions").

[7] See, e.g., Dennis W. Carlton & Daniel R. Fischel, The Regulation of Insider Trading, 35 Stan. L. Rev. 857, 866 (1983) (arguing that allowing managers to inside trade mangers' optimizes their incentives by linking their "fortunes more closely to those of the firm"); Henry G. Manne, Insider Trading: Hayek, Virtual Markets, and the Dog that Did Not Bark, 31 J. Corp. L. 167, 169 (2005) (arguing that "the argument for a strong positive relationship between market efficiency and insider trading has proved to be very robust").

[8] See, e.g., Roy A. Schotland, Unsafe at Any Price: A Reply to Manne, Insider Trading and the Stock Market, 53 Va. L. Rev. 1425, 1439 (1967) ("Even if we found that unfettered insider trading would bring an economic gain, we might still forego that gain in order to secure a stock market and intracorporate relationships that satisfy such noneconomic goals as fairness, just rewards and integrity.").

command if the inside information were publicly available.[9] If so, both society and the firm benefit through increased price accuracy. Second, he posited insider trading as an efficient way of compensating managers for having produced information.[10] If so, the firm benefits directly (and society indirectly) because managers have a greater incentive to produce additional information of value to the firm.

In the years since Manne first wrote, other scholars have advanced a third argument for deregulating insider trading. Drawing on the public choice branch of law and economics, this line of argument contends that the prohibition benefits special interest groups. The SEC had institutional incentives to sell a prohibition of insider trading, so the story goes, while certain stock market players had an incentive to purchase such a prohibition.[11]

1. Insider trading and efficient pricing of securities

Basic economic theory tells us that the value of a share of stock is simply the present discounted value of the cash flows—i.e., dividends and stock repurchases—that will be paid on the stock in the future.[12] Because the future is uncertain, however, the amount of future dividends, if any, cannot be known. In an efficient capital market, a security's current price thus is simply the consensus guess of investors as to the issuing corporation's future prospects.[13] The correct price of a security thus is that which the market would set if all information relating to the security had been publicly disclosed. Because the market cannot value nonpublic information and because corporations (or outsiders) frequently possess material information that has not been made public, however, market prices often deviate from the correct price. Indeed, if it were not for this sort of mispricing, insider trading would not be profitable.[14]

No one seriously disputes that both firms and society benefit from accurate pricing of securities. Accurate pricing benefits society by improving the economy's allocation of capital investment and by

---

[9] Manne, supra note 3, at 88–102.

[10] Manne, supra note 3, at 121–68.

[11] See Chapter 13.A.3.

[12] Franco Modigliani & Gerald A. Pogue, An Introduction to Risk and Return, 30 Fin. Anal. J. 68, 69 (1974).

[13] See Daniel R.Fischel, Use of Modern Finance Theory in Securities Fraud Cases Involving Actively Traded Securities, 38 Bus. Law. 1, 4 n.9 (1982) (defining an efficient capital market as "one in which the price of stock at a given time is the best estimate of what the price will be in the future").

[14] See generally Eugene F. Fama, Efficient Capital Markets: A Review of Theory and Empirical Work, 25 J. Fin. 383, 409–410 (1970).

decreasing the volatility of security prices.[15] The latter consideration is especially relevant to the insider trading debate, because dampening of price fluctuations decreases the likelihood of individual windfall gains and thereby increases the attractiveness of investing in securities for risk-averse investors.[16] The individual corporation also benefits from accurate pricing of its securities through reduced investor uncertainty and improved monitoring of management's effectiveness.[17]

Although U.S. securities laws purportedly encourage accurate pricing by requiring disclosure of corporate information, they do not require the disclosure of all material information. As the Second Circuit explained in *Texas Gulf Sulphur*:

> We do not suggest that material facts must be disclosed immediately; the timing of disclosure is a matter for the business judgment of the corporate officers entrusted with the management of the corporation within the affirmative disclosure requirements promulgated by the exchanges and by the SEC. Here, a valuable corporate purpose was served by delaying the publication of the K–55–1 discovery.[18]

Where disclosure would interfere with such legitimate business purposes, disclosure by the corporation is usually not required unless the firm is dealing in its own securities at the time or where a specific SEC rule requires earlier disclosure.[19]

When a firm withholds material information, the market no longer accurately prices its securities. In *Texas Gulf Sulphur*, for example, when the ore deposit was discovered Texas Gulf Sulphur common stock sold for approximately eighteen dollars per share. By the time the discovery was disclosed, four months later, the price had risen to over thirty-one dollars per share. One month after disclosure, the stock was selling for approximately fifty-eight dollars per share.[20] The difficulty, of course, is that Texas Gulf Sulphur had gone to considerable expense to identify potential

---

[15] Carlton & Fischel, supra note 7, at 866; William K. S. Wang, Trading on Material Nonpublic Information of Impersonal Stock Markets, 54 S. Cal. L. Rev. 1217, 1226 (1981).

[16] Wang, supra note 15, at 1226.

[17] Carlton & Fischel, supra note 7, at 867.

[18] SEC v. Texas Gulf Sulphur Co., 401 F.2d 833, 851 n.12 (2d. Cir. 1968), 394 U.S. 976 (1969).

[19] See, e.g., Roeder v. Alpha Industries, Inc., 814 F.2d 22 (1st Cir. 1987) (identifying three situations that could give rise to a duty to disclose material facts: (i) when an insider trades in the company's securities on the basis of material nonpublic information; (ii) when a statute or regulation requires disclosure; and (iii) when the company has previously made a statement of material fact that is false, inaccurate, incomplete, or misleading in light of the undisclosed information).

[20] See SEC v. Texas Gulf Sulphur Co., 401 F.2d 833, 847 (2d. Cir. 1968) (summarizing price movements), 394 U.S. 976 (1969).

areas for mineral exploration and to conduct the initial search. Suppose Texas Gulf Sulphur was required to disclose the ore strike as soon as the initial assay results came back. What would have happened? Landowners would have demanded a higher price for the mineral rights. Worse yet, competitors could have come into the area and bid against Texas Gulf Sulphur for the mineral rights. In economic terms, these competitors would free ride on Texas Gulf Sulphur's efforts. Texas Gulf Sulphur will not earn a profit on the ore deposit until it has extracted enough ore to pay for its exploration costs. Because competitors will not have to incur any of the search costs Texas Gulf Sulphur had incurred to find the ore deposit, they will have a higher profit margin on any ore extracted. In turn, that will allow them to outbid Texas Gulf Sulphur for the mineral rights.[21] A securities law rule requiring immediate disclosure of the ore deposit (or any similar proprietary information) would discourage innovation and discovery by permitting this sort of free riding behavior—rational firms would not try to develop new mines if they knew competitors will be able to free ride on their efforts. In order to encourage innovation, the securities laws therefore generally permit corporations to delay disclosure of this sort of information for some period of time. As we have seen, however, the trade-off mandated by this policy is one of less accurate securities prices.

Manne essentially argued that insider trading is an effective compromise between the need for preserving incentives to produce information and the need for maintaining accurate securities prices.[22] Manne offered the following example of this alleged effect. Suppose a firm's stock currently sells at fifty dollars per share. The firm has discovered new information that, if publicly disclosed, would cause the stock to sell at sixty dollars. If insiders trade on this information, the price of the stock will gradually rise toward the correct price. Absent insider trading or leaks, the stock's price will remain at fifty dollars until the information is publicly disclosed and then rapidly rise to the correct price of sixty dollars. Thus, insider trading acts as a replacement for public disclosure of the information, preserving market gains of correct pricing while permitting the corporation to retain the benefits of nondisclosure.

Despite the anecdotal support for Manne's position provided by *Texas Gulf Sulphur* and similar cases, empirical evidence on point remains scanty. Early market studies indicated insider trading had

---

[21] Suppose TEXAS GULF SULPHUR spent $2 per acre on exploration costs and is willing to pay $10 per acre to buy the mineral rights from the landowners. TEXAS GULF SULPHUR must make at least $12 per acre on extracted ore before it makes a profit. Because competitors do not incur any exploration costs, they could pay $11 per acre for the mineral rights and still make a profit.

[22] Manne supra note 3, at 77–91.

an insignificant effect on price in most cases.[23] Subsequent studies suggested the market reacts fairly quickly when insiders buy securities, but the initial price effect is small when insiders sell.[24] These studies are problematic, however, because they relied principally (indeed, in some cases, solely) on the transactions reports corporate officers, directors, and 10% shareholders are required to file under Section 16(a).[25] Because insiders are unlikely to report transactions that violate Rule 10b–5, and because much illegal insider trading activity is known to involve persons not subject to the § 16(a) reporting requirement, conclusions drawn from such studies may not tell us very much about the price and volume effects of illegal insider trading. Accordingly, it is significant that a subsequent study of insider trading cases brought by the SEC during the 1980s found that the defendants' insider trading led to quick price changes.[26] That result supports Manne's empirical claim, subject to the caveat that reliance on data obtained from SEC prosecutions arguably may not be conclusive as to the price effects of undetected insider trading due to selection bias, although the study in question admittedly made strenuous efforts to avoid any such bias.

Evaluating the efficient pricing thesis requires a brief digression into efficient capital market theory. Along with the portfolio theory and the theory of the firm, the efficient capital markets hypothesis has been one of the three economic theories most influential on corporate and securities law.[27] In brief, the hypothesis asserts that in an efficient market current prices always and fully reflect all relevant information about the commodities being traded.[28] In other words, in an efficient market, the current price is an accurate reflection of the market's consensus as to the commodity's value, such that commodities are never overpriced or underpriced in such a market.[29] Of course, there is no real world

---

[23] Schotland, supra note 8, at 1443.

[24] See, e.g., Dan Givoly & Dan Palmon, Insider Trading and the Exploitation of Inside Information: Some Empirical Evidence, 58 J. Bus. 69 (1985).

[25] See infra Chapter 14 (discussing insider transaction reporting requirements).

[26] Lisa Meulbrock, An Empirical Analysis of Illegal Insider Trading, 47 J. Fin. 1661 (1992).

[27] Michael C. Jensen, Some Anomalous Evidence Regarding Market Efficiency, 6 J. Fin. Econ. 95, 95 (1978) (opining that "there is no other proposition in economics which has more solid empirical evidence supporting it than the Efficient [Capital] Market Hypothesis").

[28] See Eugene F. Fama, Efficient Capital Markets II, 46 J. Fin. 1575, 1575 (1991) (explaining that the efficient capital markets hypothesis states that "security prices fully reflect all available information").

[29] See Eckstein v. Balcor Film Investors, 8 F.3d 1121, 1129 (7th Cir.1993) (stating that "[c]ompetition among savvy investors leads to a price that impounds all available information").

condition like this, but the securities markets are widely believed to be close to this ideal.[30]

The so-called semi-strong form of the hypothesis posits that current prices incorporate all publicly available information.[31] The semi-strong form predicts that prices will change only if the information is new.[32] If the information had been previously leaked, or anticipated, the price will not change. If correct, investors cannot expect to profit from studying available information because the market will have already incorporated the information accurately into the price.

The strong form of the hypothesis holds that prices incorporate all information, whether publicly available or not.[33] The strong form makes no intuitive sense. After all, how can the market, which after all is not some omnipotent supernatural being but simply the aggregate of all investors, value information it does not know. If the strong form were true, moreover, insider trading could not be a profitable trading strategy.[34]

---

[30] See, e.g., In re PHP Healthcare Corp., 128 F. App'x 839, 848 (3d Cir. 2005) (opining that the New York Stock Exchange is "one of the most efficient capital markets in the world").

[31] See Fama, supra note 14, at 388 (defining the semi-strong form). The weak form of the Efficient Capital Markets Hypothesis holds that all information concerning historical prices is fully reflected in the current price. Id. Put another way, the weak form predicts that price changes in securities are serially independent or random. Ronald J. Gilson & Reinier H. Kraakman, The Mechanisms of Market Efficiency, 70 Va. L. Rev. 549, 555 n.25 (1984) ("Numerous weak-form tests support the hypothesis that the history of securities prices does not yield exploitable trading opportunities. . . .") Randomness does not mean that we cannot predict whether the stock will go up or down; obviously stock prices generally go up on good news and down on bad news. What financial economists mean by randomness is simply that investors cannot profit by using past prices to predict future prices. See Michael Abramowicz, Information Markets. Administrative Decisionmaking, and Predictive Cost-Benefit Analysis, 71 U. Chi. L. Rev. 933, 935 n.10 (2004) (arguing that "markets exhibit at least weak-form efficiency, meaning that future price movements cannot be predicted solely on the basis of past prices"). Accordingly, it predicts (and the evidence appears to confirm) that charting—the attempt to predict future prices by looking at the past history of stock prices—cannot be a profitable trading strategy over time. See Dennis S. Corgill, Insider Trading, Price Signals, and Noisy Information, 71 Ind. L.J. 355, 390–91 (1996) (describing the implications of weak form market efficiency).

[32] See William O. Fisher, Does the Efficient Market Theory Help Us Do Justice in a Time of Madness?, 54 Emory L.J. 843, 850 (2005) ("At least in its simplest form, the theory does not rest on a notion that the market price is the 'right' price in the sense of correctly capturing the value of a company, but simply that the price of the company's stock moves when new information relating to the company's fortunes becomes public.").

[33] Fama, supra note 14, at 388.

[34] See James D. Cox et al., Securities Regulation: Cases and Materials 100 (4th ed. 2004) (stating that "if the strong form of market efficiency were true, then a lot of effort has been misspent recently prosecuting individuals for insider trading"); see also Corgill, supra note 31, at 392 n.177 (arguing that ("insider trading scandals of the 1980's are among the many proofs that the strong form of the ECMH is invalid").

Empirical tests of the hypothesis have generally tended to confirm the semi-strong form, while disproving the strong form.[35] To be sure, the validity of the efficient capital markets hypothesis is still hotly debated in academic circles. It is probably fair to say, however, that most scholars regard it as the best available description of how markets behave.[36]

In an efficient market, how does insider trading affect stock prices? Although Manne's assertion that insider trading moves stock prices in the "correct" direction—i.e., the direction the stock price would move if the information were announced—seems intuitively plausible, the anonymity of impersonal market transactions makes it far from obvious that insider trading will have any effect on prices.[37] Accordingly, we need to look more closely at the way in which insider trading might work its magic on stock prices.

If you studied price theory in economics, your initial intuition may be that insider trading affects stock prices by changing the demand for the issuing corporation's stock. Economics tells us that supply and demand forces set the price of a commodity. The equilibrium or market-clearing price is that at which consumers are willing to buy all of the commodity offered by suppliers. If the supply remains constant, but demand goes up, the equilibrium price rises and vice-versa.

Suppose an insider buys stock on good news. The supply of stock remains constant (assuming the company is not in the midst of a stock offering or repurchase), but demand has increased, so a higher equilibrium price should result. All of which seems perfectly plausible, but for the inconvenient fact that a given security represents only a particular combination of expected return and systematic risk, for which there is a vast number of substitutes.[38] The correct measure for the supply of securities thus is not simply the total of the firm's outstanding securities, but the vastly larger number of securities with a similar combination of risk and return.[39] Accordingly, the supply/demand effect of a relatively small

---

[35] See Daniel R. Fischel, Efficient Capital Markets, the Crash, and the Fraud on the Market Theory, 74 Cornell L. Rev. 907, 911–12 n.11 (1989) (explaining that empirical analysis tends to support the weak and semi-strong forms but not the strong form of the hypothesis).

[36] Ok-Rial-Song, Hidden Social Costs of Open Market Share Repurchases, 27 J. Corp. L. 425, 452 (2002) (stating that empirical studies have left no doubt that ECMH is still a "fundamental paradigm[ ] for analyzing modern capital markets in current studies of corporate law and financial economics" (footnotes omitted)).

[37] See Ronald J. Gilson & Reinier H. Kraakman, The Mechanisms of Market Efficiency, 70 Va. L. Rev. 549, 630 (1984) ("The increase in the correctly specified supply [of a security] caused by an insider's sell order is simply too small to have any but a transitory, and probably insignificant, impact on the price of the security.").

[38] Id.

[39] Id.

number of insider trades should not have a significant price effect. Over the portion of the curve observed by individual traders, the demand curve should be flat rather than downward sloping.

Instead, if insider trading is to affect the price of securities it is through the derivatively informed trading mechanism of market efficiency. Derivatively informed trading affects market prices through a two-step mechanism.[40] First, those individuals possessing material nonpublic information begin trading. Their trading has only a small effect on price. Some uninformed traders become aware of the insider trading through leakage or tipping of information or through observation of insider trades. Other traders gain insight by following the price fluctuations of the securities. Finally, the market reacts to the insiders' trades and gradually moves toward the correct price. The problem is that while derivatively informed trading can affect price, it functions slowly and sporadically.[41] Given the inefficiency of derivatively informed trading, the market efficiency justification for insider trading loses much of its force.[42]

2.   Insider trading as an efficient compensation scheme

Manne's other principal argument against the ban on insider trading rested on the claim that allowing insider trading was an effective means of compensating entrepreneurs in large corporations. Manne distinguished corporate entrepreneurs from mere corporate managers. The latter simply operate the firm according to predetermined guidelines. By contrast, an entrepreneur's contribution to the firm consists of producing new valuable information. The entrepreneur's compensation must have a reasonable relation to the value of his contribution to give him incentives to produce more information. Because it is rarely possible to ascertain information's value to the firm in advance, predetermined compensation, such as salary, is inappropriate for entrepreneurs. Instead, claimed Manne, insider trading is an effective way to compensate entrepreneurs for innovations. The increase in the price of the security following public disclosure provides an imperfect but comparatively accurate measure of the value of the innovation to the firm. The entrepreneur can recover the value of his discovery by purchasing the firm's securities prior to disclosure and selling them after the price rises.[43]

---

[40] The following discussion draws on id. at 572–79.

[41] Id. at 631.

[42] For a contrary argument, asserting that no one has "seriously damaged the argument of the stock-pricing benefit of insider trading," see Henry G. Manne, Insider Trading: Hayek, Virtual Markets, and the Dog that Did Not Bark, 31 J. Corp. L. 167 (2005).

[43] Manne, supra note 3, at 131–41. In evaluating compensation-based justifications for deregulating inside trading, it is highly relevant to consider

Professors Carlton and Fischel subsequently suggested a further refinement of Manne's compensation argument.[44] They likewise believed ex ante contracts fail to appropriately compensate agents for innovations. The firm could renegotiate these contracts ex post to reward innovations, but renegotiation is costly and subject to strategic behavior. One of the advantages of insider trading, they argued, is that an agent revises his compensation package without renegotiating his contract. By trading on the new information, the agent self-tailors his compensation to account for the information he produces, increasing his incentive to develop valuable innovations.

Manne argued salary and bonuses provide inadequate incentives for entrepreneurial inventiveness because they fail to accurately measure the value to the firm of innovations.[45] Query, however, whether insider trading is any more accurate. Even assuming the change in stock price accurately measures the value of the innovation, the insider's compensation is limited by the number of shares he can purchase. This, in turn, is limited by his wealth. As such, the insider's trading returns are based, not on the value of his contribution, but on his wealth.

Another objection to the compensation argument is the difficulty of restricting trading to those who produced the information. Where information is concerned, production costs normally exceed distribution costs. As such, many firm agents may trade on the information without having contributed to its production.

A related criticism is the difficulty of limiting trading to instances in which the insider actually produced valuable information. In particular, why should insiders be permitted to trade on bad news? Allowing managers to profit from inside trading reduces the penalties associated with a project's failure because trading managers can profit whether the project succeeds or fails. If the project fails, the manager can sell his shares before that information becomes public and thus avoid an otherwise certain

---

whether the corporation or the manager owns the property right to the information in question. Some of those who favor deregulating insider trading deny that firms have a property interest in information produced by their agents that includes the right to prevent the agent from trading on the basis of that information. In contrast, those who favor regulation contend that when an agent produces information the property right to that information belongs to the firm. As described § Chapter 13.F, that latter appears to be the better view. The implication of that conclusion for the compensation debate is that agents should not be allowed to set their own compensation by inside trading. Instead, if insider trading is to be used as a form of compensation, it should be so used only with the consent of the firm.

[44] See Carlton & Fischel, supra note 7, at 869–71.

[45] Manne, supra note 3, at 134–38.

WHY DO WE CARE? THE ECONOMICS
OF INSIDER TRADING

loss. The manager can go beyond mere loss avoidance into actual profitmaking by short selling the firm's stock.

A final objection to the compensation thesis follows from the contingent nature of insider trading. Because the agent's trading returns cannot be measured in advance, neither can the true cost of his reward. As a result, selection of the most cost-effective compensation package is made more difficult. Moreover, the agent himself may prefer a less uncertain compensation package. If an agent is risk averse, he will prefer the certainty of $100,000 salary to a salary of $50,000 and a ten percent chance of a bonus of $500,000 from insider trading. Thus, the shareholders and the agent would gain by exchanging a guaranteed bonus for the agent's promise not to trade on inside information.[46]

In his article *Hayek, Virtual Markets, and the Dog that Did Not Bark*,[47] Manne concedes that the compensation-based argument in favor of deregulating insider trading "is perhaps less robust than I and other proponents had originally assumed." Indeed, as Manne acknowledges, it is perhaps instructive that no company pre-*Texas Gulf Sulphur* had tried to use insider trading as a form of compensation. Manne next reminds the reader, however, that very few companies pre-*Texas Gulf Sulphur* had voluntarily adopted proscriptions of insider trading. He therefore focuses attention on the question of why insider trading, as well as that of knowledgeable outsiders, was studiously ignored by the business and investment communities pre-*Texas Gulf Sulphur*. He argues that officers, directors, and controlling shareholders were unlikely to have remained silent in the face of widespread insider trading if they had believed the practice was harmful to their firm or to its investors. Instead, drawing on an analogy to the economic work of Friedrich Hayek, Manne argues that insider trading can help resolve the inefficiencies of information flows within large corporations by allowing the stock price to serve as a proxy for transmission of valuable information to top managers and large shareholders. In a sense, he argues, when managers trade on the basis of inside information, the stock price becomes akin to the sort of "prediction" markets widely used by corporations and policymakers in decision making.

---

[46] For criticism of the compensation thesis, see Frank H. Easterbrook, Insider Trading, Secret Agents, Evidentiary Privileges, and the Production of Information, 1981 Sup. Ct. Rev. 309 (1981); Saul Levmore, Securities and Secrets: Insider Trading and the Law of Contracts, 68 Va. L. Rev. 117 (1982); Saul Levmore, In Defense of the Regulation of Insider Trading, 11 Harv. J. L. & Pub. Pol. 101 (1988).

[47] Manne, supra note 42.

3.   Public choice

Some critics of the insider trading prohibition contend that the prohibition can be explained by a public choice-based model of regulation in which rules are sold by regulators and bought by the beneficiaries of the regulation.[48] On the supply side, the federal insider trading prohibition may be viewed as the culmination of two distinct trends in the securities laws. First, as do all government agencies, the SEC desired to enlarge its jurisdiction and enhance its prestige. Administrators can maximize their salaries, power, and reputation by maximizing the size of their agency's budget. A vigorous enforcement program directed at a highly visible and unpopular law violation is surely an effective means of attracting political support for larger budgets. Given the substantial media attention directed towards insider trading prosecutions, and the public taste for prohibiting insider trading, it provided a very attractive subject for such a program.

Second, during the prohibition's formative years, there was a major effort to federalize corporation law. In order to maintain its budgetary priority over competing agencies, the SEC wanted to play a major role in federalizing matters previously within the state domain. Insider trading was an ideal target for federalization. Rapid expansion of the federal insider trading prohibition purportedly demonstrated the superiority of federal securities law over state corporate law. Because the states had shown little interest in insider trading for years, federal regulation demonstrated the modernity, flexibility, and innovativeness of the securities laws. The SEC's prominent role in attacking insider trading thus placed it in the vanguard of the movement to federalize corporate law and ensured that the SEC would have a leading role in any system of federal corporations law.

The validity of this hypothesis is suggested by its ability to explain the SEC's devotion of significant enforcement resources to insider trading during the 1980s. During that decade, the SEC embarked upon a limited program of deregulating the securities markets. Among other things, the SEC adopted a safe harbor for projections and other soft data, the shelf registration rule, the integrated disclosure system, and expanded the exemptions from registration under the Securities Act. At about the same time,

---

[48] This section focuses on slightly different, but wholly compatible, stories about insider trading told by Professor Michael Dooley and Professors David Haddock and Jonathan Macey. Dooley's version explains why the SEC wanted to sell insider trading regulation, while Haddock and Macey's explains to whom it has been sold. See Michael P. Dooley, Fundamentals of Corporation Law 816–57 (1995); David D. Haddock and Jonathan R. Macey, Regulation on Demand: A Private Interest Model, with an Application to Insider Trading, 30 J.L. & Econ. 311 (1987); see also Jonathan R. Macey, Insider Trading: Economics, Politics, and Policy (1991).

however, the SEC adopted a vigorous enforcement campaign against insider trading. Not only did the number of cases increase substantially, but the SEC adopted a "big bang" approach under which it focused on high visibility cases that would produce substantial publicity. In part this may have been due to an increase in the frequency of insider trading, but the public choice story nicely explains the SEC's interest in insider trading as motivated by a desire to preserve its budget during an era of deregulation and spending restraint.

The public choice story also explains the SEC's continuing attachment to the equal access approach to insider trading. The equal access policy generates an expansive prohibition, which federalizes a broad range of conduct otherwise left to state corporate law, while also warranting a highly active enforcement program. As such, the SEC's use of Rule 14e–3 and the misappropriation theory to evade *Chiarella* and *Dirks* makes perfect sense. By these devices, the SEC restored much of the prohibition's pre-*Chiarella* breadth and thereby ensured that its budget-justifying enforcement program would continue unimpeded.

Turning to the demand side, the insider trading prohibition appears to be supported and driven in large part by market professionals, a cohesive and politically powerful interest group, which the current legal regime effectively insulates from insider trading liability. Only insiders and quasi-insiders such as lawyers and investment bankers have greater access to material nonpublic information than do market professionals. By basing insider trading liability on breach of fiduciary duty, and positing that the requisite fiduciary duty exists with respect to insiders and quasi-insiders but not with respect to market professionals, the prohibition protects the latter's ability to profit from new information about a firm.

When an insider trades on an impersonal secondary market, the insider takes advantage of the fact that the market maker's or specialist's bid-ask prices do not reflect the value of the inside information. Because market makers and specialists cannot distinguish insiders from non-insiders, they cannot protect themselves from being taken advantage of in this way. When trading with insiders, the market maker or specialist thus will always be on the wrong side of the transaction. If insider trading is effectively prohibited, however, the market professionals are no longer exposed to this risk.

Professional securities traders likewise profit from the fiduciary-duty based insider trading prohibition. Because professional investors are often active traders, they are highly sensitive to the transaction costs of trading in securities. Prominent among these costs is the specialist's and market-maker's bid-ask spread. If a ban on insider trading lowers the risks faced by specialists and market-makers, some portion of the resulting gains should be passed on to professional traders in the form of narrower bid-ask spreads.

Analysts and professional traders are further benefited by a prohibition on insider trading, because only insiders are likely to have systematic advantages over market professionals in the competition to be the first to act on new information. Market professionals specialize in acquiring and analyzing information. They profit by trading with less well-informed investors or by selling information to them. If insiders can freely trade on nonpublic information, however, some portion of the information's value will be impounded into the price before it is learned by market professionals, which will reduce their returns.

Circumstantial evidence for the demand-side hypothesis is provided by SEC enforcement patterns. In the years immediately prior to *Chiarella*, enforcement proceedings often targeted market professionals. The frequency of insider trading prosecutions rose dramatically after *Chiarella* held insider trading was unlawful only if the trader violated a fiduciary duty owed to the party with whom he trades. Yet, despite that increase in overall enforcement activity, there was a marked decline in the number of cases brought against market professionals.

Identifying a private interest that benefits from regulation, of course, does not necessarily mean that the regulation is inconsistent with the public interest. Specialists and market makers are critical to both market efficiency and liquidity. If insider trading causes them to increase the bid-ask spread or take other precautions that reduce market efficiency and liquidity, an insider trading prohibition may be in the public interest.

Market liquidity cannot be a complete explanation for the insider trading prohibition, however. Indeed, it lacks both explanatory and normative power. Market liquidity-based theories fail to take into account the limited nature of the current prohibition. While the post-*Chiarella* framework significantly reduces the risk that market professionals will be targeted for insider trading violations, giving them a private interest in supporting that framework, the post-*Chiarella* regime does not fully insulate market makers and specialists from trading with investors having superior information. Authorized traders, brazen misappropriators, persons trading while in possession of but not on the basis of inside information, and persons trading on their own intentions all may lawfully trade. In addition, because firms benefit from having liquid and efficient markets for their securities, we would expect to observe firms bonding against insider trading. Yet, by all accounts, firms did not do so even before *Cady, Roberts*. The empirical case for market liquidity-based theories is further undermined by the well-known observation that highly liquid and efficient stock markets exist in several countries that do not prohibit insider trading or fail to enforce the laws on the books, such as Japan and Hong Kong.

The insulation the current regime gives market professionals, along with the potential protections it provides them against at least some trading by persons with superior information, suffices to explain why market professionals would support the current prohibition. In order for the allegedly deleterious effects of insider trading on market efficiency and liquidity to provide a normative justification for the current prohibition, however, several conditions need to be satisfied. First, it must be demonstrated that insider trading actually reduces liquidity. Second, a ban of insider trading must promote (or, at least, not impede) market efficiency. As we have seen, however, the evidence on the market effects of insider trading remains inconclusive. If Manne's market efficiency claims are correct, repealing the prohibition would enhance market efficiency.

B. Henry Manne: An Appreciation

Whether one agrees with Manne's views on insider trading or not, one therefore must give him due credit for helping to stimulate the outpouring of important law and economics scholarship in corporate law and securities regulation in recent decades. Manne's work on insider trading straddles what Richard Posner called the first and second generations of law and economics scholarship.[49] The first generation, which consisted of scholars such as Gary Becker, Guido Calabresi, Ronald Coase, and Aaron Director, blazed the trail by establishing the tools of microeconomics—most notably the rational choice model—as a methodology by which legal doctrines usefully may be examined.

The second generation took these tools and ran with them, applying them to a host of legal doctrines. Their projects typically entailed translation of some legal principle into economic terms. They then applied a few basic economic tools—cost-benefit analysis, collective action theory, decision making under uncertainty, risk aversion, and the like—to the problem. Finally, they translated the result back into legal terms.

---

[49] Richard A. Posner, A Review of Steven Shavell's Foundations of Economic Analysis of Law, 44 J. Econ. Lit. 405 (2006).

Manne was among those first-generation scholars who paved the way for law and economics to become an accepted jurisprudential methodology, but he also was one of the first and most important second-generation scholars. As Ronald Cass observes, "Manne was one of the first legal scholars . . . to use economics to generate a new insight into a legal issue and to do so in a way that dramatically changed discourse about that issue."[50] Indeed, Manne did it twice—once with respect to the market for the corporate control and again with respect to insider trading.

C. The Case for Regulation: Non-Economic Arguments

The arguments in favor of regulating insider trading can be separated into one set sounding in economic terms and a second set premised on fairness, equity, and other non-efficiency grounds. The non-economic arguments break down into two major sets: a claim that regulating insider trading is necessary to protect the mandatory disclosure system and a claim that insider trading is unfair. The economic arguments can be divided as follows: claims that insider trading injures investors; claims that insider trading injures firms; and claims relating to property rights in information.

1. The impact of insider trading on the mandatory disclosure regime

Mandatory disclosure is arguably the central purpose of the federal securities laws.[51] Both the Securities Act and the Exchange Act are based on a policy of mandating disclosure by issuers and others. The Securities Act creates a transactional disclosure regime, which is applicable only when a firm is actually selling securities. In contrast, the 1934 Exchange Act creates a periodic disclosure regime, which requires on-going, regular, disclosures.[52]

---

[50] Ronald A. Cass, One Among the Manne: Changing Our Course, 50 Case W. Res. L. Rev. 203, 204 (1999). See generally Stephen M. Bainbridge, Introduction, in 2 The Collected Works of Henry Manne: Insider Trading (2009) (describing Manne's contributions); see also Michael Abramowicz & M. Todd Henderson, Prediction Markets for Corporate Governance, 82 Notre Dame L. Rev. 1343, 1373–74 (2007) (calling Manne "the leading anti-establishment thinker in this area"); Douglas M. Branson, Prescience and Vindication: Federal Courts, SEC Rule 10b–5, and the Work of David S. Ruder, Nw. U. L. Rev. 613 (1991) ("The leading advocate of the view that insider trading is a benefit has always been Dean Henry Manne.").

[51] See generally Stephen M. Bainbridge, Mandatory Disclosure: A Behavioral Analysis, 68 U. Cin. L. Rev. 1023 (2000).

[52] As we have seen, of course, neither Act requires a firm to disclose all nonpublic information relating to the firm. Instead, when premature disclosure would harm the firm's interests, the firm is generally free to refrain from disclosing such information. Even proponents of the mandatory disclosure system acknowledge that it is appropriate to strike this balance between investors' need for disclosure and management's need for secrecy. See Chapter 4.B.

Some scholars argue that the federal insider trading prohibition is necessary to the effective working of this mandatory disclosure system.[53] The prohibition supposedly ensures "that confidentiality is not abused and utilized for the personal and secret profit of corporate managers and employees or persons associated with a bidder in a tender offer."[54] Many reputable corporate law scholars, of course, doubt whether mandatory disclosure is a sound policy.[55] If the latter group is correct and the mandatory disclosure system ought to be done away with, this justification for regulating insider trading collapses at the starting gate. For present purposes, however, we shall take the mandatory disclosure system as a given and limit our inquiry to whether a prohibition of insider trading is necessary to protect the mandatory disclosure system from abuse.

Insider trading seems likely to adversely affect the mandatory disclosure regime only insofar as it affects managers' incentives to manipulate the timing of disclosure. Conceivably, for example, a manager might delay making federally mandated disclosures in order to give herself more time in which to trade in her company's stock before the inside information is announced. As we shall see below, however, it is doubtful whether insider trading results in significant delays in corporate disclosures.[56]

Indeed, insider trading seems more likely to create incentives for insiders to prematurely disclose information than to delay its disclosure. While premature disclosure threatens the firm's interests, that threat has little to do with the mandatory disclosure system. Instead, it is properly treated as a breach of the insider's fiduciary duty.

In any event, concern for ensuring timely disclosure cannot justify a prohibition of the breadth it currently possesses. As we have seen, the prohibition encompasses a host of actors both within and outside the firm. In contrast, only a few actors are likely to have the power to affect the timing of disclosure. A much narrower prohibition thus would suffice if this were the principal rationale for regulating insider trading. Indeed, if this were the main concern, one need not prohibit insider trading at all. Instead, one could strike at the problem much more directly by proscribing failing to disclose material information in the absence of a legitimate corporate reason for doing so.

---

[53] Roberta S. Karmel, The Relationship Between Mandatory Disclosure and Prohibitions Against Insider Trading: Why a Property Rights Theory of Insider Trading Is Untenable, 59 Brook. L. Rev. 149, 169–70 (1993).

[54] Id. at 170–71.

[55] See, e.g., Frank H. Easterbrook & Daniel R. Fischel, The Economic Structure of Corporate Law 276–314 (1991); Roberta Romano, The Genius of American Corporate Law 91–96 (1993).

[56] See Chapter 13.E.1.

2. Insider trading is unfair

There seems to be a widely shared view that there is something inherently sleazy about insider trading. As a California state court put it, insider trading is "a manifestation of undue greed among the already well-to-do, worthy of legislative intervention if for no other reason than to send a message of censure on behalf of the American people."[57]

Given the draconian penalties associated with insider trading, however, vague and poorly articulated notions of fairness surely provide an insufficient justification for the prohibition. Can we identify a standard of reference by which to demonstrate that insider trading ought to be prohibited on fairness grounds? In my judgment, we cannot.

Fairness can be defined in various ways. Most of these definitions, however, collapse into the various efficiency-based rationales for prohibiting insider trading. We might define fairness as fidelity, for example, by which I mean the notion that an agent should not cheat her principal. But this argument only has traction if insider trading is in fact a form of cheating, which in turn depends on how we assign the property right to confidential corporate information. Alternatively, we might define fairness as equality of access to information, but this definition must be rejected in light of *Chiarella*'s rejection of the *Texas Gulf Sulphur* equal access standard.[58] Finally, we might define fairness as a prohibition of injuring another. But such a definition justifies an insider trading prohibition only if insider trading injures investors, which seems unlikely for the reasons discussed in the next section. Accordingly, fairness concerns need not detain us further; instead, we can turn directly to the economic arguments against insider trading.

D. The Case for Regulation: Protecting Investors

Insider trading is said to harm investors in two principal ways. Some contend that the investor's trades are made at the "wrong price." A more sophisticated theory posits that the investor is induced to make a bad purchase or sale.[59] Neither argument proves convincing on close examination. Equally unpersuasive is the related argument that insider trading shakes investor confidence in the integrity of the markets.

---

[57] Friese v. Superior Court, 36 Cal.Rptr.3d 558, 566 (Cal. App. 2005).

[58] See Chapter 5.A (discussing how equal access to information is no longer a recognized justification for banning insider trading).

[59] See Stanislav Dolgopolov, Insider Trading, in The Concise Encyclopedia of Economics (David R. Henderson ed., 2008) (describing arguments).

1.   Injury to investors

An investor who trades in a security contemporaneously with insiders having access to material nonpublic information likely will allege injury in that he sold at the wrong price; i.e., a price that does not reflect the undisclosed information. If a firm's stock currently sells at $10 per share, but after disclosure of the new information will sell at $15, a shareholder who sells at the current price thus will claim a $5 loss.

The investor's claim, however, is fundamentally flawed. It is purely fortuitous that an insider was on the other side of the transaction. The gain corresponding to the shareholder's loss is reaped not just by inside traders, but by all contemporaneous purchasers whether they had access to the undisclosed information or not.

To be sure, the investor might not have sold if he had had the same information as the insider, but even so the rules governing insider trading are not the source of his problem. On an impersonal trading market, neither party knows the identity of the person with whom he is trading. Thus, the seller has made an independent decision to sell without knowing that the insider is buying; if the insider were not buying, the seller would still sell. It is thus the nondisclosure that causes the harm, rather than the mere fact of trading. On an impersonal exchange, moreover, the precise identity of the seller is purely fortuitous and it is difficult to argue that the seller who happened to be matched with the insider has been hurt more than any other contemporaneous seller whose sale was not so matched.

The information asymmetry between insiders and public investors arises out of the mandatory disclosure rules allowing firms to keep some information confidential even if it is material to investor decision-making. Unless immediate disclosure of material information is to be required, a step the law has been unwilling to take, there will always be winners and losers in this situation.[60] Irrespective of whether insiders are permitted to inside trade or not, the investor will not have the same access to information as the insider. It makes little sense to claim that the shareholder is injured when his shares are bought by an insider, but not when they are bought by an outsider without access to information. To the extent the selling shareholder is injured, his injury thus is correctly attributed to the rules allowing corporate nondisclosure of material information, not to insider trading.

---

[60] Easterbrook, supra note 46, at 326–27.

Arguably, for example, the Texas Gulf Sulphur shareholders who sold from November through April were not made any worse off by the insider trading that occurred during that period. Most, if not all, of these people sold for a series of random reasons unrelated to the trading activities of insiders. The only seller we should worry about is the one that consciously thought, "I'm going to sell because this worthless company never finds any ore." Even if such an investor existed, however, we have no feasible way of identifying him. Ex post, of course, all the sellers will pretend this was why they sold. If we believe Manne's argument that insider trading is an efficient means of transmitting information to the market, moreover, selling Texas Gulf Sulphur shareholders actually were better off by virtue of the insider trading. They sold at a price higher than their shares would have commanded but for the insider trading activity that led to higher prices. In short, insider trading has no "victims." What to do about the "offenders" is a distinct question analytically.

A more sophisticated argument is that the price effects of insider trading induce shareholders to make poorly advised transactions. It is doubtful whether insider trading produces the sort of price effects necessary to induce shareholders to trade, however. While derivatively informed trading can affect price, it functions slowly and sporadically.[61] Given the inefficiency of derivatively informed trading, price or volume changes resulting from insider trading will only rarely be of sufficient magnitude to induce investors to trade.

Assuming for the sake of argument that insider trading produces noticeable price effects, however, and further assuming that those effects mislead some investors, the inducement argument is further flawed because many transactions would have taken place regardless of the price changes resulting from insider trading. Investors who would have traded irrespective of the presence of insiders in the market benefit from insider trading because they transacted at a price closer to the correct price; i.e., the price that would prevail if the information were disclosed. In any case, it is hard to tell how the inducement argument plays out when investors are examined as a class. For any given number who decide to sell because of a price rise, for example, another group of investors may decide to defer a planned sale in anticipation of further increases.

2. Investor confidence

An argument closely related to the investor injury issue is the claim that insider trading undermines investor confidence in the

---

[61] See Chapter 13.A.1 (discussing effect of derivatively informed trading on market prices).

securities market.[62] In the absence of a credible investor injury story, however, it is difficult to see why insider trading should undermine investor confidence in the integrity of the securities markets.

There is no denying that insider trading angers many investors. A Business Week poll, for example, found that 52% of respondents wanted insider trading to remain unlawful. In order to determine whether investor anger over insider trading undermines their confidence in the markets, however, one must first identify the source of that anger. Instructively, the same poll found that 55% of the respondents said they would inside trade if given the opportunity. Of those who said they would not trade, 34% said they would not do so only because they would be afraid the tip was incorrect. Only 35% said they would refrain from trading because insider trading is wrong.[63] Here lies one of the paradoxes of insider trading. Most people want insider trading to remain illegal, but most people (apparently including at least some of the former) are willing to participate if given the chance to do so on the basis of accurate information. This paradox is central to evaluating arguments based on confidence in the market. Investors who are willing to inside trade if given the opportunity obviously have no confidence in the integrity of the market in the first instance. Any anger they feel over insider trading therefore has nothing to do with a loss of confidence in the integrity of the market, but instead arises principally from envy of the insider's greater access to information.

In sum, neither investor protection nor maintenance of confidence have much traction as theoretical justifications for any prohibition of insider trading, nor do they have much explanatory power with respect to the prohibition currently on the books. An investor's rights vary widely depending on the nature of the insider trading transaction; the identity of the trader; and the source of the information. Yet, if the goal is investor protection, why should these considerations be relevant?

---

[62] See, e.g., United States v. O'Hagan, 521 U.S. 642, 658 (1997) ("Investors likely would hesitate to venture their capital in a market where trading based on misappropriated nonpublic information is unchecked by law."); SEC v. Michel, 521 F. Supp.2d 795, 830 (N.D. Ill. 2007) (opining that "insider trading causes harm to the credibility of the public markets").

[63] See Business Week/Harris Poll: Outsiders Aren't Upset by Insider Trading, Bus. Wk., Dec. 8, 1986, at 34. In contrast, a 1961 poll of business executives indicated that a large proportion did not consider insider trading immoral or unethical. Problems in Review, Harv. Bus. Rev., July–Aug. 1961, at 6 (finding that 42% of those polled would trade on the basis of material nonpublic information). Because that survey preceded the promulgation of the federal prohibition and the resulting debate, however, its conclusions are at least suspect and may no longer represent the dominant view of executives.

Recall, that in *U.S. v. Carpenter*,[64] for example, R. Foster Winans wrote the Wall Street Journal's "Heard on the Street" column, a daily report on various stocks that is said to affect the price of the stocks discussed. Journal policy expressly treated the column's contents prior to publication as confidential information belonging to the newspaper. Despite that rule, Winans agreed to provide several co-conspirators with prepublication information as to the timing and contents of future columns. His fellow conspirators then traded in those stocks based on the expected impact of the column on the stocks' prices, sharing the profits. In affirming their convictions, the Second Circuit anticipated *O'Hagan* by holding that Winans's breach of his fiduciary duty to the Wall Street Journal satisfied the standards laid down in *Chiarella* and *Dirks*.[65] From either an investor protection or confidence in the market perspective, however, this outcome seems bizarre at best. For example, any duties Winans owed in this situation ran to an entity that had neither issued the securities in question nor even participated in stock market transactions. What Winans's breach of his duties to the Wall Street Journal has to do with the federal securities laws, if anything, is not self-evident.

The incongruity of the misappropriation theory becomes even more apparent when one considers that its logic suggests that the Wall Street Journal could lawfully trade on the same information used by Winans.[66] If we are really concerned with protecting investors and maintaining their confidence in the market's integrity, the inside trader's identity ought to be irrelevant. From the investors' point of view, insider trading is a matter of concern only because they have traded with someone who used their superior access to information to profit at the investor's expense. As such, it would not appear to matter whether it is Winans or the Journal on the opposite side of the transaction. Both have greater access to the relevant information than do investors.

The logic of the misappropriation theory also suggests that Winans would not have been liable if the Wall Street Journal had authorized his trades. In that instance, the Journal would not have been deceived, as *O'Hagan* requires. Winans' trades would not have constituted an improper conversion of nonpublic information, moreover, so that the essential breach of fiduciary duty would not be present. Again, however, from an investor's perspective, it would

---

[64] U.S. v. Carpenter, 791 F.2d 1024, 1026–27 (2d Cir.1986), aff'd, 484 U.S. 19 (1987).

[65] Id. at 1031.

[66] See id. at 1033 ("Appellants' argument that this distinction would be unfair to employees illogically casts the thief and the victim in the same shoes.").

not seem to matter whether Winans's trades were authorized or not.

Finally, conduct that should be lawful under the misappropriation theory is clearly proscribed by Rule 14e–3. A takeover bidder may not authorize others to trade on information about a pending tender offer, for example, even though such trading might aid the bidder by putting stock in friendly hands. If the acquisition is to take place by means other than a tender offer, however, neither Rule 14e–3 nor the misappropriation theory should apply. From an investor's perspective, however, the form of the acquisition seems just as irrelevant as the identity of the insider trader.

All of these anomalies, oddities, and incongruities have crept into the federal insider trading prohibition as a direct result of *Chiarella*'s imposition of a fiduciary duty requirement. None of them, however, are easily explicable from either an investor protection or a confidence in the market rationale.

3. The law of conservation of securities

Some contend that insider trading results in outside investors—as a class—being injured because they reap a smaller share of the gains from new information.[67] In *Texas Gulf Sulphur*, for example, the price of Texas Gulf Sulphur's stock rose from about $18 to about $55 during the relevant time period.[68] Assuming all of that gain can be attributed to information about the ore strike, and further assuming that Texas Gulf Sulphur had 1 million shares outstanding, the total gain to be divided was about $37 million. If insiders pocketed $2 million of that gain, there will be $2 million less for outsiders to divide.

This is not a strong argument for banning insider trading, however. First, it only asserts that investors as a class are less well off by virtue of insider trading. It cannot identify any particular investor who suffered losses as a result of the insider trading. Second, if we make the traditional assumption that the relevant supply of a given security is the universe of all securities with similar beta coefficients, any gains siphoned off by insiders with respect to a particular stock are likely to be an immaterial percentage of the gains contemporaneously earned by the class of investors as a whole. (Even in *Texas Gulf Sulphur*, trading by insiders amounted to less than 10% of the trading activity in Texas

---

[67] William Wang, Trading on Material Nonpublic Information on Impersonal Stock Markets: Who Is Harmed, and Who Can Sue Whom Under SEC Rule 10b–5?, 54 S. Cal. L. Rev. 1217 (1981) (positing the "law of conservation of securities").

[68] See SEC v. Texas Gulf Sulphur Co., 401 F.2d 833, 847 (2d Cir. 1968) (summarizing price movements), 394 U.S. 976 (1969).

Gulf Sulphur stock and, of course, a vastly smaller percentage of trading activity in the class of securities with comparable betas.) Finally, although the law of conservation of securities asserts that some portion of the gains flow to insiders rather than to outside investors, that fact standing alone is legally unremarkable. To justify a ban on insider trading, you need a basis for asserting that it is inappropriate, undesirable, or immoral for those gains to be reaped by insiders. The law of conservation of securities does not, standing alone, provide such a basis.

E. The Case for Regulation: Protecting Issuers

Unlike tangible property, more than one person can use information without necessarily lowering its value to its owner. If a manager who has just negotiated a major contract for his employer then trades in his employer's stock, for example, there is no reason to believe that the manager's conduct necessarily lowers the value of the contract to the employer. But while insider trading will not always harm the employer, it may do so in some circumstances. In the sections that follow, we evaluate potential injuries to the issuer associated with insider trading.

1. Delay

Insider trading could injure the firm if it creates incentives for managers to delay the transmission of information to superiors.[69] Decision making in any entity requires accurate, timely information. In large, hierarchical organizations, such as publicly traded corporations, information must pass through many levels before reaching senior managers. The more levels, the greater the probability of distortion or delay intrinsic to the system. This inefficiency can be reduced by downward delegation of decision-making authority but not eliminated. Even with only minimal delay in the upward transmission of information at every level, where the information must pass through many levels before reaching a decision-maker, the net delay may be substantial.

If a manager discovers or obtains information (either beneficial or detrimental to the firm), she may delay disclosure of that information to other managers so as to assure herself sufficient time to trade on the basis of that information before the corporation acts upon it. Even if the period of delay by any one manager is brief, the net delay produced by successive trading managers may be substantial. Unnecessary delay of this sort harms the firm in several ways. The firm must monitor the manager's conduct to

---

[69] See generally Robert J. Haft, The Effect of Insider Trading Rules on the Internal Efficiency of the Large Corporation, 80 Mich. L. Rev. 1051, 1053–60 (1982) (discussing potential impact of delay on corporate decision making).

ensure timely carrying out of her duties. It becomes more likely that outsiders will become aware of the information through snooping or leaks. Some outsider may even independently discover and utilize the information before the corporation acts upon it.

Although delay is a plausible source of harm to the issuer, its importance is easily exaggerated. The available empirical evidence scarcely rises above the anecdotal level, but does suggest that measurable delay attributable to insider trading is rare.[70] Given the rapidity with which securities transactions can be conducted in modern secondary trading markets, moreover, a manager need at most delay corporate action long enough for a five minute telephone conversation with her stockbroker. Delay (either in transmitting information or taking action) also often will be readily detectable by the employer. Finally, and perhaps most importantly, insider trading may create incentives to release information early just as often as it creates incentives to delay transmission and disclosure of information.

2. Interference with corporate plans

Trading during the planning stage of an acquisition is a classic example of how insider trading might adversely interfere with corporate plans. If managers charged with overseeing an acquisition buy shares in the target, and their trading has a significant up-ward effect on the price of the target's stock, the takeover will be more expensive. If their trading causes significant price and volume changes, that also might tip off others to the secret, interfering with the bidder's plans, as by alerting the target to the need for defensive measures.

The risk of premature disclosure poses an even more serious threat to corporate plans. The issuer often has just as much interest in when information becomes public as it does in whether the information becomes public. Suppose Target, Inc., enters into merger negotiations with a potential acquirer. Target managers who inside trade on the basis of that information will rarely need to delay corporate action in order to effect their purchases. Having made their purchases, however, the managers now have an incentive to cause disclosure of Target's plans as soon as possible. Absent leaks or other forms of derivatively informed trading, the merger will have no price effect until it is disclosed to the market, at which time there usually is a strong positive effect. Once the information is disclosed, the trading managers will be able to reap substantial profits, but until disclosure takes place, they bear a variety of firm-specific and market risks. The deal, the stock

---

[70] Michael P. Dooley, Enforcement of Insider Trading Restrictions, supra note 66 Va. L. Rev. 1, 34 (1980).

market, or both may collapse at any time. Early disclosure enables the managers to minimize those risks by selling out as soon as the price jumps in response to the announcement.

If disclosure is made too early, a variety of adverse consequences may result. If disclosure triggers competing bids, the initial bidder may withdraw from the bidding or demand protection in the form of costly lock-ups and other exclusivity provisions. Alternatively, if disclosure does not trigger competing bids, the initial bidder may conclude that it overbid and lower its offer accordingly. In addition, early disclosure brings the deal to the attention of regulators and plaintiffs' lawyers earlier than necessary.

An even worse case scenario is suggested by *SEC v. Texas Gulf Sulphur Co.*[71] Recall that insiders who knew of the ore discovery traded over an extended period of time. During that period the corporation was attempting to buy up the mineral rights to the affected land. If the news had leaked prematurely, the issuer at least would have had to pay much higher fees for the mineral rights, and may well have lost some land to competitors. Given the magnitude of the strike, which eventually resulted in a 300–plus percent increase in the firm's market price, the harm that would have resulted from premature disclosure was immense.

Although insider trading probably only rarely causes the firm to lose opportunities, it may create incentives for management to alter firm plans in less drastic ways to increase the likelihood and magnitude of trading profits. For example, trading managers can accelerate receipt of revenue, change depreciation strategy, or alter dividend payments in an attempt to affect share prices and insider returns. Alternatively, the insiders might structure corporate transactions to increase the opportunity for secret keeping. Both types of decisions may adversely affect the firm and its shareholders. Moreover, this incentive may result in allocative inefficiency by encouraging overinvestment in those industries or activities that generate opportunities for insider trading.

Judge Frank Easterbrook has identified a related perverse incentive created by insider trading.[72] Managers may elect to follow policies that increase fluctuations in the price of the firm's stock. They may select riskier projects than the shareholders would prefer, because, if the risks pay off, they can capture a portion of the gains in insider trading and, if the project flops, the shareholders bear the loss. In contrast, Professors Carlton and Fischel assert

---

[71] 401 F.2d 833 (2d Cir.1968), cert. denied, 394 U.S. 976 (1969).

[72] Frank H. Easterbrook, Insider Trading, Secret Agents, Evidentiary Privileges, and the Production of Information, 1981 Sup. Ct. Rev. 309 (1981).

that Easterbrook overstates the incentive to choose high-risk projects.[73] Because managers must work in teams, the ability of one or a few managers to select high-risk projects is severely constrained through monitoring by colleagues. Cooperation by enough managers to pursue such projects to the firm's detriment is unlikely because a lone whistle-blower is likely to gain more by exposing others than he will by colluding with them. Further, Carlton and Fischel argue managers have strong incentives to maximize the value of their services to the firm. Therefore they are unlikely to risk lowering that value for short-term gain by adopting policies detrimental to long-term firm profitability. Finally, Carlton and Fischel alternatively argue that even if insider trading creates incentives for management to choose high-risk projects, these incentives are not necessarily harmful. Such incentives would act as a counterweight to the inherent risk aversion that otherwise encourages managers to select lower risk projects than shareholders would prefer. Allowing insider trading may encourage management to select negative net present value investments, however, not only because shareholders bear the full risk of failure, but also because failure presents management with an opportunity for profit through short-selling. As a result, shareholders might prefer other incentive schemes.

3. Injury to the issuer's reputation

It has been said that insider trading by corporate managers may cast a cloud on the corporation's name, injure stockholder relations and undermine public regard for the corporation's securities.[74] Reputational injury of this sort could translate into a direct financial injury, by raising the firm's cost of capital, if investors demand a premium (by paying less) when buying stock in a firm whose managers inside trade. Because shareholder injury is a critical underlying premise of the reputational injury story, however, this argument would appear to collapse at the starting gate. As we have seen, it is very hard to create a plausible shareholder injury story.

F. Insider Trading and Property Rights in Information

There are two ways of creating property rights in information: (1) allow the owner to enter into transactions without disclosing the information; or (2) prohibit others from using the information. In

---

[73] Dennis W. Carlton and Daniel R. Fischel, The Regulation of Insider Trading, 35 Stan. L. Rev. 857 (1983).

[74] Compare Diamond v. Oreamuno, 248 N.E.2d 910, 912 (N.Y. 1969) (discussing threat of reputational injury) with Freeman v. Decio, 584 F.2d 186, 194 (7th Cir.1978) (arguing that injury to reputation is speculative).

effect, the federal insider trading prohibition vests a property right of the latter type in the party to whom the insider trader owes a fiduciary duty to refrain from self-dealing in confidential information. To be sure, at first blush, the insider trading prohibition admittedly does not look very much like most property rights. Enforcement of the insider trading prohibition admittedly differs rather dramatically from enforcement of, say, trespassing laws. The existence of property rights in a variety of intangibles, including information, however, is well established. Trademarks, copyrights, and patents are but a few of the better-known examples of this phenomenon. There are striking doctrinal parallels, moreover, between insider trading and these other types of property rights in information. Using another's trade secret, for example, is actionable only if taking the trade secret involved a breach of fiduciary duty, misrepresentation, or theft.[75] This was an apt summary of the law of insider trading after the Supreme Court's decisions in *Chiarella* and *Dirks* (although it is unclear whether liability for theft in the absence of a breach of fiduciary duty survives *O'Hagan*).[76]

In context, moreover, even the insider trading prohibition's enforcement mechanisms are not inconsistent with a property rights analysis. Where public policy argues for giving someone a property right, but the costs of enforcing such a right would be excessive, the state often uses its regulatory powers as a substitute for creating private property rights.[77] Insider trading poses just such a situation. Private enforcement of the insider trading laws is rare and usually parasitic on public enforcement proceedings. Indeed, the very nature of insider trading arguably makes public regulation essential precisely because private enforcement is almost impossible. The insider trading prohibition's regulatory nature thus need not preclude a property rights-based analysis.

The rationale for prohibiting insider trading is the same as that for prohibiting patent infringement or theft of trade secrets; i.e., protecting the economic incentive to produce socially valuable information. As the theory goes, the readily appropriable nature of information makes it difficult for the developer of a new idea to recoup the sunk costs incurred to develop it.[78] If an inventor develops a better mousetrap, for example, he cannot profit on that invention without selling mousetraps and thereby making the new

---

[75] Edmund W. Kitch, The Law and Economics of Rights in Valuable Information, 9 J. Leg. Stud. 683, 695–96 (1980).

[76] Dooley, supra note 48, at 776.

[77] Richard A. Posner, Economic Analysis of Law 36 (4th ed. 1992).

[78] See Robert Cooter & Thomas Ulen, Law And Economics 119–28 (2d ed. 1997).

design available to potential competitors. Assuming both the inventor and his competitors incur roughly equivalent marginal costs to produce and market the trap, the competitors will be able to set a market price at which the inventor likely will be unable to earn a return on his sunk costs. Ex post, the rational inventor should ignore his sunk costs and go on producing the improved mousetrap. Ex ante, however, the inventor will anticipate that he will be unable to generate positive returns on his up-front costs and therefore will be deterred from developing socially valuable information. Accordingly, society provides incentives for inventive activity by using the patent system to give inventors a property right in new ideas. By preventing competitors from appropriating the idea, the patent allows the inventor to charge monopolistic prices for the improved mousetrap, thereby recouping his sunk costs. Trademark, copyright, and trade secret law all are justified on similar grounds.

This argument does not provide as compelling a justification for the insider trading prohibition as it does for the patent system. A property right in information should be created when necessary to prevent conduct by which someone other than the developer of socially valuable information appropriates its value before the developer can recoup his sunk costs. As we have seen, however, insider trading often has no effect on an idea's value to the corporation and probably never entirely eliminates its value. Legalizing insider trading thus would have a much smaller impact on the corporation's incentive to develop new information than would, say, legalizing patent infringement.

The property rights approach nevertheless has considerable power. Consider the prototypical insider trading transaction, in which an insider trades in his employer's stock on the basis of information learned solely because of his position with the firm. There is no avoiding the necessity of assigning a property interest in the information to either the corporation or the insider. A rule allowing insider trading assigns a property interest to the insider, while a rule prohibiting insider trading assigns it to the corporation.

From the corporation's perspective, we have seen that legalizing insider trading would have a relatively small effect on the firm's incentives to develop new information. In some cases, however, insider trading will harm the corporation's interests and thus adversely affect its incentives in this regard. This argues for assigning the property right to the corporation, rather than the insider.

That argument is buttressed by the observation that creation of a property right with respect to a particular asset typically is not dependent upon there being a measurable loss of value resulting from the asset's use by someone else. Indeed, creation of a property right is appropriate even if any loss in value is entirely subjective, both because subjective valuations are difficult to measure for purposes of awarding damages and because the possible loss of subjective values presumably would affect the corporation's incentives to cause its agents to develop new information. As with other property rights, the law therefore should simply assume (although the assumption will sometimes be wrong) that assigning the property right to agent-produced information to the firm maximizes the social incentives for the production of valuable new information.

Because the relative rarity of cases in which harm occurs to the corporation weakens the argument for assigning it the property right, however, the critical issue may be whether one can justify assigning the property right to the insider. On close examination, the argument for assigning the property right to the insider is considerably weaker than the argument for assigning it to the corporation. The only plausible justification for doing so is the argument that legalized insider trading would be an appropriate compensation scheme. In other words, society might allow insiders to inside trade in order to give them greater incentives to develop new information. As we have seen, however, this argument is unpersuasive because insider trading is an inefficient compensation scheme. The economic theory of property rights in information thus cannot justify assigning the property right to insiders rather than to the corporation. Because there is no avoiding the necessity of assigning the property right to the information in question to one of the relevant parties, the argument for assigning it to the corporation therefore should prevail.

1. Implications for the scope of the prohibition

In *Diamond v. Oreamuno*,[79] the New York Court of Appeals concluded that a shareholder could properly bring a derivative action against corporate officers who had traded in the corporation's stock. The court explicitly relied on a property rights-based justification for its holding, explaining that "[t]he primary concern, in a case such as this, is not to determine whether the corporation has been damaged, but to decide, as between the corporation and the defendants, who has a higher claim to the proceeds derived from exploitation of the information."[80] Critics of *Diamond* have

---

[79] 248 N.E.2d 910 (N.Y. 1969).

[80] Id. at 912.

frequently pointed out that the corporation could not have used the information at issue in that case for its own profit.[81] The defendants had sold shares on the basis of inside information about a substantial decline in the firm's earnings. Once released, the information caused the corporation's stock price to decline precipitously. The information was thus a historical accounting fact of no value to the corporation. The only possible use to which the corporation could have put this information was by trading in its own stock, which it could not have done without violating the antifraud rules of the federal securities laws.

The *Diamond* case thus rests on an implicit assumption that, as between the firm and its agents, all confidential information about the firm is an asset of the corporation.[82] Critics of *Diamond* contend that this assumption puts the cart before the horse. In their view, the proper question is to ask whether the insider's use of the information posed a substantial threat of harm to the corporation. Only if that question is answered in the affirmative should the information be deemed an asset of the corporation.[83]

Proponents of a more expansive prohibition might respond to this argument in two ways. First, they might reiterate that, as between the firm and its agents, there is no basis for assigning the property right to the agent. Second, they might focus on the secondary and tertiary costs of a prohibition that encompassed only information whose use posed a significant threat of harm to the corporation. A regime premised on actual proof of injury to the corporation would be expensive to enforce, would provide little certainty or predictability for those who trade, and might provide agents with perverse incentives.

2.   Implication for the choice between federal and state regulation

Even among those who agree that insider trading should be regulated on property rights grounds, there is no agreement as to how insider trading should be regulated. Some scholars favor leaving insider trading to state corporate law, just as is done with every other duty of loyalty violation, and, accordingly, divesting the

---

[81] See Victor Brudney, *O'Hagan's* Problems, 1997 Sup. Ct. Rev. 249, 254 n. 15 (1997) ("There have been common law intimations of insiders' fiduciary obligations to the 'corporation' that may be satisfied by denying gain to the insiders from transactions involving use of corporate information that they did not, or could not, lawfully disclose—even though the corporation might not be able so to use it. . . .").

[82] See *Diamond*, 248 N.E.2d at 912 (holding that "a corporate fiduciary, who is entrusted with potentially valuable information, may not appropriate that asset for his own use").

[83] See, e.g., Freeman v. Decio, 584 F.2d 186, 192–94 (7th Cir.1978).

SEC of any regulatory involvement.[84] Others draw a distinction between SEC monitoring of insider trading and a federal prohibition of insider trading. They contend that the SEC should monitor insider trading, but refer detected cases to the affected corporation for private prosecution.[85] A third set favors a federal prohibition enforced by the SEC.[86]

This debate is a wide-ranging one, encompassing questions of economics, politics, and federalism. The analysis here focuses on the question of whether the SEC has a comparative advantage relative to private actors in enforcing insider trading restrictions. If so, society arguably ought to let the SEC carry the regulatory load.

That the SEC has such a comparative advantage is fairly easy to demonstrate. Virtually all private party insider trading lawsuits are parasitic on SEC enforcement efforts, which is to say that the private party suit was brought only after the SEC's proceeding became publicly known.[87] This condition holds because the police powers available to the SEC, but not to private parties, are essential to detecting insider trading. Informants, computer monitoring of stock transactions, and reporting of unusual activity by self-regulatory organizations and/or market professionals are the usual ways in which insider trading cases come to light. As a practical matter, these techniques are available only to public law enforcement agencies. In particular, they are most readily available to the SEC.

Unlike private parties, who cannot compel discovery until a non-frivolous case has been filed, the SEC can impound trading records and compel testimony simply because its suspicions are aroused.[88] As the agency charged with regulating broker-dealers and self-regulatory organizations, the SEC also is uniquely positioned to extract cooperation from securities professionals in conducting investigations.[89] Finally, the SEC is statutorily authorized to pay bounties to informants, which is particularly important in light of the key role informants play in breaking many major insider trading cases.[90]

---

[84] See, e.g., Larry E. Ribstein, Federalism and Insider Trading, 6 Sup. Ct. Econ. Rev. 123 (1998).

[85] See, e.g., Douglas M. Branson, Discourse on the Supreme Court Approach to SEC Rule 10b–5 and Insider Trading, 30 Emory L.J. 263 (1981); Jonathan R. Macey, Insider Trading: Economics, Politics, and Policy 40–41 (1991).

[86] See, e.g., Stephen M. Bainbridge, Incorporating State Law Fiduciary Duties into the Federal Insider Trading Prohibition, 52 Wash. & Lee L. Rev. 1189 (1995).

[87] Id. at 1253.

[88] Id. at 1263.

[89] Id.

[90] Id. at 1263–64.

Internationalization of the securities markets is yet another reason for believing the SEC has a comparative advantage in detecting and prosecuting insider trading. Sophisticated insider trading schemes often make use of offshore entities or even offshore markets. The difficulties inherent in extraterritorial investigations and litigation, especially in countries with strong bank secrecy laws, probably would preclude private parties from dealing effectively with insider trading involving off-shore activities. In contrast, the SEC has developed memoranda of understanding with a number of key foreign nations, which provide for reciprocal assistance in prosecuting insider trading and other securities law violations. The SEC's ability to investigate international insider trading cases was further enhanced by the 1988 act, which included provisions designed to encourage foreign governments to cooperate with SEC investigations.[91]

In any event, although this debate has considerable theoretical interest, it is essentially mooted by the public choice arguments recounted above. There is no constituency that would support repealing the federal insider trading prohibition, while proposals to do so would meet strong opposition from the SEC and its securities industry constituencies that benefit from the current prohibition. The federal insider trading prohibition is doubtless here to stay.

G. The Special Case of Insider Trading by Legislators and Other Government Officials

Many of the issues on which the policy debate has focused are essentially irrelevant to the question of whether the insider trading prohibition should apply to legislators and other government officials. Whether or not one believes that a prohibition of insider trading by corporate insiders is necessary to ensure the effectiveness of the SEC's system of mandatory disclosure by public corporations, for example, says nothing about inside trading by Members of Congress. Whether or not one believes that insider trading causes the market price of the affected security to move toward the price which the security would command if the inside information were publicly available, to cite another example, trading by Members of Congress is unlikely to move prices very significantly.[92] Accordingly, it will be most productive to focus herein on those policy arguments directly relevant to the question of Congressional insider trading.

---

[91] Id.

[92] Matthew Barbabella et al., Insider Trading in Congress: The Need for Regulation 43, http://ssrn.com/abstract=1318682 ("The limited available empirical evidence seems to support the view that Congressional trading does not have a significant effect on pricing efficiency.").

1. Perverse incentives

As we have seen, Henry Manne famously argued that allowing corporate insiders to trade on the basis of material nonpublic information was an effective means of compensating entrepreneurs in large corporations.[93] Recall that his argument was premised on the differing roles within the corporation of managers and entrepreneurs.[94] The former simply operate the firm according to predetermined guidelines, while the latter develop new valuable information. Entrepreneurs are inherently more difficult to compensate than mere managers. As to the latter, because the service is known and easy to monitor, the manager's "service can be purchased like any commodity in the marketplace."[95] In contrast, an entrepreneur's compensation must not only compensate him for the value of his services but also incentivize him to continue producing valuable information. Because it is rarely possible to ascertain information's value to the firm in advance, however, predetermined compensation, such as salary, is inappropriate for entrepreneurs. Instead, claimed Manne, insider trading is an effective way to compensate entrepreneurs for innovations. Because the increase in the price of the security following public disclosure provides a relatively accurate measure of the value of the innovation to the firm, insider trading allows the entrepreneur to recover some substantial portion of the value of his discovery.

As we saw above, the validity of this argument vis-à-vis corporate insiders is sharply contested. Even Manne himself, however, recognized that "it has no substantial application to government" employees and officials.[96] This is so because the compensation argument rests on the need to incent entrepreneurs to produce information. Members of Congress, however, "are peculiarly in a position to *receive* valuable market information, not *create* it."[97] The information on whose basis Members of Congress thus are likely to trade "would not ordinarily reflect entrepreneurial developments for which they are responsible."[98] Accordingly, there is no socially valuable activity on their part to be incentivized.[99]

---

[93] See Chapter 13.B.

[94] See Manne, supra note 3, at 115–17; see generally Chapter 13.A.2.

[95] Manne, supra note 3, at 115.

[96] Id. at 182.

[97] Id. at 179 (emphasis in original).

[98] Id. at 183.

[99] What about creating an incentive to serve in office? An "argument can be made that government employment frequently is not financially attractive and that insider trading would encourage public service by able citizens otherwise unwilling to make the necessary financial sacrifice." Id. at 182. One suspects, however, that non-pecuniary benefits associated with the trappings of power and the potential for

To the contrary, "the ability of elected officials to profit on the basis of material nonpublic information creates perverse incentives for these officials, and introduces innumerable distortions and the potential for immeasurable harm in a legal system in which public trust and confidence is critical."[100] As Larry Ribstein observed:

> Congress's insider trading is bad because it gives our lawmakers the wrong incentives. Do we really want to give Congress more reasons to hurt and help particular firms?

> In fact, Congress's trading is worse than trading by corporate insiders, which at least might be rationalized as a way to let employees cash in on their productive efforts. It's far worse than the usual trading on non-public information by outsiders without any breach of duty, which may encourage socially productive investigation and monitoring. . . .[101]

Congressional insider trading thus is undesirable, in the first instance, because it creates incentives for members and staffers to steal proprietary information for personal gain. The massive increase in federal involvement in financial markets and corporate governance as a result of the financial crisis of 2008 has made opportunities to steal such information even more widely available to government officials. Second, it gives members and staffers incentives to game the legislative process so as to maximize personal trading profits. Third, inside information can be utilized as a pay-off device. Fourth, it gives members and staffers incentives to help or hurt firms, which distorts market competition.

2. Unfairness

"No citation is needed to assert that [giving Members of Congress the opportunity to earn abnormally high returns by virtue of their service as elected officials] strikes many people as unfair."[102] The difficulty with such a confident pronouncement is that while there is a widely shared belief that insider trading is inherently sleazy,[103] converting that impression into a coherent policy basis for developing specific legal rules has proven quite difficult.[104]As Jonathan Macey complains, "scholarship that decries

---

substantial deferred compensation provides more than adequate incentives for citizens—able or otherwise—to seek Congressional office.

[100]   Jonathan R. Macey & Maureen O'Hara, Regulation and Scholarship: Constant Companions or Occasional Bedfellows?, 26 Yale J. on Reg. 89, 108 (2009).

[101]   Larry E. Ribstein, Congress' Insider Trading, Ideoblog (Mar. 29, 2006).

[102]   Barbabella et al., supra note 92, at 34.

[103]   Cf. Michael P. Dooley, Enforcement of Insider Trading Restrictions, 66 Va. L. Rev. 1, 55 (1980) (observing that insider trading "is behavior that falls below a standard of conduct to which many, including the author, aspire").

insider trading as 'unfair' completely lacks reasoned argument. Often those who brand insider trading as unfair do not even attempt to explain what insider trading is, much less why it is unfair."[105]

In the present context, however, we may be able to put some meat on the bones of a fairness argument. Congress routinely imposes rules on the public and the executive branch that it does not impose upon itself.[106] Until recently, "one of the most notorious of these congressional exemptions' arose out of Congress exempting 'itself from federal anti-discrimination and other workforce protection laws.'"[107] In arguing in favor of the Congressional Accountability Act of 1995,[108] which ended that practice, Senator Grassley contended that;

> I hold a strong belief that we, in Congress, are merely representatives of the people. We are not better than the people we represent and we are not, by definition and determination, different from the people we represent. We are, as representative government intends, the people themselves.
>
> It is simply not fair, or good governance, for the Congress of the United States to enact laws for the American people, while exempting itself from compliance. . . . This is a democracy, and therefore, we make laws for the people, and we, too, must follow these laws.[109]

Grassley began this line of argument by quoting Madison in Federalist No. 57:

> [Members of Congress] can make no law which will not have its full operation on themselves and their friends, as well as on the great mass of society. This has always been deemed one of the strongest bonds by which human policy can connect the rulers and the people together. It creates between them that communion of interests and sympathy of sentiments of which few governments have furnished examples, but without which

---

[104]   See Frank H. Easterbrook, Insider Trading, Secret Agents, Evidentiary Privileges, and the Production of Information, 1981 Sup. Ct. Rev. 309, 324 ("I suspect that few people who invoke arguments based on fairness have in mind any particular content for the term.").

[105]   Jonathan R. Macey, Ethics, Economics, and Insider Trading: Ayn Rand Meets the Theory of the Firm, 11 Harv. J.L. & Pub. Pol'y 785, 787 (1988).

[106]   Cheryl D. Block, Congress and Accounting Scandals: Is the Pot Calling the Kettle Black?, 82 Neb. L. Rev. 365, 374 (2003).

[107]   Id.

[108]   Pub. L. No. 104–1, 109 Stat. 3 (1995) (codified as amended, at 2 U.S.C. §§ 1301–1438).

[109]   Senator Charles Grassley & Jennifer Shaw Schmidt, Practicing What We Preach: A Legislative History of Congressional Accountability, 35 Harv. J. on Legis. 33, 34–35 (1998), quoted in Block, supra note 106, at 375.

every government degenerates into tyranny.... If this spirit shall ever be so far debased as to tolerate a law not obligatory on the legislature as well as on the people, the people will be prepared to tolerate anything but liberty.[110]

As the Supreme Court has noted, Thomas Jefferson likewise believed that "legislators ought not to stand above the law they create but ought generally to the bound by it as are ordinary persons."[111]

The present exemption of Congress from the insider trading laws violates these basic principles of good government. Accordingly, even if we cannot state a universal definition of fairness in the insider trading context, the loophole through which Congressional insider trading escapes those penalties validly may be called unfair because it breaks the "bonds" of which Madison spoke. Given the harsh and Draconian penalties Congress has seen fit to impose on those who commit insider trading, moreover, the exemption of Congress from those penalties is particularly egregious.

3. Summary

The problem at hand needs no further belaboring. Indeed, it might have sufficed to note that Henry Manne advocated "a strong condemnation of [insider trading] by government officials."[112] Manne is widely acknowledged to be not just the leading critic of insider trading regulation, but also the champion of affirmatively permitting corporate insiders to trade on the basis of material nonpublic information. If Manne thinks insider trading by Members of Congress ought to be regulated, who shall gainsay him?

In sum, there is no plausible justification for allowing Members of Congress or other governmental actors to use material nonpublic information they learn as a result of their position for personal stock trading gains. To the contrary, the relevant policy arguments all come down on the side of banning such trading.

---

[110] The Federalist No. 57 (James Madison).

[111] Gravel v. U.S., 408 U.S. 606, 615 (1972).

[112] Manne, supra note 3, at 189.

Chapter 14

SECTION 16(b)

Section 16 of the Exchange Act[1] imposes three substantive obligations on specified corporate insiders:

1. *Disclosure:* Pursuant to § 16(a), insiders of an issuer must report transactions in the issuer's equity securities to the SEC.

2. *Ban on short swing profits:* In addition to the complicated insider trading rules under § 10(b), Congress also provided a much simpler prophylactic rule under § 16(b). In brief, § 16(b) provides that any profits an insider of an issuer earns on purchases and sales of the issuer's equity securities that occur within six months of each other must be forfeited to the issuer. As with all prophylactic rules, § 16(b) is both over-and under-inclusive. It captures many trades unaffected by the use of inside information, while missing many trades flagrantly based on nonpublic information.

3. *Ban on short sales:* Section 16(c) prohibits insiders of an issuer from short selling the issuer's equity securities.

As a prohibition of insider trading, § 16(b) is far more limited in scope than the regime developed by the courts under Rule 10b–5. The chief limitation is that it applies only to directors, officers, and holders of ten percent or more of a registered company's equity securities. Besides the resulting smaller class of prospective defendants, moreover, there are several other important limitations on § 16(b)'s scope relative to Rule 10b–5. Section 16(b), for example, applies only to insider transactions in their own company's stock. There is no tipping liability, no misappropriation liability, and no constructive insider doctrine. Second, § 16(b) applies only to firms that must register under the Exchange Act. Finally, it applies only to equity securities, such as stocks and convertible debt.

A. Covered Issuers

Section 16 applies only to insiders of issuers who have one or more classes of equity securities registered with the SEC under the Exchange Act.[2] Under Exchange Act § 12(a), an issuer must register any class of equity securities listed for trading on a national stock

---

[1] 15 U.S.C. § 78(p).

[2] As to the definition of equity security, see Chapter 14.C.

exchange.[3] In addition, § 12(g) requires that an issuer register its equity securities if it has more than $10 million in assets and a class of equity securities held of record by at least 2,000 persons or 500 persons who are not accredited investors.[4] In addition to § 16, a number of other Exchange Act provisions apply only to registered issuers, but they are beyond the scope of this treatise.[5]

B. Who is a § 16 Insider? Officers, Directors, and 10% Shareholders

Unlike Rule 10b–5, § 16 applies only to officers, directors, or shareholders who own more than 10% of the company's stock. Unlike the status of a director, the other two categories present certain complexities. As such, we must ask both who is a shareholder and who is an officer?

1. Who is a shareholder?

Determining whether a shareholder is subject to § 16 requires us to ask three questions. First, is the holder the beneficial owner of the shares? Second, how do we determine the appropriate numerator and denominator to calculate the holder's percentage interest? Third, does § 16 apply only to individuals or can the

---

[3] 15 U.S.C. § 78l(a). There are 16 national securities exchanges currently registered with the SEC pursuant to Exchange Act § 6(a), the most important of which historically have been the New York Stock Exchange and the NYSE MKT LLC (formerly known as the American Stock Exchange). Each exchange defines its own listing criteria, which typically include such considerations as the number of shareholders, the dollar value of the outstanding shares, the size of the company, and compliance with various corporate governance standards. Only listed securities may be traded on the exchange in question.

[4] 15 U.S.C. § 78l(g). The record holder of a security is the person or entity identified in the issuer's books as the registered owner of the company's securities, who may not necessarily be the beneficial owner of the securities. Where brokers on behalf of their clients hold shares in street name, for example, the clients are the beneficial owners of the stock even though they are not listed on the company's books as their holder of record.

Accredited investors are defined in Securities Act Rule 501 to include certain institutional investors, such as banks, mutual funds, and pension funds, top insiders of the issuer, and high income or net worth individuals. See 17 C.F.R. § 230.501.

[5] If a corporation is required to register under the Exchange Act, for example, it becomes subject to the Act's periodic disclosure rules. In addition, the corporation also becomes subject to the proxy rules under § 14, the tender offer rules under §§ 13 and 14, and certain of the Act's anti-fraud provisions. The periodic reports required by the Exchange Act include: (1) Form 10, the initial Exchange Act registration statement. It is only filed once with respect to a particular class of securities. It closely resembles a Securities Act registration statement. (2) Form 10–K, an annual report containing full audited financial statements and management's report of the previous year's activities. It usually incorporates the annual report sent to shareholders. (3) Form 10–Q, filed for each of first three quarters of the year. The issuer does not file a Form 10–Q for the last quarter of the year, which is covered by the Form 10–K. Form 10–Q contains unaudited financial statements and management's report of material recent developments. (4) Form 8–K, which must be filed within 15 days after certain important events affecting the corporation's operations or financial condition, such as bankruptcy, sales of significant assets, or a change in control of the company. See generally Stephen M. Bainbridge, Corporation law (2d ed. 2009).

holdings of certain groups of shareholders be aggregated to meet the 10% threshold?

The first question arises because Section 16 explicitly applies only to beneficial owners of equity securities.[6] As such, Congress obviously contemplated that record holders such as depository institutions and brokers holding stock for clients would not be subject to the statute. Prior to 1991, however, working out the precise parameters of beneficial ownership was left to the courts because neither the statute nor any SEC rule defined it. In that year, however, the SEC adopted Rule 16a–1(a), which defines the term beneficial owner for purposes of § 16 to "mean any person who is deemed a beneficial owner pursuant to section 13(d) of the Act and the rules thereunder."[7] In turn, Rule 13d–3 provides that:

> [A] beneficial owner of a security includes any person who, directly or indirectly, through any contract, arrangement, understanding, relationship, or otherwise has or shares: (1) Voting power which includes the power to vote, or to direct the voting of, such security; and/or, (2) Investment power which includes the power to dispose, or to direct the disposition of, such security.[8]

In addition, subsection (d) of the Rule further provides that:

> A person shall be deemed to be the beneficial owner of a security . . . if that person has the right to acquire beneficial ownership of such security, . . . including but not limited to any right to acquire: (A) Through the exercise of any option, warrant or right; (B) through the conversion of a security; (C) pursuant to the power to revoke a trust, discretionary account, or similar arrangement; or (D) pursuant to the automatic termination of a trust, discretionary account or similar

---

[6] See 15 U.S.C. § 78p(a)(1) ("Every person who is directly or indirectly the *beneficial owner* of more than 10 percent of any class of any equity security (other than an exempted security) which is registered pursuant to section 78l of this title . . . shall file the statements required by this subsection with the Commission"; emphasis supplied); Id. at § 78p(b) ("For the purpose of preventing the unfair use of information which may have been obtained by such *beneficial owner* . . . any profit realized by him from any purchase and sale, or any sale and purchase, of any equity security of such issuer . . . shall inure to and be recoverable by the issuer . . ."; emphasis supplied).

[7] 17 C.F.R. § 240.16a–1(a).

[8] 17 C.F.R. § 240.13d–3(a). In addition, subsection (b) of the Rule provides that:

> Any person who, directly or indirectly, creates or uses a trust, proxy, power of attorney, pooling arrangement or any other contract, arrangement, or device with the purpose of effect of divesting such person of beneficial ownership of a security or preventing the vesting of such beneficial ownership as part of a plan or scheme to evade the reporting requirements of section 13(d) or (g) of the Act shall be deemed for purposes of such sections to be the beneficial owner of such security.

Id. at § 240.13d–3(b).

arrangement; provided, however, any person who acquires a security or power specified in paragraphs (d)(1)(i)(A), (B) or (C), of this section, with the purpose or effect of changing or influencing the control of the issuer, or in connection with or as a participant in any transaction having such purpose or effect, immediately upon such acquisition shall be deemed to be the beneficial owner of the securities which may be acquired through the exercise or conversion of such security or power.[9]

The Rule exempts persons who hold securities solely because they are a broker who acts as record owner of shares beneficially owned by their customers, pledgees of securities, or underwriters.[10]

Some examples may be helpful:

- A stockbroker's customer beneficially owns securities held by a broker in street name.

- An insider is presumed to have beneficial ownership of shares held of record by the insider's spouse, minor children, and other relatives living in the insider's home, although the insider may disclaim ownership of such shares when filing a Form 4.[11]

- "Smith is a director of a registered company and has recently become president of a non-profit foundation which is operated exclusively for charitable purposes and is qualified under Section 501(c)(3) of the Internal Revenue Code. The foundation owns approximately 3 percent of the outstanding common stock of the registered company." If Smith's position at the foundation gives him "voting power, investment power, or other indications of control with respect to the securities held by the foundation," he can be deemed the beneficial owner of the shares held by the foundation.[12]

- "An insider is the trustee of an irrevocable trust. Neither the insider nor any member of his or her family in the beneficiary of the trust." According to the SEC, a "trustee of an irrevocable trust or a trust revocable at the discretion of another person, who has no interest in the income or corpus of the trust, is not the beneficial owner of any securities held in the trust," even if the trustee "has the power to manage the assets of the trusts, including the power to

---

[9] Id. at § 240.13d–3(d)(1).

[10] Id. at § 240.13d–3(d)(2)–(4).

[11] Interpretive Release on Rules Applicable to Insider Reporting and Trading, 23 S.E.C. Docket 856 (1981).

[12] Id.

make acquisitions and dispositions and to vote the securities held by the trusts."[13]

- In contrast to the prior example, a trustee who has an interest in the income or corpus of the trust generally will be deemed the beneficial owner of shares held by the trust.

- Where "an insider, as settlor, establishes a trust with the settlor as the sole beneficiary and in whose administration the settlor has a voice," the insider will continue to be deemed the beneficial owner of such shares.

Returning our attention to Rule 16a–1, even if someone would be deemed a beneficial owner of equity securities pursuant to Rule 13d–3, Rule 16(a)(1) exempts from Section 16's coverage a number of financial institutions unlikely to have control over the issuer:

[T]he following institutions or persons shall not be deemed the beneficial owner of securities of such class held for the benefit of third parties or in customer or fiduciary accounts in the ordinary course of business (or in the case of an employee benefit plan specified in paragraph (a)(1)(vi) of this section, of securities of such class allocated to plan participants where participants have voting power) as long as such shares are acquired by such institutions or persons without the purpose or effect of changing or influencing control of the issuer or engaging in any arrangement subject to Rule 13d–3(b) (§ 240.13d–3(b)):

(i) A broker or dealer registered under section 15 of the Act (15 U.S.C. 78o);

(ii) A bank as defined in section 3(a)(6) of the Act (15 U.S.C. 78c);

(iii) An insurance company as defined in section 3(a)(19) of the Act (15 U.S.C. 78c);

(iv) An investment company registered under section 8 of the Investment Company Act of 1940 (15 U.S.C. 80a–8);

(v) Any person registered as an investment adviser under Section 203 of the Investment Advisers Act of 1940 (15 U.S.C. 80b–3) or under the laws of any state;

(vi) An employee benefit plan as defined in Section 3(3) of the Employee Retirement Income Security Act of 1974, as amended, 29 U.S.C. 1001 et seq. ("ERISA") that is subject to the provisions of ERISA, or any such plan that is not subject to ERISA that is maintained primarily for the benefit of the

---

[13] Id.

employees of a state or local government or instrumentality, or an endowment fund;

(vii) A parent holding company or control person, provided the aggregate amount held directly by the parent or control person, and directly and indirectly by their subsidiaries or affiliates that are not persons specified in § 240.16a–1(a)(1)(i) through (x), does not exceed one percent of the securities of the subject class;

(viii) A savings association as defined in Section 3(b) of the Federal Deposit Insurance Act (12 U.S.C. 1813);

(ix) A church plan that is excluded from the definition of an investment company under section 3(c)(14) of the Investment Company Act of 1940 (15 U.S.C. 80a–30);

(x) A non-U.S. institution that is the functional equivalent of any of the institutions listed in paragraphs (a)(1)(i) through (ix) of this section, so long as the non-U.S. institution is subject to a regulatory scheme that is substantially comparable to the regulatory scheme applicable to the equivalent U.S. institution and the non-U.S. institution is eligible to file a Schedule 13G pursuant to § 240.13d–1(b)(1)(ii)(J); and

(xi) A group, provided that all the members are persons specified in § 240.16a–1 (a)(1)(i) through (x).[14]

Now that we have defined the class of persons potentially deemed beneficial owners of equity securities, we must turn to determining what percentage of the relevant class of equity securities they hold. As for the numerator, Rule 13d–3 provides that "all securities of the same class beneficially owned by a person, regardless of the form which such beneficial ownership takes, shall be aggregated in calculating the number of shares beneficially owned by such person."[15] The denominator normally will be number of shares of the class outstanding. Where the individual in question is deemed a beneficial owner by virtue of subsection (d), however, that subsection provides that "[a]ny securities not outstanding which are subject to such options, warrants, rights or conversion privileges shall be deemed to be outstanding for the purpose of computing the percentage of outstanding securities of the class owned by such person but shall not be deemed to be outstanding for the purpose of computing the percentage of the class by any other person."[16]

---

[14] 17 C.F.R. § 240.16a–1(a)(1)(i)–(xi).

[15] 17 C.F.R. § 240.13d–3(c).

[16] Id. at § 240.13d–3(d)(1).

We come finally to the question of whether the holdings of a group of shareholders acting together can be aggregated so that they are collectively subject to Section 16's requirements. Recall that Rule 16a–1(a) defines the term beneficial owner for purposes of § 16 to "mean any person who is deemed a beneficial owner pursuant to section 13(d) of the Act and the rules thereunder."[17] In turn, Section 13(d)(3) provides that when two or more persons act as a group for the purpose of acquiring, holding or disposing of shares of the issuer they will collectively be deemed a "person" under the statute. Accordingly, such a group must file a Schedule 13D report if the members' aggregate holdings exceed the 5% threshold.

Generally speaking, some kind of agreement is necessary before it can be said that a group exists. Not only must there be an agreement, but the agreement must go to certain types of conduct. The relevant statutory provision, Exchange Act § 13(d)(3) identifies "acquiring, holding, or disposing" of stock as the requisite purposes. Shortly after the Williams Act was adopted, the question arose whether two or more persons acting together for the purpose of voting shares, as when they cooperate in conducting a proxy contest, form a group for purposes of this provision. The courts split on that question.[18] The SEC subsequently adopted Rule 13d–5(b)(1), which expanded the statutory list of purposes to include voting. Consequently, a group is formed when two or more shareholders agree to act together for the purposes of voting their shares, even if they do not intend to buy any additional shares. The rule's adoption seems to have resolved the controversy, even if the SEC's authority to effectively amend the statute remains somewhat obscure.

Proving the existence of the requisite agreement is a complex and potentially difficult question of fact. On the one hand, "Section 13(d) allows individuals broad freedom to discuss the possibilities of future agreements without filing under securities laws."[19] On the other hand, an agreement to act in concert need not be formal or

---

[17] Id. at § 240.16a–1(a).

[18] Compare GAF Corp. v. Milstein, 453 F.2d 709 (2d Cir.1971) (group exists) with Bath Indus., Inc. v. Blot, 427 F.2d 97 (7th Cir.1970) (no group).

[19] Pantry Pride, Inc. v. Rooney, 598 F.Supp. 891, 900 (S.D.N.Y.1984). See also Lane Bryant, Inc. v. Hatleigh Corp., 1980 WL 1412 at *1 (S.D.N.Y.1980) ("Section 13(d) seems carefully drawn to permit parties seeking to acquire large amounts of shares in a public company to obtain information with relative freedom, to discuss preliminarily the possibility of entering into agreements and to operate with relative freedom until they get to the point where they do in fact decide to make arrangements which they must record under the securities laws"). Hence, for example, merely showing the existence of a relationship or the sharing of information or advice between the alleged group members, will not suffice absent some additional evidence that indicates an intention to act in concert. Similarly, investment analysts who follow one another's trades without any agreement so to do, tacit or otherwise, will not be held to be a group. See, e.g., K N Energy, Inc. v. Gulf Interstate Co., 607 F.Supp. 756 (D.Colo.1983).

written.[20] The existence of such an agreement may be proven by circumstantial evidence.[21]

In *Segen ex rel. KFx Inc. v. Westcliff Capital Management, LLC*,[22] the defendants were part of two § 13(d) groups that both collectively owned more than 10% of the issuer's stock. The court explained that:

> [E]ach individual member of the [groups], even though considered a member of their respective "groups" for the purposes of aggregation to determine ownership percentage vis-à-vis the ten percent insider threshold, is only liable for its own short-swing profits resulting from its own trades. See SEC Release No. 34–28869, 56 Fed.Reg. at 7245 ("[O]nly those securities in which a member of a group has a direct or indirect pecuniary interest would be . . . subject to short-swing profit recovery. Thus, while securities holdings of group members may subject the group members to section 16, if the group member does not have or share a pecuniary interest in securities held by other group members, the transactions of the other group members do not create section 16 obligations for that member.").[23]

In other words, while the holdings of members of a § 13(d) group can be aggregated for purposes of determining whether each member of the group is a 10% shareholder, the individual group members generally will have liability only for short swing profits made by trading their own shares.

2. Who is an officer?

Determining whether one is an officer can be tricky. Exchange Act Rule 3b–2 defines an officer as a "president, vice president, secretary, treasury or principal financial officer, comptroller or principal accounting officer, and any person routinely performing corresponding functions. . . ."[24] The latter catchall phrase is the potential trouble spot. Should the statutory term "officer" be construed narrowly so that objective factors, especially one's title, determine whether one was subject to § 16(b)? Or should the term be interpreted more broadly, so as to take into account subjective considerations such as the nature of one's functions and/or whether one's role gave one access to inside information?

---

[20] Morales v. Quintel Entertainment, Inc., 249 F.3d 115, 124 (2d Cir.2001); Wellman v. Dickinson, 682 F.2d 355, 362–63 (2d Cir.1982).

[21] Morales v. Quintel Entertainment, Inc., 249 F.3d 115, 124 (2d Cir.2001); SEC v. Savoy Indus., 587 F.2d 1149, 1163 (D.C.Cir.1978).

[22] 299 F.Supp.2d 262 (S.D.N.Y. 2004).

[23] Id. at 272.

[24] 17 C.F.R. § 240.3b–2.

An early decision, *Colby v. Klune*,[25] expressed doubt as to whether the SEC had authority to adopt Rule 3b–2. Instead, the court adopted a formulation that looked to subjective considerations, which defined an officer as "a corporate employee performing important executive duties of such character that he would be likely, in discharging those duties, to obtain confidential information that would aid him if he engaged in personal market transactions."[26] The Ninth Circuit later concurred with the view that title alone is not dispositive, but focused on access to information as the relevant consideration, holding that § 16(b) "is not based simply upon a person's title within his corporation; rather, liability follows from the existence of a relationship with the corporation that makes it more probable than not that the individual has access to inside information."[27]

The SEC ultimately intervened in the debate by adopting Rule 16a–1(f), under which either one's title or one's function could result in officer status:

> The term "officer" shall mean an issuer's president, principal financial officer, principal accounting officer (or, if there is no such accounting officer, the controller), any vice president of the issuer in charge of a principal business unit, division or function (such as sales, administration or finance), any other officer who performs a policy making function, or any other person who performs similar policy making functions for the issuer. Officers of the issuer's parent(s) or subsidiaries shall be deemed officers of the issuer if they perform such policy making functions for the issuer. In addition, when the issuer is a limited partnership, officers or employees of the general partner(s) who perform policy making functions for the limited partnership are deemed officers of the limited partnership.[28]

Someone who holds one of the listed titles is likely to be deemed an officer, whether or not he has access to inside information, subject to a "very limited exception applicable only where the title is essentially honorary or ceremonial."[29] An executive with

---

[25] 178 F.2d 872 (2d Cir. 1949).

[26] Id. at 873.

[27] Merrill Lynch, Pierce, Fenner & Smith, Inc. v. Livingston, 566 F.2d 1119 (9th Cir.1978).

[28] 17 C.F.R. § 240.16a–1(f).

[29] National Medical Enterprises, Inc. v. Small, 680 F.2d 83 (9th Cir.1982). Conversely, the mere fact that one's position is described in, say, the corporate bylaws as that of an officer does not suffice to make one an officer for this purpose. See Lockheed Aircraft Corp. v. Campbell, 110 F.Supp. 282 (S.D.Cal.1953) (holding that assistant treasurer and assistant secretary were not officers for § 16(b) purposes even though their positions were described in the bylaws as those of officers).

policymaking functions that give the executive access to inside information, however, will be deemed an officer even if the executive lacks one of the formal titles usually associated with that position.

3. Indirect insiders

In *Blau v. Lehman*,[30] Lehman Brothers held a substantial (albeit less than 10%) number of shares in Tide Water Associated Oil Company. At that time, Lehman Brothers was a partnership engaged in investment banking, securities brokerage, and trading for its own account. Tide Water was a reporting company and, as such, its officers, directors, and 10% shareholders were subject to § 16.

Joseph A. Thomas was a Lehman Brothers partner and served as a Tide Water director. Plaintiff Blau, a Tide Water shareholder, claimed "Lehman Brothers 'deputed . . . Thomas, to represent its interests as a director on the Tide Water Board of Directors.'" Accordingly, Blau argued, Lehman Brothers could be held liable under § 16(b) as though the entity—i.e., Lehman Brothers—were a director.

The Supreme Court agreed that, in principle, that so-called "deputization" could result in one being indirectly treated as an insider:

> No doubt Lehman Brothers, though a partnership, could for purposes of § 16 be a "director" of Tide Water and function through a deputy, since § 3(a)(9) of the Act provides that "person" means . . . partnership' and § 3(a)(7) that "'director' means any direct or of a corporation or any person performing similar functions with respect to any organization, whether incorporated or unincorporated." Consequently, Lehman Brothers would be a "director" of Tide Water, if as petitioner's complaint charged Lehman actually functioned as a director through Thomas, who had been deputized by Lehman to perform a director's duties not for himself but for Lehman.[31]

On the facts before it, however, the Supreme Court concluded that there had been no such deputization and, accordingly, "Thomas, not Lehman Brothers as an entity, . . . was the director of Tide Water."[32]

---

[30] 368 U.S. 403 (1962).

[31] Id. at 409–410 (footnotes omitted).

[32] Id. at 410.

Later cases have identified a number of factors to be considered in determining whether an entity has become a director by deputization, including:

—The director took part in the decision to trade the issuer's securities. . . .

—The director succeeded another employee of the deputing entity as a director of the issuer.

—The director joined the issuer's board, thinking it would be in the interests of the deputing entity.

—The management of both the issuer and the deputing entity believed the director to be a deputy.

—The director admitted in writing that he was representing the interests of the deputing entity.

—The deputing entity's board consented to the director serving as a director of the issuer.

—The deputing entity had deputies on boards of other corporations.

—The director had a duty to report to the deputing entity.

—The deputing entity owned a controlling block of the issuer's stock.

—A majority of the issuer's directors were officers of the deputing entity.

Other factors that tend to indicate that a person is not a deputy include:

—The director never discussed operating details of the issuer with the deputing entity.

—The director disclaimed any interest in the deputing entity's profit.

—The issuer, not the deputing entity, initiated the invitation to join the issuer's board.

—The issuer initially invited the director to join its board before the deputing entity began purchasing the issuer's stock.

—The director turned down an offer to become a director after the deputing entity already owned a sizable block of the issuer's stock.

—No other representative of the deputing entity was ever mentioned for the directorship if the director declined to be elected.

—The director's professional experience was the prime motivation for choosing him.

—The director was not protecting any affairs of the deputing entity or seeking to promote any policies for that entity.[33]

C. Covered Securities

All three of Section 16's substantive provisions apply only to equity securities. In turn, Exchange Act § 3(a)(11) defines "equity security" as "any stock or similar security; or any security future on any such security; or any security convertible, with or without consideration, into such a security, or carrying any warrant or right to subscribe to or purchase such a security; or any such warrant or right."[34] In addition, Rule 3a11–1 includes limited partnership interests, interests in a joint venture, voting trust certificates, and options as equity securities.[35] Accordingly, equity security broadly encompasses corporate stock—whether common or preferred—and equivalent ownership interests in some other forms of limited liability entities, as well as instruments convertible into or derived from them.

In contrast, none of § 16's substantive provisions apply to exempt securities. Exchange Act § 3(a)(12) defines exempted securities to include a wide range of instruments, such as U.S. government notes and bonds, state and local government bonds, some types of investment fund securities, specified pension plans, and some securities issued by churches.[36] Many of these instruments, of course, would not fall within the definition of an equity security in any event. In addition, § 3(a)(12) authorizes the SEC to exempt such other securities as it deems appropriate "in the public interest and for the protection of investors." In exercising that power, the SEC, has specifically exempted from § 16 asset-backed securities and those issued by foreign private issuers.[37]

D. Reporting Obligation

Section 16(a) requires insiders to report their holdings in the issuer's equity securities within 10 days after they first become subject to Section 16.[38] Thereafter, an insider must report any

---

[33] Arnold S. Jacobs, An Analysis of Section 16 of the Exchange Act of 1934, 32 N.Y.L. Sch. L. Rev. 209, 283–85 (1987) (footnotes omitted).

[34] 15 U.S.C. § 78c(a)(11).

[35] 17 C.F.R. § 240.3a11–1.

[36] 15 U.S.C. § 78c(a)(12).

[37] See 17 C.F.R. § 240.3a12–12 (asset-backed securities); 17 C.F.R. § 240.3a12–3(b) (foreign private issuers).

[38] Section 16(a) provides that:

transactions in the issuer's equity securities within two business days of their occurrence. The report must be filed electronically with the SEC. In addition, the report must be posted to the issuer's corporate website.

E. Ban on Short-Swing Profits

Under § 16(b), any profits earned on purchases and sales within a six month period must be disgorged to the issuer.[39]

---

(1) Directors, officers, and principal stockholders required to file: Every person who is directly or indirectly the beneficial owner of more than 10 percent of any class of any equity security (other than an exempted security) which is registered pursuant to section 78l of this title, or who is a director or an officer of the issuer of such security, shall file the statements required by this subsection with the Commission.

(2) Time of filing: The statements required by this subsection shall be filed—

(A) at the time of the registration of such security on a national securities exchange or by the effective date of a registration statement filed pursuant to section 78l (g) of this title;

(B) within 10 days after he or she becomes such beneficial owner, director, or officer, or within such shorter time as the Commission may establish by rule;

(C) if there has been a change in such ownership, or if such person shall have purchased or sold a security-based swap agreement involving such equity security, before the end of the second business day following the day on which the subject transaction has been executed, or at such other time as the Commission shall establish, by rule, in any case in which the Commission determines that such 2–day period is not feasible.

(3) Contents of statements: A statement filed—

(A) under subparagraph (A) or (B) of paragraph (2) shall contain a statement of the amount of all equity securities of such issuer of which the filing person is the beneficial owner; and

(B) under subparagraph (C) of such paragraph shall indicate ownership by the filing person at the date of filing, any such changes in such ownership, and such purchases and sales of the security-based swap agreements or security-based swaps as have occurred since the most recent such filing under such subparagraph.

(4) Electronic filing and availability: Beginning not later than 1 year after July 30, 2002—

(A) a statement filed under subparagraph (C) of paragraph (2) shall be filed electronically;

(B) the Commission shall provide each such statement on a publicly accessible Internet site not later than the end of the business day following that filing; and

(C) the issuer (if the issuer maintains a corporate website) shall provide that statement on that corporate website, not later than the end of the business day following that filing.

15 U.S.C. § 78p(a).

[39] Exchange Act § 16(b) provides that:

For the purpose of preventing the unfair use of information which may have been obtained by such beneficial owner, director, or officer by reason of his relationship to the issuer, any profit realized by him from any purchase and sale, or any sale and purchase, of any equity security of such issuer (other than an exempted security) or a security-based swap agreement (as defined in section 206B of the Gramm-Leach-Bliley Act) involving any such equity security within any period of less than six months, unless such security or security-based swap agreement was acquired in good faith in connection with a debt previously contracted, shall inure to and be recoverable by the issuer, irrespective of any intention on the part of such beneficial owner, director, or

Shareholders of the issuer may sue insiders derivatively and a shareholder's lawyer can get a contingent fee out of any recovery or settlement:

> To enforce this strict liability rule on insider trading, Congress chose to rely solely on the issuers of stock and their security holders. Unlike most of the federal securities laws, § 16(b) does not confer enforcement authority on the Securities and Exchange Commission. It is, rather, the security holders of an issuer who have the ultimate authority to sue for enforcement of § 16(b). If the issuer declines to bring a § 16(b) action within 60 days of a demand by a security holder, or fails to prosecute the action "diligently," then the security holder may "institut[e]" an action to recover insider short-swing profits for the issuer.[40]

1. Standing

In *Gollust v. Mendell*,[41] the Supreme Court defined the class of issuer shareholders with standing to sue under Section 16(b) quite liberally. Noting that the "only textual restrictions on the standing of a party to bring suit under § 16(b) are that the plaintiff must be the 'owner of [a] security' of the 'issuer' at the time the suit is 'instituted,'" the court stressed that "Congress intended to grant enforcement standing of considerable breadth."[42] Interestingly, while liability is limited to short swing profits earned on transactions in equity securities, the standing provision of § 16(b) is not limited to holders of such securities. Instead, while "plaintiffs seeking to sue under the statute must own a 'security,' § 16(b) places no significant restriction on the type of security adequate to confer standing."[43] Accordingly, not just shareholders of the issuer have standing, but so do the holders of the issuer's bonds, debentures, warrants, and other securities. Only a "note, draft, bill

---

officer in entering into such transaction of holding the security or security-based swap agreement purchased or of not repurchasing the security or security-based swap agreement sold for a period exceeding six months. Suit to recover such profit may be instituted at law or in equity in any court of competent jurisdiction by the issuer, or by the owner of any security of the issuer in the name and in behalf of the issuer if the issuer shall fail or refuse to bring such suit within sixty days after request or shall fail diligently to prosecute the same thereafter; but no such suit shall be brought more than two years after the date such profit was realized. This subsection shall not be construed to cover any transaction where such beneficial owner was not such both at the time of the purchase and sale, or the sale and purchase, of the security or security based swap agreement (as defined in section 206B of the Gramm-Leach-Bliley Act) involved, or any transaction or transactions which the Commission by rules and regulations may exempt as not comprehended within the purpose of this subsection.

15 U.S.C. § 78p(b).

[40] Gollust v. Mendell, 501 U.S. 115, 122 (1991) (citations omitted).

[41] 501 U.S. 115 (1991).

[42] Id. at 122–23.

[43] Id. at 123.

of exchange, or banker's acceptance which has a maturity at the time of issuance of not exceeding nine months" is excluded.[44]

In contrast to standard corporate derivative lawsuits, where the representative plaintiff must satisfy a contemporaneous ownership standard, there is no such requirement under § 16. "In fact, the terms of the statute do not even require that the security owner have had an interest in the issuer at the time of the defendant's short-swing trading, and the courts to have addressed this issue have held that a subsequent purchaser of the issuer's securities has standing to sue for prior short-swing trading."[45] Although the statute does not expressly require that the plaintiff retain ownership of a security of the issuer until final judgment is rendered, the Court in *Gollust* held that "Congress understood and intended that, throughout the period of his participation, a plaintiff authorized to sue insiders on behalf of an issuer would have some continuing financial interest in the outcome of the litigation, both for the sake of furthering the statute's remedial purposes by ensuring that enforcing parties maintain the incentive to litigate vigorously, and to avoid the serious constitutional question that would arise from a plaintiff's loss of all financial interest in the outcome of the litigation he had begun."[46]

In order to have standing, a plaintiff must own a security issued by the same company that issued the equity securities traded by the insider. Accordingly, holders of securities issued by a parent or subsidiary of the issuer lack standing.[47]

2. Matching transactions

Although there must be both a sale and a purchase within six months of each other in order to trigger § 16(b), it applies whether the sale follows the purchase or vice versa.[48] Accordingly, shares are fungible for § 16(b) purposes.[49] The trader thus need not earn his or her gains from buying and selling specific shares of stock. Instead, if the trader unloads 10 shares of stock and buys back 10 different

---

[44] Id. There is no minimum number or value of securities someone must own in order to have standing. See Portnoy v. Revlon, Inc., 650 F.2d 895, 897 (CA7 1981) (granting plaintiff standing even though plaintiff owned just a single share); Magida v. Continental Can Co., 231 F.2d 843, 847–848 (CA2) (same where plaintiff owned 10 shares), cert. denied, 351 U.S. 972 (1956).

[45] *Gollust*, 501 U.S. at 123.

[46] Id. at 126.

[47] See id. at 123 ("An 'issuer' of a security is defined under § 3(a)(8) of the 1934 Act as the corporation that actually issued the security . . . and does not include parent or subsidiary corporations.").

[48] See Robert Charles Clark, Corporate Law 295–95 (1986) (explaining that § 16(b) "requires at least two transactions within six months: a purchase followed by a sale or a sale followed by a purchase").

[49] See, e.g., Gratz v. Claughton, 187 F.2d 46, 51 (2d Cir.1951) (noting "the fungible nature of shares of stock").

shares of stock in the same company at a cheaper price, he or she is liable.[50]

Examples: (1) Susan is chief financial officer of Acme, Inc. She buys 1,000 Acme shares at $8 on February 1. She sells 1,000 shares at $10 on May 1. Because the sale and purchase took place within six months, § 16(b) is triggered. She has earned a $2 profit per share and therefore must disgorge $2,000 to Acme.

(2) Sam is senior vice president of Ajax, Inc. He has owned 10,000 shares for many years. On June 1 he sells 1,000 shares at $10. On September 15 he buys 1,000 shares at $8. He also must disgorge $2,000 to Ajax ($2 per share times 1000 shares).

Courts interpret the statute to maximize the amount the company recovers.[51] They do not use any of the standard accounting tools (e.g., FIFO: first in, first out). Much less do they let shareholders identify specific shares of stock; for example, courts will not allow the defendant to argue that "in November I sold the share I bought in January, not the share I bought in October." Instead, they match the lowest priced purchases and the highest priced sales.[52] Again, an example will be helpful:

Example: Shania is president of Acme, Inc. Her transactions were as follows:

- March 1: bought 100 shares at $10
- April 1: sold 70 shares at $12
- May 1: bought 50 shares on May 1 at $9
- May 15: sold 25 shares at $13
- December 31: sold 35 shares at $20

The December 31 sale cannot be matched with either the March 1 or May 1 purchase, because they are more than six months apart. The other transactions are all matchable. A court will match them in the way that maximizes Acme's recovery:

- Match the 25 shares sold on May 15 with 25 of the shares bought on May 1, because they have the largest price differential. With a $4 profit per share ($13 minus $9) times 25 shares, Shania owes Acme $100.

---

[50] See Smolowe v. Delendo Corp., 136 F.2d 231, 237 n.13 (2d Cir.1943) (holding that § 16(b) is not limited to "the purchase and sale of the same certificates of stock").

[51] See Mayer v. Chesapeake Ins. Co., 877 F.2d 1154, 1164 (2d Cir.1989) ("To effectuate the remedial purposes of § 16(b), courts should compute the amount of profit from short-swing sales in a manner that will maximize the plaintiff's recovery."), cert. denied, 493 U.S. 1021 (1990).

[52] See, e.g., Smolowe v. Delendo Corp., 136 F.2d 231 (2d Cir.), cert. denied, 320 U.S. 751 (1943).

• Next match 25 of the shares sold on April 1 with the remaining 25 shares purchased on May 1 for a profit of $75 ($3 per share ($12 minus $9) times 25 shares).

• Now match the remaining 45 shares sold on April 1 with 45 of the shares bought on March 1 for a profit of $90 ($2 per share ($12 minus $10) times 45 shares).

• Shania therefore owes Acme a total of $265.

3.   Different matching rules for shareholders

Section 16(b) treats officers and directors on the one hand and shareholders on the other hand differently, by providing that:

> This subsection shall not be construed to cover any transaction where such beneficial owner was not such both at the time of the purchase and sale, or the sale and purchase, of the security . . . involved. . . .

A shareholder thus has § 16(b) liability only if she owned more than 10 percent of the company's shares both at the time of the purchase and of the sale. In contrast, although pursuant to Rule 16a–2, you cannot match a transaction by an officer or director made prior to his or her appointment as an officer or director to one made after he or she is appointed,[53] you can match transactions that occur after he or she ceases to be an officer or director with those made while he or she still held office.

The Supreme Court first took up this distinction in *Reliance Electric Co. v. Emerson Electric Co.*[54] Emerson bought 13.2 percent of Dodge Manufacturing Co. stock in a hostile tender offer. To avoid being taken over by Emerson, Dodge agreed to merge with Reliance. Emerson gave up the fight and decided to sell its Dodge shares. In an attempt to minimize any potential § 16(b) liability, Emerson first sold Dodge shares representing 3.24 percent of the outstanding common stock. It then sold the remainder, which represented 9.96 percent of the outstanding. When Reliance sued under § 16(b), the Supreme Court held that shareholders are subject to the statute only if they own more than 10 percent of the stock immediately before the sale. Emerson therefore had no liability with respect to its sale of the final 9.96 percent. *Reliance* is a good example of how form prevails over substance in § 16(b)—even though Emerson's two sales were part of a related series of transactions effected pursuant to a single plan, which plausibly could have been deemed a step transaction, the court treated the second sale as having independent legal significance.

---

[53] 17 C.F.R. § 240.16a–2.

[54] 404 U.S. 418 (1972).

Notice that Emerson did not raise, and the Supreme Court thus did not address, the significance of the fact that Emerson had not been a 10 percent shareholder at the time it made its initial tender offer. Instead, that issue came up in *Foremost-McKesson, Inc. v. Provident Securities Co.*,[55] in which the Supreme Court held that a purchase by which a shareholder crosses the 10% threshold cannot be matched with subsequent sales for § 16(b) purposes. Again, an example may be helpful.

Example: Selena is not an officer or director of Ajax, Inc. At all relevant times, Ajax has 1,000 shares outstanding. Selena's transactions are as follows:

- January 1: buys 50 shares at $10
- February 1: buys 55 shares at $10
- April 1: buys 50 shares at $10.
- May 1: sells 60 shares at $15
- May 2: sells 55 shares at $20

Liability equals $250 (50 shares times ($15–$10)). The January 1 purchase cannot be matched with either sale, because on January 1 Selena was not yet a 10 percent shareholder. The February 1 purchase cannot be matched with either sale because it is the transaction by which Selena became a (more than) 10 percent shareholder. Only the April 1 purchase is potentially matchable, because only at the time of that purchase did Selena own more than 10 percent of Ajax's stock. As to the sales, only the May 1 sale can be matched with the April 1 purchase. On May 2, Selena owned less than 10 percent of Ajax's stock.

4. Form versus substance

Form usually triumphs over substance in § 16(b) cases. There are some exceptions, however, the most notable of which is the unconventional transaction doctrine. The Exchange Act defines "sale" very broadly: it includes every disposition of a security for value. For purposes of § 16(b), however, certain transactions are not deemed sales; namely, so-called unconventional transactions.

The leading case in this area is *Kern County Land Co. v. Occidental Petroleum Corp.*[56] In 1967, Occidental launched a tender offer for 500,000 shares of Kern County Land Co. (Old Kern). The offer later was extended and the number of shares being sought was increased. When the offer closed in June, Occidental owned more than 10% of Old Kern's stock. To avoid being taken over by

---

[55] 423 U.S. 232 (1976).

[56] 411 U.S. 582 (1973).

Occidental, Old Kern negotiated a defensive merger with Tenneco. Under the merger agreement, Old Kern stock would be exchanged for Tenneco stock. In order to avoid becoming a minority shareholder in Tenneco, Occidental sold to a Tenneco subsidiary an option to purchase the Tenneco shares Occidental would acquire in the merger, which could not be exercised until the § 16(b) six-month period had elapsed. Tenneco and Old Kern merged during the six-month period following Occidental's tender offer. Somewhat later, more than 6 months after the tender offer, Occidental sold Tenneco stock pursuant to the option.

The successor corporation to Old Kern (New Kern) sued under § 16(b). It offered two theories. First, the merger and resulting exchange of Old Kern for Tenneco stock constituted a sale, which had occurred less than six months after the purchase effected by the tender offer. Second, the tender offer constituted a purchase and that the grant of the option (rather than the exercise of the option) constituted a sale. Because the option was granted less than six months after the tender offer, New Kern argued that Occidental was liable for any profit earned on the shares covered by the option. The Supreme Court rejected both of New Kern's arguments, holding that Occidental had no § 16(b) liability. Both the merger and the grant of the option were unconventional transactions and, as such, were not deemed a sale for § 16(b) purposes.

Courts consider three factors in deciding whether a transaction is conventional or unconventional: (1) whether the transaction is volitional; (2) whether the transaction is one over which the beneficial owner has any influence; and (3) whether the beneficial owner had access to confidential information about the transaction or the issuer.[57] In the case at bar, Occidental was a hostile bidder with no access to confidential information about Old Kern or Tenneco. In addition, as to the merger, the exchange was involuntary—because the other shareholders had approved the merger, Occidental had no option but to exchange its shares.

Although *Kern* still stands for the proposition that substance sometimes triumphs over form even in § 16(b), it no longer states the rule for options. Instead, the SEC treats the acquisition of an option as the purchase (or sale) of the underlying stock. Thus, the purchase of an option to buy stock (a call) could be matched either with a sale of the underlying stock or with the purchase of an option to sell the stock (a put). For example, suppose an investor bought

---

[57] See, e.g., Heublein, Inc. v. Gen. Cinema Corp., 722 F.2d 29, 31 (2d Cir.1983) (listing as factors hostility, involuntariness, and the lack of any likelihood of access to material inside information); At Home Corp. v. Cox Commc'ns, Inc., 446 F.3d 403, 408 (2d Cir.2006) ("This Circuit has suggested that these factors—an involuntary transaction by an insider having no access to inside information—are prerequisites to use of the *Kern County* analysis").

call options on 10 shares for $1 each, exercisable at $50 per share. If he exercised the options and sold the stock for $60 a share, he would have § 16(b) liability of $60x10—(10x$1 + 10x$50) = $90. A purchase of stock could similarly be matched with the purchase of a put.

F. Important Exemptions

Section 16 itself contains two exemptions. Section 16(d) exempts market making activities from subsections (b) and (c) of the statute.[58] Section 16(e) exempts arbitrage transactions made in compliance with the SEC rules governing such transactions.[59] In addition, the SEC has carved out numerous exemptions by rule.

The most important of these exemptions is provided by Rule 16b–3, which broadly exempts from the definition of "purchase" any transaction, other than a discretionary transaction,[60] in which an officer or director of the issuer acquires an equity security of the issuer from the issuer. At least one of the following conditions must be satisfied in order for the exemption to be available: the transaction is approved by the issuer's board of directors or a board committee comprised solely of two or more non-employee directors; the transaction was approved or ratified, in compliance with the proxy rules under Exchange Act Section 14, by the issuer's shareholders; or the officer or director is required to hold the acquired securities for a period of six months after acquiring the securities. Because such transactions are exempted from the definition of "purchase," they cannot be matched with a corresponding sale within 6 months. Although the Rule is not

---

[58] 15 U.S.C. § 78p(d) provides that:

The provisions of subsection (b) of this section shall not apply to any purchase and sale, or sale and purchase, and the provisions of subsection (c) of this section shall not apply to any sale, of an equity security not then or theretofore held by him in an investment account, by a dealer in the ordinary course of his business and incident to the establishment or maintenance by him of a primary or secondary market . . . for such security. The Commission may, by such rules and regulations as it deems necessary or appropriate in the public interest, define and prescribe terms and conditions with respect to securities held in an investment account and transactions made in the ordinary course of business and incident to the establishment or maintenance of a primary or secondary market.

[59] 15 U.S.C. § 78p(e) provides that:

The provisions of this section shall not apply to foreign or domestic arbitrage transactions unless made in contravention of such rules and regulations as the Commission may adopt in order to carry out the purposes of this section.

[60] A discretionary transaction is defined by Rule 16b–3(b)(1) as one effected pursuant to an employee benefit plan transaction that "is at the volition of a plan participant" and "results in either an intra-plan transfer involving an issuer equity securities fund, or a cash distribution funded by a volitional disposition of an issuer equity security." 17 C.F.R. 240.16b–3(b)(1).

limited to transactions effected with a compensatory purpose,[61] as a practical matter the rule's main importance is to facilitate stock-based employee compensation plans.

Rule 16b–3(e) likewise exempts from the definition of "sale" any transaction, excluding discretionary transactions, in which an officer or director sells or otherwise disposes of equity securities of the issuer to the issuer. At least one of the following conditions must be satisfied in order for the exemption to be available: the transaction is approved by the issuer's board of directors or a board committee comprised solely of two or more non-employee directors; or the transaction was approved or ratified, in compliance with the proxy rules under Exchange Act Section 14, by the issuer's shareholders. Because any such disposition is exempted from "sale," it cannot be matched with a purchase within the six-month period.[62]

Rule 16b–5 exempts from § 16(b) an acquisition or disposition of an issuer's equity securities by a bona fide gift, pursuant to a will, or under the laws of descent and distribution.[63] Any such transactions, however, are reportable under Section 16(a).

Rule 16b–7 exempts from Section 16(b) transactions effected pursuant to a merger, consolidation, reclassification, and similar transactions that do not result in a significant change in the issuer's business or assets. In order to qualify for the exemption, the insider must surrender a security in exchange for the acquired security. In addition, the security surrendered must have been issued by a company that, before the transactions, owned 85% or more of the equity securities of all other companies party to the merger or consolidation, or 85% or more of the combined assets of all of the companies undergoing merger or consolidation. In other words, the entities involved must have at least 85% cross-ownership.[64]

G. Ban on Short Sales

Section 16(c) provides that:

> It shall be unlawful for any such beneficial owner, director, or officer, directly or indirectly, to sell any equity security of such issuer (other than an exempted security), if the person selling the security or his principal

---

[61] See, e.g., Tinney v. Geneseo Communications, Inc., 2006 WL 2917388 (D. Del. 2006) (holding that "that the SEC had the power to enact the exemptions listed in Rule 16b–3 (as well as the 2005 amendment stating that transactions need not have a compensatory element in order to be eligible for such exemptions)").

[62] 17 C.F.R. 240.16b–3(e).

[63] 17 C.F.R. 240.16b–5.

[64] 17 C.F.R. 240.16b–7.

(1) does not own the security sold, or

(2) if owning the security, does not deliver it against such sale within twenty days thereafter, or does not within five days after such sale deposit it in the mails or other usual channels of transportation; but no person shall be deemed to have violated this subsection if he proves that notwithstanding the exercise of good faith he was unable to make such delivery or deposit within such time, or that to do so would cause undue inconvenience or expense.[65]

Subsection 16(c)(1) prohibits insiders from selling the issuer's stock short. In a short sale, the investor sells stock that he does not currently own for delivery at a subsequent date agreed upon with the buyer. The investor hopes that the price of the stock will have fallen by the delivery date, so as to make a profit. Suppose John sold short 100 shares at a price of $10 for delivery in 60 days. When the 60 days expires, John must transfer 100 shares to the buyer and will receive $1,000 in return. Because John did not own the shares at the time he entered into the transaction, he will have to go out and buy them on the market. If the stock price has fallen, say to $9 per share, John can buy the 100 shares for $900 and will have earned a $100 profit (the difference between the $1,000 he received from the buyer and the $900 it cost him to buy the shares for delivery). If the stock price has risen, say to $11 per share, however, John will have to pay $1,100 buy the 100 shares for delivery to the buyer and will therefore lose $100.

An insider who knows that bad news is forthcoming may be tempted to sell the issuer's stock short to profit on the anticipated drop in the issuer's stock price expected to occur when the bad news is made public. Indeed, the insider may even be tempted to generate bad news, so as to create short selling opportunities. Section 16(c)(1) is intended to eliminate that temptation by banning insiders from selling their issuer's shares short.

Section 16(c)(2) prohibits a related practice known as "short sales against the box." These are hedging transactions, in which "an owner of stock resorts to a short sale in order to avoid the risk of future price fluctuations. He owns sufficient securities to make delivery, but chooses to make a short sale involving the borrowing of shares for delivery, rather than to sell and make delivery of the shares which he owns."[66]

---

[65] 15 U.S.C. § 78p(c). Congress later added § 16(f) to the statute so as to make clear that subsection (c)—like subsections (a) and (b), as well—applies to transactions involving the use of securities futures. 15 U.S.C. § 78p(f) ("The provisions of this section shall apply to ownership of and transactions in security futures products.").

[66] Fisher v. Comm'r, 1938 WL 8197 (Board of Tax Appeals 1938).

TABLE OF CASES

INDEX

239